Do you find it difficult to approach God with the questions that are tugging at your heart?

When speaking of God, Elisabeth Elliot writes, "He is not only the Almighty. He is also our Father, and what a father does is not by any means always understood by the child."

On Asking God Why reminds us that as children of God we can bring our questions to Him with all the trust of a child in his earthly parent. We are encouraged to search the Scriptures for God's answers. Among the issues Elliot contemplates are singleness, risk taking, and being judgmental of others. When we overcome our fears and decide to ask God why, He will surely give us all the answers we need.

Barbara Neri
25 Tarkiln Road
Chepachet, RI 0

OTHER BOOKS BY THE SAME AUTHOR

Through Gates of Splendor
Shadow of the Almighty
Love Has a Price Tag
Discipline: The Glad Surrender
Passion and Purity
A Lamp for My Feet
The Savage My Kinsman
These Strange Ashes
The Mark of a Man
Let Me Be a Woman
A Chance to Die
All That Was Ever Ours
Loneliness

ELISABETH ELLIOT

♦

On Asking God Why

FLEMING H. REVELL COMPANY
OLD TAPPAN, NEW JERSEY

Scripture quotations identified NEB are from The New English Bible.
Copyright © The Delegates of the Oxford University Press and the Syndics of
the Cambridge University Press 1961, 1970. Reprinted by permission.

Scripture quotations identified PHILLIPS are from THE NEW TESTAMENT
IN MODERN ENGLISH, Revised Edition—J. B. Phillips, translator. © J. B.
Phillips 1958, 1960, 1972. Used by permission of Macmillan Publishing Co.,
Inc.

Scripture quotations identified KJV are from the King James Version of the
Bible.

Scripture quotations identified RSV are from the Revised Standard Version of
the Bible, Copyrighted © 1946, 1952, 1971, by the Division of Christian
Education of the National Council of the Churches of Christ in the United States
of America, and are used by permission. All rights reserved.

"Tenderness" is from *The Mark of a Man* by Elisabeth Elliot. Copyright ©
1981 by Elisabeth Elliot. Published by Fleming H. Revell Company. Used by
permission.

Library of Congress Cataloging-in-Publication Data
Elliot, Elisabeth.
On asking God why / Elisabeth Elliot.
p. cm.
Essays originally published in Christian herald and other journals.
ISBN 0-8007-5303-8
1. Christian life—1960– I. Title.
BV4501.2.E372 1989
248.4—dc19

Copyright © 1989 by Elisabeth Elliot
Published by the Fleming H. Revell Company
Old Tappan, New Jersey 07675
Printed in the United States of America

To my husband
Lars Gren
who builds the
fences around me
and
stands on all sides

CONTENTS

CONTENTS

FOREWORD

God does many things which we do not understand. Of course he does—he is God, perfect in wisdom, love, and power. We are only children, very far from perfect in anything. A true faith must rest solidly on his character and his Word, not on our particular conceptions of what he ought to do. The word *ought* presupposes an idea of justice. When God's actions do not seem to conform to our idea of justice, we are tempted at least to ask *why,* if not actually to charge him with injustice.

Thousands of years ago one of God's faithful servants, having lost practically everything, sat on an ash heap surrounded by weeping friends who were tearing up their clothes and tossing dust into the air for grief. For seven days and seven nights they were speechless in the face of Job's suffering. It was Job who broke the silence—with a long and eloquent curse. He asked the question men have asked ever since: *Why?*

Why was I not still-born?
Why did I not die when I came out of the womb?
Why was I ever laid on my mother's knees?
Why should the sufferer be born to see the light?

Why is life given to men who find it so bitter?
Why should a man be born to wander blindly, hedged in by God
on every side?

See Job 3:11, 12, 20, 23 NEB

Written centuries later, the Psalms express similar agonized
cries:

I will say to God my Rock, "Why hast thou forgotten me?"
Why hast thou cast us off, O God? Is it for ever?

Psalms 74:1 NEB

There would be no sense in asking *why* if one did not believe
in anything. The word itself presupposes *purpose*. Purpose
presupposes a purposeful intelligence. *Somebody* has to have
been responsible. It is because we believe in God that we address
questions to him. We believe that he is Just and that he is Love,
but that belief is put to severe strain as we wrestle with our pains
and perplexities, with our very position in his ordered universe.

"Whence knowest thou that this thing is unjust, unless thou
know what is just?" wrote St. Augustine. "Hast thou that which
is just from thyself, and canst thou give justice to thyself?
Therefore when thou art unjust, thou canst not be just except by
turning thee to a certain abiding justice, wherefrom if thou
withdrawest, thou art unjust, and if thou drawest near to it, thou
art just. . . . Look back therefore, rise to the heights, go to that
place where once God hath spoken, and there thou wilt find the
fountain of justice where is the fountain of life. 'For with thee is
the fountain of life' [Psalms 36:9]."

The pieces in this book make up a somewhat mongrel
collection. Essays? Sketches? "Cautionary tales"? Those, perhaps, and some less classifiable. They touch lightly on matters of
considerable weight—the mystery of suffering (losses, cancer,
despair, death), the mystery of evil (abortion, divorce, euthana-
sia, the cult of rock "music"), and on the mystery of our

ordinary human condition (loneliness, hopelessness, tenderness, confusion, aging, the need for forgiveness). All but one are the expression of a single writer who owes a special debt to the author of the second chapter, "On Brazen Heavens. He is my brother, eight years my junior, to whom for the first decade or so of his life I taught everything I knew. He has been teaching me ever since. He wrote the abovementioned chapter while my husband Addison Leitch was dying. I think we share the same vision, seeking always to see things in the light of "a certain abiding justice." It is my hope that this collection will help some to "rise to the heights, go to that place where once God hath spoken," and find that Fountain of Life.

On Asking God Why

ON
ASKING GOD
WHY

One of the things I am no longer as good at as I used to be is sleeping through the night. I'm rather glad about that, for there is something pleasant about waking in the small hours and realizing that one is, in fact, in bed and need not get up. One can luxuriate. Between two and three o'clock yesterday morning I luxuriated. I lay listening to the night sounds in a small house on the "stern and rockbound" coast of Massachusetts. The wind whistled and roared, wrapping itself around the house and shaking it. On the quarter hour the clock in the living room softly gave out Whittington's chime. I could hear the tiny click as the electric blanket cut off and on, the cracking of the cold in the walls, the expensive rumble of the oil burner beneath me, and the reassuring rumble of a snoring husband beside me. Underneath it all was the deep, drumming rhythm of the surf, synchronized with the distant bellow of "Mother Ann's Cow," the name given the sounding buoy that guards the entrance to Gloucester Harbor.

I was thinking, as I suppose I am always thinking, in one way or another, about mystery. An English magazine which contained an interview with me had just come in the mail, and of course I read it, not to find out what I'd said to the man last spring in Swanwick, but to find out what he said I'd said. He had asked me about some of the events in my life, and I had told him that because of them I had had to "come to terms with mystery." That was an accurate quotation, I'm sure, but as I lay in bed I knew that one never comes to any final terms with mystery—not in this life, anyway. We keep asking the same unanswerable questions and wondering why the explanations are not forthcoming. We doubt God. We are anxious about everything when we have been told quite clearly to be anxious about nothing. Instead of stewing we are supposed to pray and give thanks.

Well, I thought, *I'll have a go at it.* I prayed about several things for which I could not give thanks. But I gave thanks in the middle of each of those prayers because I was still sure (the noise of the wind and ocean were reminding me) that underneath are the everlasting arms.

My prayers embraced four things:

1. Somebody I love is gravely ill.
2. Something I wanted has been denied.
3. Something I worked very hard for failed.
4. Something I prized is lost.

I can be specific about three of the things. A letter from a friend of many years describes her cancer surgery and its aftermath—an incision that had to be scraped and cleaned daily for weeks.

It was so painful that Diana, Jim, Monica, and I prayed while she cleaned it, three times and some days four times. Monica would wipe my tears. Yes, Jesus stands right there as the pain takes my breath away and my toes curl to keep from crying out loud. But I haven't asked, Why me, Lord? It is only now that I can pray for cancer patients and know how the flesh hurts and how relief, even for a moment, is blessed.

16

The second thing is a manuscript on which I have spent years. It is not, I believe, publishable now, and I can see no way to redeem it. It feels as though those years of work have gone down the drain. Have they? What ought I to do about this failure?

The other thing is my J.B. Phillips translation of the New Testament, given to me when I lived in the jungle in 1960 and containing nineteen years' worth of notes. I left this book on an airplane between Dallas and Atlanta several weeks ago. The stewardess brought my breakfast as I was reading it, so I laid it in my lap and spread my napkin on top of it. I suppose it slipped down beside the seat. (Stupid of me, of course, but on the same trip my husband did just as stupid a thing. He left his briefcase on the sidewalk outside the terminal. We prayed, and the prayers were almost instantly answered. Someone had picked the briefcase up and turned it in to the airline, and we had it back in a couple of hours.) I am lost without my Phillips. I feel crippled. It is as though a large segment of the history of my spiritual pilgrimage has been obliterated. It was the one New Testament in which I knew my way around. I knew where things were on the page and used it constantly in public speaking because I could refer quickly to passages I needed. What shall I do?

I have done the obvious things. Prayer is the first thing—asking God to do what I *can't* do. The second thing is to get busy and do what I *can* do. I prayed for my friend, of course, and then I sat down and wrote her a letter. I don't know what else to do for her now. My husband and I prayed together about the lost New Testament (and many of my friends prayed too). We went to the proper authorities at the airline and have been assured that everything will be done to recover it, but it has not turned up. We prayed about the bad manuscript and asked for editorial advice. It looks quite irremedial. I continue to pray repeatedly, extensively, and earnestly about all of the above. And one more thing: I seek the lessons God wants to teach me, and that means that I ask why.

There are those who insist that it is a very bad thing to question God. To them, "why?" is a rude question. That depends, I believe, on whether it is an honest search, in faith, for his meaning, or whether it is a challenge of unbelief and rebellion. The psalmist often questioned God and so did Job. God did not answer the questions, but he answered the man—with the mystery of himself.

He has not left us entirely in the dark. We know a great deal more about his purposes than poor old Job did, yet Job trusted him. He is not only the Almighty—Job's favorite name for him. He is also our Father, and what a father does is not by any means always understood by the child. If he loves the child, however, the child trusts him. It is the child's ultimate good that the father has in mind. Terribly elementary. Yet I have to be reminded of this when, for example, my friend suffers, when a book I think I can't possibly do without is lost, when a manuscript is worthless.

The three things are not all in the same category. The second and third things have to do with my own carelessness and failure. Yet in all three I am reminded that God is my Father still, that he does have a purpose for me, and that nothing, absolutely nothing, is useless in the fulfillment of that purpose if I'll trust him for it and submit to the lessons.

"God disciplines us for our good *that we may share his holiness.*" That is a strong clue to the explanation we are always seeking. God's purpose for us is holiness—his own holiness which we are to share—and the sole route to that end is discipline.

Discipline very often involves loss, diminishment, "fallings from us, vanishings." Why? Because God wills our perfection in holiness, that is, our *joy.* But, we argue, why should diminishments be the prerequisite for joy? The answer to that lies within the great mystery that underlies creation: the principle of life out of death, exemplified for all time in the Incarnation ("that a vile Manger his low Bed should prove, who in a Throne of stars

Thunders above," as Crashaw expressed it) and in the cross and resurrection ("who, for the joy that was set before him, endured a cross"). Christ's radical diminishments—his birth as a helpless baby and his death as a common criminal—accomplished our salvation.

It follows that if we are to share in his destiny we must share in his death, which means, for us sinners, the willingness to offer up to him not only ourselves but all that goes with that gift, including the simplest, down-to-earth things. These things may be aggravating and irritating and humiliating as well as mysterious. But it is the very aggravation and irritation and humiliation that we can offer—every diminishment of every kind—so that by the grace of God we may be taught his loving lessons and be brought a little nearer to his loving purpose for us and thus be enlarged.

Somehow it's easy to understand the principle of control and denial and loss in the matter of *self*-discipline. It is perfectly plain to anyone who wants to do a difficult and worthwhile thing that he's got to deny himself a thousand unimportant and probably a few hundred important things in order to do the one thing that matters most. Bishop Stephen Neill said that writing is almost entirely a matter of self-discipline. "You must make yourself write." I know. Alas. Sit yourself down, shut yourself up, restrict your enthusiasms, control your maunderings. Think. (Sir Joshua Reynolds wrote, "There is no expedient to which a man will not resort to avoid the real labor of thinking.") Diminishments. Then put things on paper—carefully. Then (and this is the part I resist most strenuously) rewrite. Cut things. Drop things you've spent hours on into the wastebasket.

I lay in bed, luxuriating in the physical bliss, cogitating on the spiritual perplexities. I could not explain why God would restore Lars' lost briefcase and not my New Testament. I could not fathom my friend's suffering or the "waste" of time. But God could. It's got something to do with that great principle of loss being the route to gain, or diminishments being the only way we can finally be enlarged, that is, conformed to the image of Christ.

"Who watched over the birth of the sea?"

The words from God's dialogue with Job came to mind as I listened to the throbbing of the ocean from my bed.

"Have you descended to the springs of the sea, or walked in the unfathomable deep?"

No, Lord, but you have. Nothing in those dark caverns is mysterious to you. Nor is anything in my life or my friend's life. I trust you with the unfathomables.

But you know I'll be back—with the usual question.

ON BRAZEN HEAVENS

Thomas Howard

For about a year now I have been witness to a drama that is all too familiar to us mortal men. Someone finds he has cancer; the medical treadmill begins, with its implacable log of defeat; hope is marshalled, begins the march, is rebuffed at every juncture, flags, rouses, flags again, and is finally quietly mustered out.

And meanwhile, because the people in the drama are Christian believers, everyone is dragged into the maelstrom that marks the place where our experience eddies into the sea of the Divine Will. The whole question of prayer gapes open.

The promises are raked over. And over and over. "Is the primary condition enough faith on our part?" "We must scour our own hearts to see that there is no stoppage there—of sin or of unbelief." "We must stand on the promise." "We must *claim* thus and such." "We must resist the Devil and his weapons of doubt."

And we leap at and pursue any and all reports and records of healings. "Look at what happened to so-and-so!" "Listen to this!" "I've just read this wonderful pamphlet." We know the Gospel accounts by heart. We agree that this work of healing did not cease with the apostolic age. We greet gladly the tales of healing that pour in from all quarters in the Church—no longer only from those groups that have traditionally "specialized" in healing, but from the big, old, classic bodies in Christendom—Rome, Anglicanism, Lutheranism, Presbyterianism, and so forth. "God is doing something in our day," we hear, and we grasp at it eagerly.

And meanwhile the surgery goes on its horrific way, and the radiation burns on, week after grim week; and suffering sets in, and the doctors hedge and dodge into the labyrinthine linoleum and stainless-steel bureaucracy of the hospital world, and our hearts sicken, and we try to avert our eyes from the black flag that is fluttering wildly on the horizon, mocking us.

And the questions come stealing over us: "Where is now their God?" "Where is the promise of his coming?" "He trusted in God that he would deliver him . . ." and so on. And we know that we are not the first human beings into whose teeth the Tempter and his ilk have flung those taunts.

We look for some light. We look for some help. Our prayers seem to be vanishing, like so many wisps, into the serene aether of the cosmos (or worse, into the plaster of the ceiling). We strain our ears for some word from the Mount of God. A whisper will do, we tell ourselves, since clearly no bolts or thunderings have been activated by our importunity (yes, we have tried that tactic, too: the "nonfaith" approach).

But only dead silence. Blank. Nothing. "But Lord, how are we supposed to know if we're on the right track at all if we don't get some confirmation from you—some corroboration—in *any* form, Lord—inner peace maybe, or some verse springing to life for us, or some token. Please let us have some recognizable attestation to what you have said in your Book." Nothing. Silence. Blank.

Perhaps at this point we try to think back over the experience of the people of God through the millennia. There has been a whole spectrum of experience for them: glorious deliverances, great victories, kingdoms toppled, widows receiving their dead back, men wandering about in sheepskins and goatskins—

"Men wandering about in sheepskins and goatskins? What went wrong there?"

"That's in the record of faith."

"But then surely something went wrong."

"No. It is part of the log of the faithful. That is a list of what happened to the people of faith. It is about how they proved God."

The whole spectrum of experience is there. The widow of Nain got her son back and other mothers didn't. Peter got out of prison and John the Baptist didn't. Elijah whirled up to heaven with fiery horses and Joseph ended in a coffin in Egypt. Paul healed other people, but was turned down on his own request for healing for himself.

A couple of items in the Gospels seem to me to suggest something for the particular situation described in this article, where deliverance did not, in fact, come, and where apparently the juggernaut of sheer nature went on its grim way with no intervention from Heaven.

One is the story of Lazarus and the other is the Emmaus account. You object immediately: "Ah, but in both those cases it turned out that the dead *were* raised." Well, perhaps there is something there for us nonetheless.

For a start, the people involved in those incidents were followers of Jesus, and they had seen him, presumably, heal dozens of people. Then these followers experienced the utter dashing of all their expectations and hopes by death. God did not, it seemed, act. He who had been declared the Living One and the Giver of Life seemed to have turned his back in this case. What went wrong? What did the household at Bethany *not* do that the Widow of Nain had done? How shall we align it all? Who rates and who doesn't? Whatever it is that we might have chosen to say to them in the days following their experience of death, we would have had to come to terms somehow with the bleak fact that God had done something for others that he had not done for them.

From the vantage point of two thousand years, we later believers can, of course, see that there was something wonderful in prospect, and that it emerged within a very few days in both cases. The stories make sense. They are almost better than they would have been if the deaths had not occurred. But of course this line would have been frosty comfort for Mary and Martha, or for the two en route to Emmaus, if we had insisted to them, "Well, surely God is up to something. We'll just have to wait."

And yet what else could we have said? Their experience at that point was of the utter finality of death, which had thrown everything they had expected into limbo. For them there was no walking and leaping and praising God. No embracing and ecstatic tears of reunion. Only the silence of shrouds and sepulchres, and then the turning back, not just to the flat routines of daily life, but to the miserable duel with the tedious voices pressing in upon their exhausted imaginations with "Right! *Now* where are you? Tell us about your faith now! What'd you do wrong?"

The point is that for *x* number of days, their experience was of defeat. For us, alas, the "*x* number of days" may be greatly multiplied. And it is small comfort to us to be told that the difference, then, between us and, say, Mary and Martha's experience of Lazarus' death, or of the two on the road to Emmaus, is only a quantitative difference. "They had to wait four days. You have to wait one, or five, or seventy years. What's the real difference?" That is like telling someone on the rack that his pain is only quantitatively different from mine with my hangnail. The quantity *is* the difference. But there is, perhaps, at least this much of help for us whose experience is that of Mary and Martha and the others, and not that of the widow of Nain and Jairus and that set: the experience of the faithful *has,* in

ON BRAZEN HEAVENS

fact, included the experience of utter death. That seems to be part of the pattern, and it would be hard indeed to insist that the death was attributable to some failure of faith on somebody's part.

There is also this to be observed: that it sometimes seems that those on the higher reaches of faith are asked to experience this "absence" of God. For instance, Jesus seemed ready enough to show his authority to chance bystanders, and to the multitudes; but look at his own circle. John the Baptist wasn't let off—he had his head chopped off. James was killed in prison. And the Virgin herself had to go through the horror of seeing her Son tortured. No legions of angels intervened there. There was also Job, of course. And St. Paul—he had some sort of healing ministry himself, so that handkerchiefs were sent out from him with apparently healing efficacy for *others,* but, irony of ironies, his own prayer for *himself* was "unanswered." He had to slog through life with whatever his "thorn" was. What do these data do to our categories?

But there is more. Turning again to the disclosure of God in Scripture, we seem to see that, in his economy, there is no slippage. Nothing simply disappears. No sparrow falls without his knowing (and, one might think, caring) about it. No hair on anybody's head is without its number. Oh, you say, that's only a metaphor; it's not literal. A metaphor of *what,* then, we might ask. Is the implication there that God *doesn't* keep tabs on things?

And so we begin to think about all our prayers and vigils and fastings and abstinences, and the offices and sacraments of the Church, that have gone up to the throne in behalf of the sufferer. They have vanished, as no sparrow, no hair, has ever done. Hey, what about that?

And we know that this is false. It is nonsense. All right then—we prayed, with much faith or with little; we searched ourselves; we fasted; we anointed and laid on hands; we kept vigil. And nothing happened.

Did it not? What angle of vision are we speaking from? Is it not true that again and again in the biblical picture of things, the story has to be allowed to *finish*?

Was it not the case with Lazarus' household at Bethany, and with the two en route to Emmaus? And is it not the case with the Whole Story, actually—that it must be allowed to finish, and that this is precisely what the faithful have been watching for since the beginning of time? In the face of suffering and endurance and loss and waiting and death, what is it that has kept the spirits of the faithful from flagging utterly down through the millennia? Is it not the hope of Redemption? Is it not the great Finish to the Story—and to all their little stories of wandering about in sheepskins and goatskins as well as to the One Big Story of the whole creation, which is itself groaning and waiting? And is not that Finish called glorious? Does it not entail what amounts to a redoing of all that has gone wrong, and a remaking of all that is ruined, and a finding of all that has been lost in the shuffle, and an unfolding of it all in a blaze of joy and splendor?

A finding of all that is lost? All sparrows, and all petitions and tears and vigils and fastings? Yes, all petitions and tears and vigils and fastings.

"But where *are* they? The thing is over and done with. He is dead. They had no effect."

Hadn't they? How do you know what is piling up in the great treasury kept by the Divine Love to be opened in that Day? How do you know that this death *and* your prayers and tears and fasts will not *together* be suddenly and breathtakingly displayed, before all the faithful, and before angels and archangels, and before kings and widows and prophets, as gems in that display? Oh no, don't speak of things being lost. Say rather that they are hidden—received and accepted and taken up into the secrets of the divine mysteries, to be transformed and multiplied, like everything else we offer to him—loaves and fishes, or mites, or bread and wine—and given back to you and to the one for whom

ON BRAZEN HEAVENS

you kept vigil, in the presence of the whole host of men and angels, in a hilarity of glory as unimaginable to you in your vigil as golden wings are to the worm in the chrysalis.

But how does it *work?* We may well ask. How *does* Redemption work?

Thomas Howard is a college professor, author of Christ the Tiger, Splendor in the Ordinary, *and other books.*

SINGLENESS
IS A GIFT

Nearly a hundred years ago a twenty-eight-year-old woman from a windy little village on the north coast of Ireland began her missionary work in India. Amy Carmichael was single, but on the very eve of her leaving the docks, an opportunity "which looked towards 'the other life' " was presented.

Amy, with the combined reticence of being a Victorian and being Irish, never said how or by whom this "opportunity" was presented. She spoke very little of matters of the heart. She was also a thoroughgoing Christian, with a soldier's determination to carry out her Commander's orders. Single life, she believed, was not only a part of those orders; it was also a gift.

She tried not to suggest in any way that her gift was superior. "Remember," she wrote, "our God did not say to me, 'I have something greater for you to do.' This life is not greater than the other, but it is different." It was simply God's call to her.

The oldest of seven children, she had been full of ideas to amuse, educate, inspire, and spiritually edify her brothers and sisters. One of these ideas was a family magazine called *Scraps*, beautifully handwritten, illustrated, and published monthly for

family and friends. Before Amy was twenty, one brother knew
the direction her life was taking. In a series of sketches for *Scraps*
he wrote:

> *Our eldest sister is the*
> *light of our life.*
> *She says that she will never*
> *be a wife.*

Amy took as her guide the ideal set forth by the apostle Paul:
"The unmarried (woman) concerns herself with the Lord's affairs,
and her aim is to make herself holy in body and in spirit. . . .
I am not putting difficulties in your path, but setting before you an
ideal, so that your service of God may be as far as possible free
from worldly distractions" (1 Corinthians 7:34, 35 PHILLIPS).

With all her heart she determined to please him who had
chosen her to be his soldier. She was awed by the privilege. She
accepted the disciplines.

"A Touch of Disappointment"

Loneliness was one of those disciplines. How—the modern
young person always wants to know—did she "handle" it? Amy
Carmichael would not have had the slightest idea what the
questioner was talking about. "Handle" loneliness? Why, it was
part of the cost of obedience, of course. Everybody is lonely in
some way, the single in one way, the married in another; the
missionary in certain obvious ways, the schoolteacher, the
mother, the bank teller in others.

Amy had a dear co-worker whom she nicknamed Twin. At a
missions conference they found that in the posted dinner lists,
Twin and a friend named Mina had been seated side by side.

"Well, I was very glad that dear Mina should have Twin,"
Amy wrote to her family, "and I don't think I grudged her to her

one little bit, and yet at the bottom of my heart there was just a touch of disappointment, for I had almost fancied I had somebody of my very own again, and there was a little ache somewhere. I could not *rejoice* in it . . . . I longed, yes *longed*, to be glad, to be filled with such a wealth of unselfish love that I should be far gladder to see those two together than I should have been to have had Twin to myself. And while I was asking for it, it came. For the very first time I felt a rush, a real joy in it, His joy, a thing one cannot pump up or imitate or force in any way. . . . Half-unconsciously, perhaps, I had been saying, 'Thou and Twin are enough for me'—one so soon clings to the gift instead of only to the Giver.''

Her letter then continued with a stanza from the Frances Ridley Havergal hymn:

> *Take my love, my Lord, I pour*
> *At Thy feet its treasure-store.*
> *Take myself and I will be*
> *Ever, only, all for thee.*

After writing this, Amy felt inclined to tear it out of the letter. It was too personal, too humiliating. But she decided the Lord wanted her to let it stand, to tell its tale of weakness and of God's strength. She was finding firsthand that missionaries are not apart from the rest of the human race, not purer, nobler, higher.

"Wings are an illusive fallacy," she wrote. "Some may possess them, but they are not very visible, and as for me, there isn't the least sign of a feather. Don't imagine that by crossing the sea and landing on a foreign shore and learning a foreign lingo you 'burst the bonds of outer sin and hatch yourself a cherubim.' ''

The Single "Mother"

Amy landed in India in 1897 and spent the first few years in itinerant evangelism. She began to uncover a secret traffic in little girls who were being sold or given for temple prostitution. She prayed that God would enable her find a way to rescue some of them, even though not one had ever been known to escape.

Several years later, God began to answer that prayer. One little girl actually escaped and came (led by an angel, Amy believed) straight to Amy. Then in various ways babies were rescued. Soon she found that little boys were being used for homosexual purposes by dramatic societies connected with Hindu temple worship. She prayed for the boys, and in a few years Amy Carmichael was *Amma* ("Mother") to a rapidly growing Indian family that, by the late 1940s, numbered about 900. In a specially literal way the words of Jesus seemed to have been fulfilled: "Everyone who has left houses or brothers or sisters or father or mother or children or fields for my sake will receive a hundred times as much and will inherit eternal life" (Matthew 19:29).

In answer to a question from one of her children who years later had become a close fellow worker, Amy described a transaction in a cave. She had gone there to spend the day with God and face her feelings of fear about the future. Things were all right at the moment, but could she endure years of being alone?

The Devil painted pictures of loneliness that were vivid to her years later. She turned to the Lord in desperation. "What can I do, Lord? How can I go on to the end?"

His answer: "None of them that trust in me shall be desolate" (from Psalms 34:22 KJV). So she did not "handle" loneliness— she handed it to her Lord and trusted his Word.

"There is a secret discipline appointed for every man and woman whose life is lived for others," she wrote. "No one escapes that discipline, nor would wish to escape it; nor can any shelter another from it. And just as we have seen the bud of a flower close round the treasure within, folding its secret up, petal by petal, so we have seen the soul that is chosen to serve, fold

31

round its secret and hold it fast and cover it from the eyes of man. The petals of the soul are silence.''

Her commitment to obedience was unconditional. Finding that singleness was the condition her Master had appointed for her, she received it with both hands, willing to renounce all rights for his sake and, although she could not have imagined it at the time, for the sake of the children he would give her—a job she could not possibly have done if she had had a family of her own.

Many whose houses, for one reason or another, seem empty, and the lessons of solitude hard to learn, have found strength and comfort in the following Amy Carmichael poem:

> *O Prince of Glory, who dost bring*
> *Thy sons to glory through Thy Cross,*
> *Let me not shrink from suffering,*
> *Reproach or loss . . . .*
>
> *If Thy dear Home be fuller, Lord,*
> *For that a little emptier*
> *My house on earth, what rich reward*
> *That guerdon* were.*

*recompense; something earned or gained

A LOOK
IN THE MIRROR

Most of us are rather pleased when we catch sight of ourselves (provided the sight is sufficiently dim or distant) in the reflection of a store window. It is always amusing to watch people's expressions and postures change, perhaps ever so slightly, for the better as they look at their images. We all want the reflected image to match the image we hold in our minds (e.g. a rugged, casual slouch goes well with a Marlboro Country type; an erect, distinguished carriage befits a man of command and responsibility). We glimpse ourselves in a moment of lapse, and quickly try to correct the discrepancies.

A close-up is something else altogether. Sometimes it's more than we can stand. The shock of recognition makes us recoil. "Don't tell me that's *my* voice!" (on the tape recorder); "Do I really look *that* old?" (as this photograph cruelly shows). For me it is a horrifyingly painful experience to have to stand before a three-way mirror, in strong light, in a department-store fitting room. ("These lights—these mirrors—they distort, surely!" I tell myself.) I have seen Latin American Indians whoop with laughter upon first seeing themselves on a movie screen, but I have never seen them indignant, as "civilized" people often seem to be. Perhaps it is that an Indian has not occupied himself very much with trying to be what he is not.

What is it that makes us preen, recoil, laugh? It must be the degree of incongruity between what we thought we were and what we actually saw.

People's standards, of course, differ. Usually, in things that do not matter, we set them impossibly high and thus guarantee for ourselves a life of discontent. In things that matter we set them too low and are easily pleased with ourselves. (My daughter came home from the seventh grade one day elated. "Missed the honor roll by two C's!" she cried, waving her report card happily.) Frequently we judge by standards that are irrelevant to the thing in question. You have to know what a thing is for, first of all, before you can judge it at all. Take a can opener—how can I know whether it's any good unless I know that it was made for opening cans?

Or a church. What is it for? Recently the one I belong to held a series of neighborhood coffee meetings for the purpose of finding out what the parishioners thought about what the church was doing, was not doing, and ought to be doing. The results were mailed to us. Eighty people participated and came up with one hundred and five "concerns and recommendations." These revealed considerable confusion as to what the church is meant to be about. "Should have hockey and basketball teams." "There is too much reference to the Bible in sermons." "The ushers should stop hunching at the doors of the church and seek out unfamiliar faces." "The rear parking lot is messy." "A reexamination of spirtual goals should be carried out." I was glad there were a few like that last one. The range of our congregational sins was pretty well covered (we didn't get into the mire of our personal ones), and as I read them over I thought, If we just managed to straighten out these one hundred and five things we'd have—what? Well, something, I suppose. But not a perfect church. Not by a long shot. If by our poor standards (some of them obviously applicable to things other than churches) we picked out over a hundred flaws, how many were visible to God, "to whose all-searching sight the darkness shineth as the light"?

There are times when it is with a kind of relief that we come upon the truth. A man passing a church one day paused to see if he could catch what it was the people were mumbling in unison. He moved inside and heard the words:"We have erred and strayed from thy ways like lost sheep. We have followed too much the devices and desires of our own hearts. We have offended against thy holy laws."

"Hmm," thought the man, "they sound like my kind of people."

"We have left undone those things which we ought to have done, and we have done those things which we ought not to have done."

"This is the church for me," he decided. (I don't suppose a basketball team or a blacktopped parking lot would have persuaded him.)

"Put up a complaint box and you'll get complaints," my husband says. There is something to be said for airing one's grievances, and there is a great deal to be said for not airing them, but one thing at least seems good to me—that we be overwhelmed, now and then, with our sins and failures.

We need to sit down and take stock. We need mirrors and neighborhood coffees and complaint boxes, but our first reaction may be despair. Our second, "Just who does so-and-so think he is, criticizing the church when he never even comes to church?" And we find ourselves back where we started, setting our own standards, judging irrelevantly and falsely, excusing ourselves, condemning an institution for not being what it was never meant to be, and so on.

Then there is Lent. It is a time to stop and remember. All year we have had the chance in the regular communion service to remember the death and passion of the Lord Jesus, and this once during the year we are asked, for a period of six weeks, to recall ourselves, to repent, to submit to special disciplines in order that we may understand the meaning of the Resurrection.

We are indeed "miserable offenders." We have done and left undone. We are foolish and weak and blind and self-willed and men of little faith. We run here, we run there, we form committees and attend meetings and attack the church and its organization and its isolation and its useless machinery and its irrelevance and ineffectiveness. But all the time it stands there, holding the Cross, telling us that there is forgiveness, that we have not been left to ourselves, that no matter how shocking the image that we finally see of ourselves in the light of God's truth, God himself has done something about it all.

"He was wounded for our transgressions. He was bruised for our iniquities." For the very things we've been discussing. For the things that make us moan and groan and ask, "What's the use?"

And so Lent, simply because it is another reminder of him who calls us to forgiveness and refreshment, makes me glad.

HAPPY BIRTHDAY—
YOU'RE HEADING HOME!

The cards on the racks simply won't fill the bill. I wander disconsolately past the "Relative," "Comic," and other categories of birthday cards, even a rack labeled, "These cards are outrageous. Prepare for shock!" What I want to wish on your birthday is not the sort of happiness that depends on the denial of the passing years, or on your undiminished power to get ever bigger and better thrills out of tall bottles or other people's beds. The cartoons are crazy. In fact, they're horrifying, in that they show what a dead-end street the desperate search for happiness usually is. The only cards that suggest the possibility of any other kind of happiness make such exaggerated claims for my feelings for you, in such soupy, mawkish language, and with such wispy or misty illustrations—no, I'm sorry, I can't bring myself to buy them.

What I want to wish you today is joy. I want you to have the happiest birthday ever. Not because you're just exactly the age you've always dreamed of being: the perfect age. Not because you'll be having the splashiest, roaringest party ever, or because you're surrounded by all your favorite fans, feeling marvelous, getting a vast pile of gorgeous gifts. I could merely wish you a happy birthday, but I'll do more than that. I'll turn my wish into prayer, and ask the Lord to give you the happiest birthday ever. I'll ask him for the kind of joy that isn't dependent on how you feel or who's there to celebrate or what's happening.

The people who write those awful cards are doing the best they can, but they haven't much to fall back on. Best to try to forget the hard facts: time *is* passing, people *are* actually growing old, happiness *is* pretty hard to come by in this old world. What is there to fall back on? Can't do a thing about the facts. The misery and loneliness and disintegration and horror are there (Edna St. Vincent Millay put it bluntly: "Death beating the door in"), but who wants to put things like that into a birthday card? Isn't it good enough to settle for cute comics, sweet sentiments, and just have fun? We can at least pretend we're happy. Forget the truth for a day. It's your birthday, and by George, we're gonna *frolic!*

That's one way to do it, but why frolic for all the wrong reasons? I love celebrations and gifts, a little dinner by candlelight in a quiet place with loved friends is my idea of a happy evening. But it's specially nice to have somebody remind me of something even happier than the bouquets, the balloons, and the bubbly, something that will last out the day, the week, even the coming year, if there is any such thing. There is, you know. Here's joy:

> *The wretched and the poor look for water*
> *and find none,*
> *their tongues are parched with thirst;*
> *but I the Lord will give them an answer,*
> *I the God of Israel will not forsake them.*
> *I will open rivers among the sand-dunes*
> *and wells in the valleys;*

HAPPY BIRTHDAY—YOU'RE HEADING HOME!

> *I will turn the wilderness into pools*
> *and dry land into springs of water;*
> *I will plant cedars in the wastes,*
> *and acacia and myrtle and wild olive*
> *the pine shall grow on the barren heath.*

> *Isaiah 41:17–19* NEB

A birthday is a milestone. It's a place to pause. Look back now for a minute over the way the Lord has brought you. There has been thirst, hasn't there? You've been over some sand dunes, through some valleys, some wilderness, out on a barren heath once in a while. I have too. Sometimes it seemed that there weren't any rivers, wells, pools, or springs. Nothing but sand. No lovely acacias or wild olives, only barrenness. The trouble was I hadn't learned to find them. I was trying to travel alone. I made the same mistake when I first went to live as a missionary in the South American jungle. After one bad experience of getting lost, I learned to follow an Indian guide. He knew the trails. He could find water to drink (inside a bamboo, for example, if there wasn't a river handy), honey in a hollow tree, fruit where there seemed to be no fruit. I couldn't see them. I didn't know where to look. The Indian did. He could make a cup out of a palm leaf, build a fire in the rain, construct a shelter for the night in an hour or so. I was helpless. He was my helper.

A milestone is not only a place to look back to where you've come from. It's a place to look forward to where you're going. We don't always want to do that on birthdays. If we look back it seems such a long time, the good old days are over, and (here's the hard part) so much guilt clogs the memories. If we look forward—alas. How many more birthdays? What will happen before the next one? Thoughts of the future are full of fear.

*I the Lord your God
take you by the right hand;
I say to you, Do not fear;
It is I who help you.*

Isaiah 41:13 NEB

Parties and presents won't do much for a checkered past or a frightening future. Only the God who was loving you then, loves you today on your birthday, and will keep right on loving you till you see him face-to-face, can possibly do anything about them. "It is I who help you," he says. There is help for all the guilt. Confess it in full. He'll forgive it in full. And I mean *forgive.* That doesn't mean he denies its reality, sweeps it under the rug, or bathes it in sentiment. There was once an old rugged cross. You know where it was—on a hill far away. And you know what it means—nothing sentimental at all, but forgiveness, freely offered to all of us, the whole price paid in blood by the Dearest and Best.

There is help for your fear too. Express it in full. Let the Lord take you by your right hand and help you. I had to do that with my Indian guide. I simply could not make it across those slippery log bridges, laid high over jungle ravines, without help. I was scared to death. The Indian, who had been over them many more times than I had, held me by the hand.

You've heard those bad news/good news jokes. Well, this isn't cheap birthday card humor. The bad news is that another year has gone by and we haven't done all we meant to do and it's not going to come back to give us another chance. The good news is the Gospel. We can be reconciled to God—sins forgiven, fears taken care of. That old cross, the emblem of suffering and shame, stands between us and our sins and fears, our past and future, and on its outstretched arms we see Love. The Love that would die for us is the Love that lives for us—Jesus Christ, Lord, Master, Savior of the World, wanting to give you (for your birthday if you'll take it) something that will really quench your thirst, rivers among the sand dunes and wells in the valley; wanting to hold your hand, help you, give you—not only a happy birthday, but everlasting joy.

I'm not the least bit bashful about telling my age. I'm glad for every birthday that comes, because it is the Lord, my faithful Guide, who "summoned the generations from the beginning." I look in the mirror and see the increasingly (and creasingly) visible proofs of the number of years, but I'm reconciled. Christ reconciles me to God and to God's wonderful plan. My life is his life. My years are his years. To me life *is* Christ, and death is nothing but gain. When I remember that, I really can't think of a thing I ought to be afraid of. I can't be sorry I'm a year older and nearer to absolute bliss.

I pray for you on your birthday, that your path, as is promised to the just man, will shine not less and less but more and more; that you will still bring forth fruit in old age; that the Lord will give you a thankful heart like the psalmist's who sang,

> *O God, thou hast taught me from boyhood,*
> *all my life I have proclaimed thy marvellous works:*
> *and now that I am old and my hairs are gray,*
> > *forsake me not, O God. . . .*
> *Songs of joy shall be on my lips;*
> *I will sing thee psalms, because*
> > *thou has redeemed me.*
> *All day long my tongue shall tell*
> > *of thy righteousness.*

Psalms 71:17, 18, 23, 24 NEB

So—happy birthday! If you have friends and parties and presents, be thankful for such bonuses. If you have no friends with you today, no party, not a package to open, you still have a long list of things to thank God for, things that matter much more. A birthday filled with thanksgiving and hope is the happiest kind of birthday. Have one of those! Deck yourself with joy!

I WON'T BOTHER
WITH A FACE-LIFT

Because tomorrow I will begin the last of threescore years, and because my mother is now closer to ninety than to eighty, I do a lot of thinking about old age. Has any of my friends called me "spry" yet, or remarked, "She's amazing—still got all her faculties"?

If they have, of course, it means they see me as over the hill, i.e., *old*. When I look in the mirror, I have to admit the evidence is all on their side, but otherwise it's hard to remember. I *feel* as "spry" and energetic as I did twoscore years ago.

I don't mind getting old. Before the day began this morning I was looking out at starlight on a still, wintry sea. A little song we used to sing at camp came to mind—"Just one day nearer Home." That idea thrills me. I can understand why people who have nothing much to look forward to try frantically and futilely to hang on to the past—to youth and all that. Get a face-lift, plaster the makeup on ever more thickly (but Estee Lauder says false eyelashes can add ten years to your looks), wear running shoes and sweat suits, dye your hair—anything to create the illusion you're *young*. (The illusion is yours, of course, nobody else's.)

Let's be honest. Old age entails suffering. I'm acutely aware of this now as I watch my mother, once so alive and alert and quick, now so quiet and confused and slow. She suffers. We who love her suffer. We see the "preview of coming attractions," ourselves in her shoes, and ponder what this interval means in terms of the glory of God in an old woman.

It would be terrifying if it weren't for something that ought to make the Christian's attitude toward aging utterly distinct from all the rest. *We know it is not for nothing.* "God has allowed us to know the secret of his plan: he purposes in his sovereign will that all human history shall be consummated in Christ, that everything that exists in Heaven or earth shall find its perfection and fulfillment in him" (Ephesians 1:9, 10 PHILLIPS).

In the meantime, we look at what's happening—limitations of hearing, seeing, moving, digesting, remembering; distortions of countenance, figure, and perspective. If that's all we could see, we'd certainly want a face-lift or something.

But we're on a pilgrim road. It's rough and steep, and it winds uphill to the very end. We can lift up our eyes and see the unseen: a Celestial City, a light, a welcome, and an ineffable Face. We shall behold him. We shall be like him. And that makes a difference in how we go about aging.

WHY FUNERALS MATTER

When a dear friend died recently I found myself unexplainably disappointed when I learned that there would be only a memorial service. I wanted a funeral, and I was not sure why. Even more unexplainably, I wished there had been a "viewing" or wake—a chance to see her face. Is this wholly indefensible? I am sure that it is wholly human, but is it mere idle curiosity? Is it crass, or childish, or pagan, or materialistic? Is it hideously ghoulish?

"Christians do not need to make much of the body. We believe in the Resurrection. We know the person is not here but There." Thus I argued with myself.

"Who wants to see somebody dead? Wouldn't you rather remember him as you knew him, strong and healthy and alive?" That makes sense too.

"Funerals are meaningless ordeals, pompous, expensive, emotionally costly, and serve no purpose other than conventional and commercial. And as for viewings—what can possibly be the point of coiffing, painting, powdering, and dressing up a corpse, stretching it out lugubriousy in a satin-lined mahogany box with its head on a fancy pillow, for people to stare at?" What indeed?

I could not come up with immediate rejoinders. There did not seem much logic in my protest. Didn't it spring from emotions alone, and those perhaps crude and primeval? Yes, very likely. But crude and primeval emotions may be eminently human and not necessarily sinful. They may even be useful. How do we know? Well, back to the Bible. What does it say?

The Bible does not say "Thou shalt have funerals," or "Thou shalt not have memorial services."

When Jacob died there was the final scene in which he blessed each of his sons, then drew up his feet into the bed, breathed his last, and was "gathered to his people." Then Joseph threw himself on his father's body and wept over him and kissed him and commanded that he be embalmed. The Egyptians went through the customary seventy days of mourning. Then Joseph carried the body to Canaan, accompanied by a huge retinue of servants, elders, relatives, friends, chariots, and horsemen. Seven more days were spent in "a very great and sorrowful lamentation."

When Moses died God buried him, but the people of Israel wept for him thirty days. Joseph's bones were carried by the people of Egypt to be buried at Shechem.

Stephen was the first martyr, stoned to death, and it says "devout men buried Stephen and made great lamentation over him." It was right and proper that a man killed for his Christian witness should be buried by those who shared his faith—devout men. It was right and proper that they should grieve greatly, that they should grieve together, and that they should grieve "over him," which I take to mean literally over the grave.

Only last week my friend Van found her little black dog which had been lost ten days before. But she was dead—drowned in a pond where she had apparently fallen through the ice. Little Nell was Van's friend, and Van grieved for her, but she thanked God she found her and knew at last what had become of her. She lifted the wet furry thing in her arms and looked into her face and talked to her. Then, of course, giving her back to death, she buried her.

That was what we had been deprived of in my late friend's decision not to have a funeral. The memorial service was held eleven days after her death, and when we entered the church there was nothing of her there. It would only have been a body, of course—but it would have been the "earthly house of this tabernacle" in which our friend had lived, through which we had known her, and it would have been the resurrectible body. It was long since deposited miles away in a mausoleum. We could not see her face. We could not even see a closed box with the knowledge that what was left of her was inside it. She had died of that most feared of diseases and no doubt its ravages were great. She had not wanted any of us to come near her during the last four or five weeks of her life. We understood her feeling. It is doubtful that she was in a position to understand ours. It was too late. I write this so that thoughtful people can consider the matter before it is too late.

We longed for the privilege of entering into her suffering insofar as it would have been possible. She was too ill to talk. We understood that. We would not have asked her to. If we had been allowed only to slip into the room for a minute, hold her hand, pray briefly or be silent, we would have been grateful. Perhaps a little of the loneliness of dying would have been assuaged for her, and a little of our sorrow and love communicated. I am sure that we, at least, would have been helped. But it was not to be. Even after she died, we to whom she had meant so much needed to establish a last link. That, too, was denied.

Several months ago a friend from New York wrote of the death of a child she had been close to. "I have mixed feelings about private funerals. Does that seem harsh to you? I so badly wanted to be with them in their grief, and I think a lot of others felt the same way. It was almost more than I could do, having an errand at the church, to walk past the hearse and out of sight before the family arrived. There will be a memorial service, but not for several weeks. I guess I am very old-fashioned or something. It is not a morbid hankering to 'view' the body, but the sight of a coffin brings home the reality and gives an outlet for grief, in my experience, as nothing else can.''

Yes, my heart said, she is right. Now, after many years, I have sorted out why it mattered to me that we had only a memorial service for my first husband and real funeral for the second. In the first case, we had no choice. He was murdered, and the body was not found for five days. It was deep in uninhabited jungle from which transportation would have been nearly impossible. My second husband knew he was going to die, and we had time to discuss the funeral together. I don't remember his saying anything about a viewing, but I made that decision without difficulty as soon as he died. I knew that I had missed something when Jim died. Add had been beaten down by cancer and the last weeks were horrifying. Somehow it was a relief to see his face one more time in a different setting from his sickroom. The face was thin and aged and pallid, of course, but this time free from pain. The strength of the features was still there, the brow, as somebody observed, still noble. I could say good-bye to him then in my heart and resign him to the grave.

When I was nine years old, my best and almost my only friend died. I remember the hot July day when I was playing in the side yard and my mother came out to tell me that Essie had gone. I remember my parents driving me up Broad Street in Philadelphia to the funeral parlor where she lay in a white dress with her golden curls around her face. She was nine years old too.

Nobody said to me, "But it's only a body. The spirit has flown, you know." Nobody needed to. I could see that. But I could also see my friend who had led me on many a wild chase through vacant lots and back alleys and had scared the wits out of me with terrible tales of giants she had run across. She was very quiet now, very subdued. My playmate was dead. The sight was very real to me. It was not a shock. Children are not shocked at things. It is their elders who cannot face reality. I was awed and solemn, and I thought about it for years afterward. It was a very wise decision of my parents to take me to the funeral.

I appeal to Christians. Plan your funeral now. If you are "getting on in years" it may be possible even to choose the minister and discuss things with him. If death seems more remote, at least write down the fact that you want a funeral, and choose hymns and Scripture passages to be used. Don't be too dogmatic about the practical arrangements. Leave those to whoever is responsible for disposing of you, so that it will be easiest for them.

But please remember your friends. They are the people to whom it will matter greatly to be allowed to bid you farewell, and to grieve in company with others who love you. Don't make light of that.

C. S. Lewis, that wise man who seems to have thought *through* almost everything, writes in his *Preface to Paradise Lost:* "Those who dislike ritual in general—ritual in any way and every department of life—may be asked most earnestly to reconsider the question. It is a pattern imposed on the mere flux of our feelings by reason and will, which renders pleasures less fugitive and griefs more endurable, which hands over to the power of wise custom the task (to which the individual and his moods are so inadequate) of being festive or sober, gay or reverent, when we choose to be, and not at the bidding of chance" (Oxford University Press, 1952, p. 21).

If it is a Christian funeral, we will be reminded in word and hymn that we do not "grieve like the rest of men, who have no hope. We believe that Jesus died and rose again; and so it will be for those who died as Christians; God will bring them to life with Jesus," and "we who are left alive shall join them, caught up in clouds to meet the Lord in the air" (1 Thessalonians 4:13, 14, 17 NEB). Let funerals be, then, for Christians, celebrations in the presence of the mortal remains, visible signs of those glorious invisible realities which we believe with all our hearts.

HOPE FOR A
HOPELESS FAILURE

Olive trees are not much good for leaning against. Too knobby. I kick away a few stones and sit down on the ground, knees braced in my arms. The other two stand for a while, eyeing the one who has gone off alone.

"Might as well sit down," I say. They don't answer.

Long day. Tired. I look up through the trees. Ragged clouds, thin moon. Enough wind to move the olive leaves. My head's too heavy to hold up. I stare at my old sandals, one of them with a loose thong. Then I notice my feet and remember—at supper—"altogether clean." Dusty again now, but they were clean, all right. Never had them so clean. "Do you understand what I have done for you?" he asked. Maybe the rest understood. Not me. And what was all that about being *slaves?*

My two friends sit down a little way off. Can't hear much of the conversation (they're almost whispering). His body. His blood. (Strange things he said to us tonight at the table.) How he longed to eat with us, but would never do it again—until . . . something about a *kingdom.*

Yawn. Too tired to think now. I push away a few more stones

51

and lie down in the grass. No pillow. Well, my arm will have to do.

What do I hear? Not my friends—they're flat out on the ground now, like me. Some movement. Wind? An animal? No, over *there*, where *he* is. A sort of gasp, was it? I strain my ears. Can't tell. Maybe they can, they're nearer, but they don't say anything. Silence now. Never mind. Have a little snooze.

"Asleep, Simon?" I jump. He did ask us to stay awake, now that I think of it. He's standing over us and here we all are, snoring away. Poor show. "Pray that you may be spared the test." Yes, Lord. (Test?)

He goes off again. We sit up, shake ourselves. (It's colder now, my tunic's clammy with dew.) We pray. We can see, from the silhouette over by the rock, that something is very wrong. Wonder if we should do something? But he said stay here.

"You will all fall from your faith." We talk about that. What could he mean? *All* of us? The other two lie down. I sit here, thinking of what he said to me—about Satan, sifting me like wheat. He said he prayed especially for me. My faith fail? I told him I'd even go to prison with him. Die, if it came to that. Judas now—that's another story. Wonder what he's up to? Left the table in an awful hurry. Never did trust him. Shifty-eyed. Slick.

Ah-oh. Must have fallen asleep again. I can sense his presence, standing close, but I'll keep my eyes shut. What can I say? I wait. He says nothing, goes away.

"You awake?" I poke the others. I remember he told me I was to "lend strength to the brothers." They pull themselves up, and again we talk. He said he was going away. Somewhere where we could not come. Peace . . . love . . . the Prince of this world . . . persecution . . . the breakdown of faith. Doesn't sound good.

"What's that?" (I'm the one who's whispering now.) A soft noise—like wings. There's somebody there, bending over him in the moonlight. We peer through the trees. Can't tell who it is. It's not good, his being here in this garden. Too many people know they can find him here. What! Whoever was there has—why, vanished! Just like that! He is standing now, his face lifted up.

"That's the third time he's prayed the same prayer," my friend says. I didn't hear it.

We keep talking, trying to stay awake this time. He needs me, I guess. We'd better be on our toes. Not sure what's going on. Is he in danger? But he doesn't seem to know fear. Has his own ways of getting out of trouble when he wants to—remember the time he slipped through the crowd that was about to dump him over the precipice? Yes, but we told him this time he ought not to come up to the city. Bad timing.

What about what he said about our needing purse, pack, and sword now, after sending us out *barefoot*, without a *coin* or a *crust*, the first time? Said he had a good many other things he couldn't tell us now, but would send a spirit—Spirit of Truth, that was it—who would explain things that were going to happen.

Hours go by. We lose track of how long we talk. Yawn, relax.

"Still sleeping? Up, let's go forward." On our feet like a shot. What's happening? "My betrayer is upon us." Mob surging through the garden. Lanterns, torches, swords, cudgels.

"Master! Here, quickly, get behind. . . ." He doesn't hear me. Walks straight up to them. "What is it you want?" I grab my sword, swing it at one of the gang, only get his ear.

"Put up your sword," he tells me. "This is the cup the father has given me. Don't you realize I must drink it?"

What could we do? I follow him partway, but I can see it's all over. No point getting involved.

Years have passed now. The memory of what happened during the rest of that night is still sharp. A very dark night it was. But could I know what I know now, could I write things I write in my letters, if it had not happened?

Praise be to the God and Father of our Lord Jesus Christ, who in his great mercy gave us new birth into a living hope by the resurrection of Jesus Christ from the dead! The inheritance to which we are born is one that nothing can destroy or spoil or wither. It is kept for you in heaven, and you, because you put your faith in God, are under the protection of his power . . . (1 Peter 1:3–5 NEB).

I know that mercy. I've been given that new birth. A hopeless failure, I know that living hope. No one deserved them less than I. No one can be more grateful than I, to whom so much was forgiven. Where would I be if he had not risen?

O LITTLE TOWN OF NAZARETH

There is a town in Galilee called Nazareth. Years ago I passed through it very briefly at about noon on a chilly day in November. It seemed a dull place on the surface, but far from dull to me as I thought of the stunning happening in one of its dull little houses one day nearly two millennia ago. The written account is excessively spare.

"The angel Gabriel was sent from God to a town in Galilee called Nazareth." A simple declarative sentence. Nothing superfluous, no superlatives. No lights, no sound effects, no advance publicity of coming attractions. An angel made a journey—think of it—"from God to a town." The fact is put (for us anyway) in words of one syllable.

Who was this angel? Not just any angel, but one with a name: Gabriel. We have met him before. About five hundred years earlier, in the first year of the reign of Darius, King of the Chaldeans, Gabriel had been sent to a man named Daniel. The divine Author of Scripture, who is also the divine Commissioner, pinpointed the precise place, the specific man, the exact era of human history and, most incredibly, the time of day. Daniel was praying, at the hour of evening sacrifice, when Gabriel came close to him, "flying swiftly."

How swiftly? Amy Carmichael, later to become a renowned missionary to India and author of dozens of books, recorded a conversation she had in 1887 with the Reverend James Gall, who imagined Gabriel's journey earthwards as taking

perhaps six, certainly not more than ten hours. In the first hour he would have left behind him the firmament of his native world, and entered the great wilderness of the universe, where no single star was visible, and where the black vault above, beneath, around was sprinkled only with its distant nebulae. He is alone with God, and, probably, in the solemn silence of his solitary flight, is receiving upon his inmost spirit the prophetic message that he was to bear to earth.

For hours together the same dread grandeur of nebulous scenery would continue, and yet the inconceivable swiftness of his progess would produce, as it were, a moving panorama around him.

To the close of his voyage, his course is directed to one particular nebula. It is our Milky Way, although as yet, it is no more than a mere speck in the distant night. Having entered the firmament of the Milky Way his eye is now directed to a feeble undistinguished star, upon which all his interest is concentrated. On he flies, passing Sirius, brighter than all beside, Orion, with his cloudy sword, the Pleiades, that vast system of congregated suns around which our own appears to be revolving, the Southern Cross, Neptune, Uranus, Saturn, Jupiter, Mars—on and on swifter than the light flies the "Pilgrim Angel" till at last he lays his hand upon the prostrate Daniel. It is the time of the evening oblations.

Mere speculation? But then, what was his route, if not on this wise? "But angels are ministering *spirits,*" you say, "they need not travel physically, as we do." Perhaps not. But at some point Gabriel had to become aware of the physical. Was it when he entered the universe, or only when he entered the poor stone house? Such was his journey, I believe, to our planet when he was assigned to go to Nazareth. Unerringly he found the little dull town, the dusty street, the right house. In obedience he went in, stood before the astonished girl, and spoke—*in her own language.* "Greetings, most favored one! The Lord is with you." She is "deeply troubled." She wonders what this strange greeting means. The angel looks into her face, understands what is in her heart, and—can we try to imagine the sound of his voice? An angel's voice, speaking in the accents of Nazareth, speaking quietly, I suppose, for Mary's parents were no doubt nearby. Surely he speaks also tenderly to the frightened girl. "Do not be afraid, Mary [he knows her *name!*], for God has been gracious to you; you shall conceive and bear a son, and you shall give him the name Jesus . . . Son of the Most High . . . King over Israel forever . . . Son of God. God's promises can never fail."

Mary was not a feeble girl, weak and without spunk, imagination, or initiative. Subsequent action proves that. But she was meek. Never confuse weak with meek. She was meek as Moses was meek—strong enough and holy enough to recognize her place under God. Thoughts of what people would say, what Joseph her fiance would say, or how she would ever convince them that she had not been unfaithful were instantly set aside. "Here I am, the Lord's handmaid," she said. "I will accept whatever he gives me."

Mission accomplished. The angel left her, the account says. Back he flies, past Mars, Jupiter, Saturn, Uranus, beyond the Southern Cross and the Milky Way into the black vault which Mr. Gall conceived as starless, and finally to the firmament of his native world where the will of the God of all those heavens and firmaments is always done, and always done perfectly.

Gabriel, too, had obeyed. He delivered the message. He brought back a message: on that planet, in Galilee, in a town called Nazareth, in the house to which God had sent him, the girl named Mary had said yes.

I cannot tell why He whom angels worship
should set His love upon the sons of men. . . .
But this I know: that He was born of Mary.

W. Y. Fullerton, *Keswick Hymnal*
Marshall, Morgan, and Scott

A NO-RISK
LIFE

The risks people are prepared to take these days are certainly a different set from what they used to be. I have been reading what Dickens and Kipling said about travel in their times. The reason I have been reading Dickens and Kipling just now when I am also trying to catch up with Solzhenitsyn and C. S. Lewis (I never catch up with Lewis—I have to start over as soon as I've finished one of his books because while I am always completely convinced by his argument I find I can't reproduce it for somebody else so I have to go back) is that a friend asked me to take care of some books she had just inherited from a rich aunt.

But it was risks I started out to write about. Dickens describes a journey into the Scottish Highlands:

> When we got safely to the opposite bank, there came riding up a wild highlander, his great plaid streaming in the wind, screech-ing in Gaelic to the post-boy on the opposite bank, making the most frantic gestures. . . . The boy, horses and carriage were plunging in the water, which left only the horses' heads and boy's body visible. . . . The man was perfectly frantic with panto-mime. . . . The carriage went round and round like a great stone,

the boy was pale as death, the horses were struggling and plashing and snorting like sea animals, and we were all roaring to the driver to throw himself off and let them and the coach go to the devil, when suddenly it all came right (having got into shallow water) and, all tumbling and dripping and jogging from side to side, they climbed up to the dry land.

Kipling, in a speech made more than sixty years ago to the Royal Geographic Society, looks forward to the possibilities of air travel:

> Presently—very presently—we shall come back and convert two hundred miles across any part of the Earth into its standardized time equivalent, precisely as we convert five miles with infantry in column, ten with cavalry on the march, twelve in a Cape cart [which I found is a strong, two-wheeled carriage used in South Africa], or fifty in a car—that is to say, into two hours. And whether there be one desert or a dozen mountain ranges in that two hundred miles will not affect our timetable by five minutes.

Traveling nowadays means what it has always meant: facing risks. Take air travel, for example. There is of course the total risk—a crash—but most of us, when it comes to actually getting on a plane, are not preoccupied with that possibility. We are much more conscious of the sort of risk that calls forth no very high courage. Weather, topography, sources of food and water along the way hardly concern us at all. We expect the aircraft itself, the radar, the pilots, the mechanics, the caterers, and the stewardesses to do their jobs and we forget about them from the start. We worry instead about whether we will get stuck in the middle seat between two (perhaps fat) people who use both arms of their seats, whether we'll have legroom after we've stuffed our bag underneath the seat in front of us, and whether a talkative seatmate will ruin our plans to get some serious reading done on a coast-to-coast flight.

There is a white paper bag in the seat pocket reminding us of another risk, "motion discomfort," which has superseded what sounds like a worse one, airsickness. The stewardess's voice comes over the intercom at takeoff, while another stewardess goes through a pantomime, telling us where to find the emergency exits and what to do in "the extremely unlikely event of a change in cabin pressure," and we pay no attention.

The apostle Paul was shipwrecked three times. He had to spend twenty-four hours in the open sea. He wrote to the Corinthians:

> In my travels I have been in constant danger from rivers and floods, from bandits, from my own countrymen and from pagans. I have faced danger in city streets, danger in the desert, danger on the high seas, danger among false Christians. I have known exhaustion, pain, long vigils, hunger and thirst, doing without meals, cold and lack of clothing.

Well, Paul, once in a transoceanic flight in something called a jumbo jet my daughter watched a movie for a whole hour before she realized that the sound track she had plugged into her ears was for another movie. (What do I mean by "flight"? "Movie"? "Sound track"? Never mind. They're all of them hazards you never had to cope with.) On top of that, the reading lights didn't work, there was no soap in the lavatories, no pillows or blankets on board although the air-conditioning was functioning only too well, and they served dinner at eleven o'clock at night and breakfast at one in the morning.

We take risks, all right. But what acquaintance have we with the physical hardships which used to be the testing ground for a man's character and stamina? We know nothing of the necessity of covering ground with our own two feet for days or weeks or months at a time, every step of which must be retraced on those same two feet if we're ever to get back to civilization again. We haven't felt the panic of isolation beyond help. When a book like

Alive: The Story of the Andes Survivors appears, it becomes a best-seller for we recognize then the hermetic seal of our civilization.

An ancient longing for danger, for challenge, and for sacrifice stirs in us—us who have insulated ourselves from weather by heating and air-conditioning and waterproofing and Thermopane; from bugs, germs, pests, and odors by screening, repellants, insecticides, weed killers, disinfectants, and deodorizers; from poverty by insurance, Medicare, and Social Security; from theft by banks, locks, Mace, and burglar alarms; from having to watch others suffer by putting them where somebody else will do the watching; and from guilt by calling any old immorality a "new morality," or by joining a group that encourages everybody to do whatever feels good.

We don't risk involvement if we can help it. We try not to turn around if anybody screams. Responsibility for others we'd rather delegate to institutions, including the government, which are supposed to make it their business to handle it.

I saw a man on television just a few days after Mr. Ford became President telling us that what America needs is a little more honesty. Because of technology, the man said, people have to be more dependent on each other than they used to be (Oh?) and therefore we need more honesty (Oh). Probably, he allowed, our standards have never been quite what they ought to be and it's time to hike them up a notch or two.

How do we go about this? Take a deep breath and—all together now—start being honest? Ah, the man had a plan. I waited, tense and eager, to hear what it might be. Popularization was what he proposed. Make honesty the In Thing. If everybody's doing it, it will be easy. In fact, the bright-eyed man told us, it would take the *risk* out of it.

Funny, I always thought righteousness was supposed to be risky. I was taught it wasn't easy, and I found it hard when I tried it. It's never likely to be either easy or popular.

"But I'm not asking for a change in human nature or anything," the man on the TV insisted, "only a change in attitude." And the round-eyed artlessness with which the remark was made and with which it was received by the TV host was breathtaking.

I'm for civilization. I'm all for certain kinds of progress and I accept quite gladly most of today's means of avoiding the risks that Dickens and Kipling and all of mankind before them had to run, but to imagine that we shall whip off the dishonesty that is characteristic of fallen human nature everywhere as painlessly as we whip off one garment and put on another, to imagine that by simply taking a different view we shall come up with a no-risk brand of honesty, is a piece of self-deception and fatuity to make the mind reel.

Plato, three hundred years before Christ, predicted that if ever the truly good man were to appear, the man who would tell the truth, he would have his eyes gouged out and in the end be crucified.

That risk was once taken, in its fullest measure. The man appeared. He told the world the truth about itself and even made the preposterous claim "I am the Truth." As Plato foresaw, that man was crucified.

He calls us still to follow him, and the conditions are the same: "Let a man deny himself and take up his cross."

SHORTCUT
TO PEACE

"Later he said to Marjorie, 'Brenda tried to be confidential about Beaver this evening.'
" 'I didn't know you knew.'
" 'Oh, I knew all right. But I wasn't going to let her feel important by talking about it.' "
Lines from Evelyn Waugh's A Handful of Dust

*   *   *

A Christian man who for many years has been helping alcoholics who want to be helped: *"I make it clear from the start that I don't want to know where they've been. I've heard all that. I only want to know where they're going."*

*   *   *

"She's been seeing a psychiatrist for months, and says he's really fantastic, says she's just beginning to understand why she's been acting that way toward her husband."
"But does she really need to know all that?"

*   *   *

Most of us enjoy talking about ourselves, our problems, our escapades. We want to defend our mistakes ("I was really down that day") and explain our failures ("Couldn't get my head together"). People who are willing to listen make us feel important. Analysis not only exonerates us of full responsibility for bad behavior but even lends dignity. Sin, of course, is highly undignified. We dignify it by calling it something else. Trauma, hurts, "syndromes," and the whole pattern of ordinary human reaction to them are respectable. We would far rather discuss processes and symptoms than make the radical turnaround that means repentance. It is nicer to be soothed than summoned. As long as we are "undergoing treatment," or "in counselling" we can postpone decision.

I don't want to knock psychology, unless theology is being put at the *mercy* of psychology. That's dangerous.

Psychology may be a science, but it is certainly not an exact science. Psychiatry is even less exact, though it has risen almost to the place of supreme authority in our time. One theologian has called it "the anti-Christ of the twentieth century." I know one psychiatrist who has quit the field altogether and returned to general practice because, he says, "psychiatry does not exist. It is a pseudoscience."

Science at best is only science, and while we thank God for every realm of knowlege he has allowed men to enter, it is one thing to give it place. It is another to own its sovereign sway. Lewis Thomas, in an essay entitled, "On Science and Uncertainty" (*Discover* magazine, October 1980), wrote, "It is likely that the twentieth century will be looked back at as the time when science provided the first close glimpse of the profundity of human ignorance. . . . Science is founded on uncertainty. . . . We are always, as it turns out, fundamentally in error. I cannot think of a single field in biology or medicine in which we can claim genuine understanding."

It would be well to keep Dr. Thomas's statement in mind when we are tempted to think that we shall, through psychological treatment or counselling, arrive at an understanding of ourselves which is deeper and closer to the truth than that which the writer of the Book of Proverbs, for example, perceived.

When my father was editor of a religious weekly a reader once wrote, "What is philosophy? Is it good or bad?" I have no record of his reply but I suppose he told her it was a method of inquiry, and in itself neither good nor bad. Psychology is also a method of inquiry, but P. T. Forsyth said that it cannot go beyond method, has no machinery for testing reality, and no jurisdiction in ultimates. In the sixty or seventy years since he wrote that, we have moved much closer to the edge of the precipice where we abandon the protection, restraint, and control of the everlasting Word and plunge over into the abyss of subjectivism. We need a control.

To change the metaphor: a certain psychological approach which seems to have gained tremendous popularity among Christians reminds me of the jungle rivers that I used occasionally to travel by canoe. They meandered. It was possible to get where you wanted to go by following the tortuous curves and loops, some of them doubling back almost on themselves. It was also possible to get there on foot by cutting straight through a curve, covering in ten minutes what it would take hours to cover by canoe.

To search out and sort out and "hang out" all the whys and wherefores of what we call our problems (a few of which just might be plain sins) may be one route to the healing of certain kinds of human difficulties, but I suggest that it may be the longest way home. I say this, I know, at the risk of being labeled simplistic, reductionist, obscurantist. But where, I want to know, does the *genuine understanding* which Dr. Thomas says science cannot claim begin? Where does it *begin?*

> No man knows the way to it:
> It is not found in the land of living men.
> The depths of the ocean say, "It is not in us,"

and the sea says, "It is not with me."
Red gold cannot buy it,
nor can its price be weighed out in silver. . . .
Where then does wisdom come from,
and where is the source of understanding?
. . . God understands the way to it,
he alone knows its source.
And he said to man:
 The fear of the Lord is wisdom,
and to turn from evil is understanding.

Job 28:13–15, 23, 28 NEB

The ancient and tested source is revealed in a Book whose reliability, relevance, and accuracy all fields of human knowledge continue to corroborate. It is the Bible. My plea is not that we reject the findings of psychology or any other field of study. It is that we *start* instead with theology, with the knowledge of God. Without that knowledge (given only to those who turn from evil) there is "no jurisdiction in ultimates," no knowledge even of ourselves, no certainty of any kind. My plea is that we give the Word a first hearing, take our bearings there, and turn only after that to whatever branch of science may apply to the need in question. Chances are it will be a more direct route to the truth, a shortcut to peace.

The Scriptures encompass the whole man, his whole world, and reveal the Lord of the universe. In them we have not only a perfect frame of reference, but specific and practical instruction, reproof when it's reproof we need, correction when we've gone wrong.

I have found this to be true every time I have tried it. Recently I was in turmoil about some things somebody said to me. I lay awake at night, mentally enacting whole scenes and conversations in which we would "have it out," dragging everything into consciousness, saying everything that was in our minds, pitting

what she said against what I said, what she did against what I did,
defending and offending, complaining and explaining. I had
heard this was what we are supposed to do—get it out, get it up
front, express it. But what a devastating business! What a
crashing bore! What a way to consume time, not to mention
emotional and spiritual energy! The very process itself gives me
the chance to add to my own list of sins against her. "When men
talk too much," says Proverbs 10:19, "sin is never far away.
Common sense holds its tongue."

Psychology describes. The Bible prescribes. "Turn from evil.
Let that be the medicine to keep you in health" (Proverbs 3:7, 8
NEB).

"Love is kind. Love is never quick to take offense. Love keeps
no score of wrongs. There is nothing love cannot face; there is no
limit to its faith, its hope, and its endurance" (1 Corinthians
13:4, 5, 7 NEB).

"Help one another to carry these heavy loads, and in this way
you will fulfil the law of Christ" (Galatians 6:2 NEB).

"Let your bearing toward one another arise out of your life in
Christ Jesus. . . . He made himself nothing . . . humbled himself
. . . accepted death" (Philippians 2:5, 7, 8 NEB).

The woman who had hurt me had plenty of heavy burdens to
bear. I knew that very well. How could I help her to bear them?
Well, for one thing, by "being offended without taking offense,"
that is, by following my Master.

What a relief! I no longer had to plot and plan and cogitate
about how to handle my feelings or how to confront my friend or
just what to say. My bearing toward her would arise *out of my life
in Christ Jesus*. I couldn't do it myself. He could, and he would
enable me.

To cut the straight path a good deal of the jungle of my
selfishness had to be slashed through. But it was a much shorter
way home.

TO JUDGE
OR NOT
TO JUDGE

"But everybody's being so judgmental! And you're another one," she complained. "Since you have chosen to be my judge, you can never be my friend."

For months Lisa had been watching Joan's behavior, which seemed to her to be very wrong. She had prayed about mentioning it. When she felt at last that she could no longer keep silent she approached her dear friend in the spirit of Galatians 6:1.

> Even if a man should be detected in some sin, my brothers, the spiritual ones among you should quietly set him back on the right path, not with any feeling of superiority but being yourselves on guard against temptation. Carry each other's burdens and so live out the law of Christ.

Joan, in response, was bitter, angry, and hurt. The wrong, she insisted, was Lisa's. Lisa was being "judgmental." The right, she felt, was on her side, for neither Lisa nor anyone else knew "the whole story."

The only verse about judgment in the Bible which anyone seems to have heard of these days is "Judge not." There the discussion usually ends. It is tacitly assumed that negative judgments are forbidden. That positive judgments would also come under the interdict escapes the notice of those who assume it is a sin to judge.

One morning long before dawn I sat staring out onto a starlit sea, thinking of Joan and Lisa's story and of what Christian judgment ought to be. My thoughts ran like this:

If one does right and is judged to be right, he will be neither angry nor hurt. He may, if he is humble, be pleased (is it not right to be glad that right is done?) but he will not be proud.

If one who is proud does wrong and is judged to be wrong he will be both angry and hurt.

If one who is proud does right and is judged to be wrong he also will be both angry and hurt.

If one who is truly humble does wrong and is judged to be wrong, he will not resent it but will in gratitude and humility, no matter what it costs him, heed the judgment and repent.

If one who is truly humble does right and is judged to be wrong he will not give the judgment a second thought. It is his Father's glory that matters to him, not his own. He will "rejoice and be exceeding glad," knowing for one thing that a great reward will be his, and, for another, that he thus enters in a measure into the suffering of Christ—"when he suffered he made no threats of revenge. He simply committed his cause to the One who judges fairly."

Joan was outraged that her close friend should judge her, thus disqualifying herself, Joan felt, from ever again being her friend. She failed to see that one as close as Lisa ought in fact to be the first to rebuke her, since she loves her and will be the first to notice that she needs to be rebuked. Joan, however, was sure that if Lisa could have seen the whole picture as God sees it she would have judged differently: because what she was doing *was* right, both God and Lisa would see it to be right. That kind of "judgment" Joan would not have minded, nor would the word *judgmental* have entered her head. *Perceptive* or *discerning* are words which perhaps would have come to her mind.

Joan was right, of course, that Lisa did not see the whole picture. No one but God ever sees it, for only to him are all hearts open, all desires known. We mortals often fail to see right as right, wrong as wrong. We look on the outward appearance. It is all we have access to. We therefore know only in part.

In the meantime we are given the book of standards by which to judge our own actions and those of others. "By their fruits" we know them. If we were not to judge at all we would have to expunge from our Christian vocabulary the word *is,* for whatever follows that word is a judgment: Jack is a fine yachtsman, Mrs. Smith is a cook, Harold is a bum. It depends on how one sees Jack, Mrs. Smith, and Harold.

Jesus told us to love our enemies. How are we to know who they are without judging? He spoke of dogs, swine, hypocrites, liars, as well as of friends, followers, rich men, the great and the small, the humble and the proud, "he who hears you and he who rejects you," old and new wineskins, the things of the world and the things of the Kingdom. To make any sense at all of his teachings requires, among other things, the God-given faculty of judgment, which includes discrimination.

The current popular notion that judging others is in itself a sin leads to such inappropriate maxims as "I'm o.k. and you're o.k." It encourages a conspiracy of moral indifference which says "If you never tell me that anything I'm doing is wrong, I'll never tell you that anything you're doing is wrong." "Judge not that ye be not judged" has come to mean that if you never call anything sin nobody can ever call you a sinner. You do your thing and let me do mine and let's accept everybody and never mind what they're up to.

There is a serious misunderstanding here. The Bible is plain that we have no business trying to straighten out those who are not yet Christians. That's God's business. Alexander the copper-smith did Paul "much evil," and was "an obstinate opponent" of Paul's teaching. That description is a straightforward judg-ment, but Paul did not consider it his duty to deal with that man. "The Lord will reward him for what he did."

"But surely it is your business to judge those who are inside the church," he wrote to the Christians at Corinth, and com-manded them to expel a certain immoral individual from the church:

> Clear out every bit of the old yeast. . . . Don't mix with the immoral. I didn't mean, of course, that you were to have no contact at all with the immoral of this world, nor with any cheats or thieves or idolaters—for that would mean going out of the world altogether! But in this letter I tell you not to associate with any professing Christian who is known to be an impure man or a swindler, an idolater, a man with a foul tongue, a drunkard, or a thief. My instruction is: Don't even eat with such a man.

That's pretty clear. And pretty hard to obey. I have seldom heard of its being obeyed in this country, but a missionary named Herbert Elliot tells me that he has seen it obeyed many times in the little Peruvian churches he visits in remote regions of the Andes and the jungle, where Christians simply believe the Word and put it into practice. In the majority of cases, he tells me, this measure has led to repentance, reconciliation, restoration, and healing.

The key to the matter of judgment is meekness. Childlikeness might be just as good a word. Meekness is one of the fruits of the Spirit. No one who does not humble himself and become like a little child is going to get into the Kingdom. We can never set ourselves up as judges, for we ourselves are sinners and inclined to be tempted exactly as those we judge are tempted. But if we are truly meek (caring not at all for self-image or reputation) we shall speak the truth as we see it (how else can a human being speak it?). We shall speak it in love, recognizing our own sinful capabilities and never-ending need for grace, as well as the limitations of our understanding. If we are to do the will of God in this matter, as in all other matters, we must do it by faith, taking the risk of being at times mistaken. We may misjudge, but let us be at least honest and charitable. We ourselves may be misjudged. Let us be charitable then, too, and accept it in humility as our Lord did. "When He was reviled, He reviled not in return."

I said we cannot set ourselves up as judges. It is God who sets us this task, who commands us Christians to judge other Christians. It is not pride that causes us to judge. It is pride that causes us to judge *as though* we ourselves are not bound by the same standards or tempted by the same sins. It was those who were trying to remove "specks" from a brother's eye when they themselves had "logs" in their own eyes to whom Jesus said "Judge not."

"You fraud!" he said to them. "Take the plank out of your own eye first, and then you can see clearly enough to remove your brother's speck of dust." The dust must indeed be removed, not tolerated or ignored or called by a polite name. But it must be removed by somebody who can see—that is, the humble, the childlike, the pure, the meek. If any of us are inclined to excuse ourselves from the responsibility to judge, pleading that we do not belong in that lovely company, let us not forget that it is those of that company and only those who are of any use in the Kingdom, in fact, who will even enter it. We must take our stand with them beneath the cross of Jesus, where, as the hymn writer says:

. . . my eyes at times can see
The very dying form of One
Who suffered there for me.
And from my smitten heart, with tears,
Two wonders I confess:
The wonders of His glorious love,
And my own worthlessness.

HAVE IT YOUR WAY—
OR GOD'S

When Lars and I lived in Georgia he took me one Saturday night to a place called "Swampland" in the little country town of Toomsboro. It comprised a barnlike eating place and a barnlike auditorium where there was a gospel singing jamboree from four until midnight.

As we sat at a long table with a lot of people we didn't know, eating our catfish and hush puppies (there wasn't much else on the menu), we noticed an odd person standing by the fireplace. He was a kind of middle-aged hippie. He had long gray hair like a broom. He was wearing baggy patched pants, a jacket with fringes (some of them on purpose and some just tatters), a pistol belt, and a hat that was so greasy Lars said it would burn for a week if it ever caught fire. Every now and then he gave the logs on the fire a poke or two, but seemed to be otherwise unoccupied.

When the manager of the restaurant came by, table-hopping, we asked about the local character.

"You mean old Rusty Russell there? You don't know Rusty Russell?"

We said no. We asked if he was the official fire-poker.

"Nope."

"What does he do?"

"Do? Don't do nothin'. Come with the place." The manager went on to tell us a little more. Seems he was from Alabama originally. His old daddy used to live with him, and when he died, Rusty wanted to bury him back home in Alabama. Dressed him up in his Sunday suit, put a Sunday hat on his head, belted him into the front seat of his old Ford car, and headed out of town.

"Health authorities caught up with him, though. It was summertime. No way was they gonna let him drive that corpse outa state.

"Old Rusty had a wife once, too. Next-door neighbor took a shine to 'er. Rusty goes over, says, 'See you like ma wife.'

" 'Yup,' he says.

" 'Want 'er?' Rusty says.

" 'Yup,' he says.

" 'What'll you give me for 'er?'

" 'Stove,' he says.

"Old Rusty says 'I'll take it.'

"He did. Traded his wife for a wood stove. Good one, too. Rusty still uses that stove, by golly. Got a good deal. Better'n the neighbor got, I reckon."

We loved that story. We did not love the story we heard last week—three stories, in fact, depressingly familiar, of three ministers of the Gospel who, like Rusty's neighbor, let their eyes wander to their neighbors' wives. All three liked what they saw next door (or, more accurately, in one of the pews of their churches) and, hearkening to current commercials ("You can have it all," "Do yourself a favor," "Have it your way") opted out.

Among the processes accelerating the breakdown of human structures is the flooding of imagery, produced by the mass media, "sweeping us into a chaotic and unassimilable whirlpool of influences," writes Dr. James Houston in *I Believe in the Creator* (Eerdmans, 1980). "We are overwhelmed by undigested data, with endlessly incomplete alternatives to every sphere of living."

Christians, encouraged by the example of Christian leaders everywhere, have begun to regard divorce as an option. There is nothing new about marital difficulties. If a man who is a sinner chooses as a life partner a woman who is a sinner they will run into trouble of some sort, depend upon it. Paul was realistic about this in 1 Corinthians 7: "Those who marry will have worldly troubles and I would spare you that."

Jill Briscoe says that she and her husband Stuart are incompatible. She told a whole audience this. "And we live with incompatible children and an incompatible dog and an incompatible cat." The point she makes is: when it comes right down to it, aren't all human beings incompatible? It takes grace for any of them to get along on an every-day-of-the-year basis. The apostle Peter, who was married, reminded us that a husband and wife are "heirs together of the grace of life." God knows our frame, remembers we're nothing but dust, and we need grace, lots of grace. This God supplies—plenteous, sufficient, enough—to those willing to receive.

If we receive that grace with thanksgiving he will enable us to make the sacrifice of self without which no human relationship will work very well. The refusal of grace is like the refusal to put oil in an engine. The machinery will break down. Prolonged friction between the parts will result in the whole thing's grinding to a halt. When, for lack of grace in one or both partners, a marriage grinds to a halt, the "world," coming at us loud, clear, and without interruption via television and other media, persuades us that we have plenty of alternatives. The Church, always in danger of pollution by the spirit of the world, begins to choose the proffered alternatives in preference to grace, to replace "I believe" with "I feel."

There is an Eternal Word which has been spoken. For thousands of years Christians have taken their stand on that Word, have driven into it all the stakes of their faith and hope, believing it to be a liberating Word, a *saving* Word. They have arranged their lives within its clear and bounded context.

The trouble with television is that it has no context. We sit in our living rooms or stand, as I often do, dicing carrots in our kitchens with the Sony on the counter. The program comes to us from New York or Hollywood or Bydgoszcz or Virginia Beach. The set—a corner of an elegant living room, a city street, a desk high in some skyscraper, or perhaps Cypress Gardens or a "crystal" cathedral—seems fake even if it is real. It has nothing to do with us or with what is being spoken. There is no context which embraces both my life and theirs, or it is "the context of no-context," as George W. S. Trow argued brilliantly in a *New Yorker* article (November 17, 1980):

> The work of television is to establish false contexts and to chronicle the unravelling of existing contexts; finally to establish the context of no-context and to chronicle it. . . . The New History was the record of the expression of demographically significant preferences: the lunge of demography *here* as opposed to *there*. . . . Nothing was judged, only counted. The preferences of the child carried as much weight as the preferences of an adult, so the refining of preferences was subtracted from what it was necessary for a man to learn to do.

Divorce has become "demographically significant" among Christians. So have too many other things. It is because we have forgotten that our context is the Kingdom of God, not the kingdom of this world (which is the kingdom of self). In the Kingdom of God the alternatives are not boundless, not so long as we live in this mortal coil. You can't have it all. You are not there to do yourself a favor. You may not have it your way. You opted out of all that when you made up your mind to follow a Master who himself had relinquished all rights, all equality with the Father, and his own will as well. You are called not to be served but to serve, and you can't serve two masters. You can't operate in two opposing kingdoms. These kingdoms *are* the alternatives. Settle it once for all. It is, quite simply, a life-and-death choice. Pay no attention to what is demographically significant.

I receive a good many letters from young people who are utterly at sea about their life's choices—college, career, marriage. They are faced with too many alternatives. The seeming limitlessness overwhelms, unsettles, often even paralyzes them. (Can I have marriage *and* a career? Can I have marriage and a career *and* babies? Can I be really feminine and be an initiator? Can I be really a man and not the head of my home?) Twenty years ago they were faced with a whole cupboard full of packaged breakfast foods and were asked by a well-meaning but unwise mother what they wanted for breakfast. They didn't know. They have been going to McDonald's ever since, gobbling up those (how many billions is it now?) hamburgers with or without onion, with or without mustard, relish, catsup, everything. They still think they can have it all, and they still don't know what they want. Why not stop bothering about what *you* want, I suggest to them. Find out what your Master wants.

The three ministers think they know. They married the wrong woman. A youthful mistake. They've grown apart now. The children will not be hurt if they "handle" it properly, they say. They owe it to themselves to take this daring and creative step. God wants them to be happy. It's a leap and a risk and there's a price to pay, but look how liberating, how stretching, how redemptive. Why be threatened by traditional morality? Why be hung up? The other woman has understood and affirmed and fulfilled them as the poor wife was never equipped to do and—a line from an old song reminds them—"to waste our lives would be a sin."

Twirl those television dials. Look, for a minute, at the suffering of the world on the evening news. Twirl it off. Look at the beautiful people if you want to. There they are. You can be beautiful too. You can do what they do, go where they go. TWA will take you up, up and away. Delta is ready when you are. Become a legend. Charm a holiday party. Enhance your fragrance image. Give to thyself. Wear the Mark of Success. Try everything. Experience all the thrills.

> *Now it may be the flower for me*
> *Is this beneath my nose,*
> *But how shall I tell unless I smell*
> *The Carthaginian rose?*

So wrote Edna St. Vincent Millay (*Collected Lyrics*, Washington Square Press) decades ago. In the 1980s the possibilities seem even more endless and enticing, the unreached corners of the world ever more reachable, the pleasures of sin more innocuous. In fact, we suspect, they are not even luxuries. They have become, for the self-respecting man or woman, requirements.

There is plenty of room on the road that leads to that kingdom, and many go that way, but it is still true that the gate that leads to Life is small and the road is narrow and those who find it are few.

PERSON
OR THING?

Not long ago *Time* magazine reported another triumph of modern medical technology. An unborn child, found, by means of a process called amniocentesis, to suffer from Down's syndrome, was aborted (terminated? quietly done away with? killed?). It was all very safe and scientific and sterile. Not only was there little danger to the mother, there was no harm to the other twin in the mother's womb. The affected child (Is that an acceptable word? Should I say afflicted? unwanted? undesirable? useless? disposable?) was relieved of its life by being relieved of its lifeblood, which was slowly withdrawn through a long needle which pierced its beating heart. This was called a therapeutic abortion. The word *therapeutic* means serving to cure or heal. The strange part about this case was that nobody except the aborted child was ill. Who then was cured? Who was healed?

It seemed a huge irony that only a few weeks later the same magazine hailed another medical breakthrough: surgery to correct an abnormal kidney condition known as hydronephrosis. The amazing part about this case was that the patient was an unborn child, again one of twins. Again, a needle was inserted—through the mother's abdominal wall, through the uterus, through the amniotic sac lining, through the abdominal wall of the fetus, into the bladder. The needle was not used to withdraw blood but to insert a catheter which would drain urine, thus saving little Michael's life.

"For all its promise," *Time* comments, "fetal surgery poses some difficult ethical dilemmas."

Difficult indeed but only if we refuse to call the thing operated on a child.

In the first case, the mother did not want it. Whatever she called it, it had every possibility of becoming a person, and only as a person posed a threat. When it was rendered harmless, that is, when the heart no longer beat, when it was, in fact, dead, she continued to carry it to term. Then, along with its twin, it was born. Its twin had been very like itself to begin with, fully capable of becoming a person, but now very different indeed— wanted, desirable, "useful"—and alive.

In the second case, the mother wanted both the twins, the well one and the sick one with the swollen bladder and kidneys. To her, what was in her womb was her children. Could they possibly save the tiny thing? Was there anything they could do for her baby? It was (Did the mother ever question it?) a baby.

Dr. Leonie Watson said, "If they can do surgery on a fetus, then it is in fact a baby."

We recognize how far we have departed from what nature has always told any prospective mother, when we realize that *arguments* must be adduced, some of them even from technical procedures like fetal surgery, to prove that the living, moving, creature about to come forth into the world is a human baby. *If* surgery is possible, *then* it's a baby.

This is, of course, where the battle lines are drawn. Is it, or is it not? What is the thing to be aborted? What is the thing to be born? What is the thing on which surgery was done? If we call it a fetus does it make the ethical dilemmas less difficult?

PERSON OR THING?

Dr. Phillip Stubblefield, a gynecologist at Boston's Massachusetts General Hospital, argues that a fetus is only a baby if it can live outside the womb.

If we can accept this assertion, may we also assume that a patient is not a person unless "it" can survive without, for example, dialysis or a heart pump? Is a machine somehow more humanizing than a womb? Is it possible seriously to believe that successful detachment from the mother is what turns an otherwise disposable and expendable mass of tissue into what we may legitimately call a baby?

Katharine Hepburn recently sent out a letter (I suppose to nearly everybody, otherwise I don't know how I would have gotten on her list) appealing for $3.6 million to stand up against what she called "repressive legislation" to limit individual rights and reproductive freedom. She listed eight reasons a certain amendment which would prevent abortion on demand should be defeated. Not a single one of her eight reasons would stand up in any court as a valid argument against the amendment *if* the thing aborted were called a person.

That is the question.

That is the only relevant question.

When what Miss Hepburn calls "individual rights and reproductive freedom" impinge on the rights of a person other than the pregnant woman, that is, on a person who happens to be hidden, helpless, and at the mercy of the one entrusted with its life, are we who object hysterical, illogical, bigoted, fanatic? Are we duped by what she calls "simple outdated platitudes of television preachers" if we cry aloud against her and her kind?

Last week there was another scandal. A woman had been running nursing homes which turned out to be what an investigator called "human sewers." She made a great deal of money off another group of defenseless human beings—the elderly, who had something in common with the "fetuses" Miss Hepburn claims the right to dispose of. They, too, were hidden, helpless, and at the mercy of the one entrusted with their lives. People were outraged. These victims had not been treated as human beings.

Why all the fuss? Suppose we apply some of the arguments used in favor of abortion to the treatment of the indigent, the friendless, the senile.

If there is brain damage or deformity, the fetus (read also the senile or the crippled) may be terminated.

If the fetus's becoming a person, i.e., being born, would be a serious inconvenience to the mother, or to other members of the family, it may be terminated. As has often been observed, there is no such thing as a "convenient" time to have a baby. All babies (and many disabled or bedridden people) are an inconvenience. All are at times what might be called a serious inconvenience. Love alone "endures all things."

If a baby is allowed to be born, it may become the victim of brutality. One solution offered for the "battered child syndrome" is abortion. What about the "neglected octogenarian syndrome"?

A sixteen-year-old high school student who has no prospect for a stable home and whose pregnancy will end her chance for an education is counseled to abort her baby. How shall we counsel a fifty-eight-year-old divorced man about what to do with his invalid mother? Taking care of her might end his chances for a lot of things.

If we refuse to allow medically "safe" abortions, we are told that we thereby encourage "back-alley butchery," self-induced procedures of desperate women, even suicide. By the same token, if we outlaw sterile injections of, say, an overdose of morphine administered to an old man in a nursing home whose "quality of life" does not warrant continuation, do we thereby encourage less humane methods of getting people out of the way?

Miss Hepburn deplores "cold constitutional prohibitions," prefers instead individual choice based on "sound advice from the woman's personal physician." Some of those cold constitutional prohibitions happen to deal with the question of human life and what we citizens of these United States are allowed to do for or against it.

That is still the question. What do we do with the gift of life? Shall we acknowledge first of all its Creator, and recognize the sanctity of what is made in his image? Shall we hold it in reverence? If any human life, however frail, however incapable of retaliation, is entrusted to us shall we nourish and cherish it, or may we—by some enormously civilized and educated rationalization—convince ourselves either that it is not a person, or that, although it is a person, its life is not worth living, and that therefore what we do with it is a matter of individual choice?

What *is* this thing?

We are faced with only one question. Are we talking about an object, or might it by any stretch of the imagination be a person? If we cannot be sure of the answer, at least we may pick up a clue or two from the word of the Lord which came to Jeremiah: "Before I formed you in the womb I knew you for my own; before you were born I consecrated you, I appointed you a prophet to the nations." To God, at least, Jeremiah was already a person. For my part, I will try to regard whatever bears the marks of humanity as God's property and not mine.

TO A MAN
WHO CHOSE DIVORCE*

Dear Dick:

It was like a kick in the stomach to hear that you decided to get rid of Sally and the babies. We had heard some months ago that there was trouble. We did not know the nature or the seriousness of it, but we prayed. You opted for divorce and now it's all over. Or is it? You have your "freedom," such as it is, you live in the bachelor officers' quarters, and you can do what you like, without sacrifice or responsibility, while Sally is looking for a job and her parents have stepped in to help with the job you once promised to do—taking care of your wife and your babies.

I wrote to you, asking you to call, but no call came. I can understand why you did not want to talk to me or anyone else who might try to talk you out of what you had made up your mind to do. Your explanation for the decision, I am told, was that you did not want to be a husband, you did not want to be a father. As simple as that. But very poor timing, if I may say so.

---

* This and the following two chapters were never sent to anyone. They were written as a means of sorting through what I would say if a couple were to allow me the opportunity to counsel them while reconciliation was still possible.

"Wait a minute," you say. "You don't know the whole story." That's true. There is much on each side that I know nothing about. But I know this: you took a vow to cleave to Sally in sickness or in health, for richer, for poorer, for better *or for worse*, as long as you both should live. What did you think you meant by those words? A real man (that is, a true man) is always a man of his word.

You are a child of your generation. I can hear your answer: "But I've changed. Sally's changed. She's not the woman I married. I'm no longer the same man who mouthed those words (and they were only words, a tradition, a ceremony we went through to satisfy society). Things have happened to alter everything. Will you get off my back?"

You have grown up in a time when people are declaring their independence of what they choose to call "other people's morality." "What right do they have to tell me what to do? I have to do what's right for *me*," they whine, as though selfishness may be destructive for one man and constructive for another, as though putting the happiness of another before your own really need not be a part of the marriage contract in the 1980s.

You have your freedom, I said a moment ago, but it is only a manner of speaking. There is no freedom anywhere in the universe apart from the freedom we were created for in the very beginning: to glorify God. I'm not telling you anything you have not grown up knowing. You know also that the choices in life resolve themselves ultimately to this one: God or self. You are searching for some place in God's world where you need not face so stark a choice. You will never find it.

You have supposed that you can elect to stop being a husband and father. It is like saying "Stop the world, I want to get off," because the truth is that you and Sally became one flesh. Divorce papers do not undo that. You begot two sons. Abandoning them cannot nullify your fatherhood. Your children will always be yours, and they will always know that you discarded them. I have no idea what the legal arrangements are, whether you have "visiting rights" or whatever, but no matter. Those are nothing more than legal arrangements. The cold fact stands that you rejected the gift of fatherhood along with the gift of being husband and head and priest in the home you chose under God to establish.

"Sally can marry somebody else," you are quoted to have said. Perhaps she will. Your children will then have a stepfather who may love them as you ought to have loved them, and accept responsibility for their care which you have shrugged off. No protests that you love them, that you do indeed want to see them from time to time and pay their bills, can ever change the fact that you quit. Things were tough, so you bugged out.

You are in the military service now, Dick. Things might get tough there, too, but I would imagine you were sworn in. You pledged your word to serve, to obey the rules, to be loyal. Have we, the citizens of the United States, any reason to expect you to keep your word if you find, after a while, that you've changed, circumstances have changed, things were not exactly what you bargained for? Will you confront the difficulties by breaking the promises you swore to keep? Is your word to your country worth any more than your word to God, or to the witnesses before whom you plighted your troth to Sally?

You are holding imaginary dialogues with those who condemn your action (people like me), proving that you had to do it, you couldn't take it any longer, it will turn out all right in the end, it will be much better for Sally and the boys. I hope you *are* holding such dialogues, because it would show that you needed to justify your action. Action that is clearly right needs no justification.

I dare to hope, too, that in some predawn hour of sleeplessness in your solitary bed you have admitted that you have not found the freedom you were looking for. You face, in saner moments, the sad truth: you have been irrevocably changed by quitting. If you are half the man we thought you were you are hating yourself for what you have done. The arguments you have adduced—you are being honest, you were living a lie while you were married, you finally got in touch with your real feelings and summoned the courage to defy convention and the expectations of all who love you—those arguments are beginning to ring hollow. You know that the "real feelings" of all of us nearly all the time are selfish, and what we conveniently call convention might be (in this case *is*) the clear command of God: What God has joined together, man must not separate (Matthew 19:6 NEB).

I earnestly hope that you have not fallen so far as not to be ashamed of yourself.

"In trying to extirpate Shame," wrote C. S. Lewis, "we have broken down one of the ramparts of the human spirit, madly exulting in the work as the Trojans exulted when they broke their walls and pulled the Horse into Troy. I do not know that there is anything to be done but to set about rebuilding as soon as we can. It is mad work to remove hypocrisy by removing the temptation to hypocrisy: the 'frankness' of people sunk below shame is a very cheap frankness" (*The Problem of Pain,* p. 45).

What you have done is detestable. Understandable, of course, but detestable. I know that from the Book. It says, "God hates divorce." If we do not also hate it we are not on God's side. I dare to hope that you still think of yourself as on his side, and are therefore, at least when you are not paying attention to the Enemy's suggestions, thoroughly ashamed. This is your hope of salvation. Until you accept God's estimate of the thing done, you will never seek his remedy.

Your present discontent is a mercy, affording opportunity to repent. Any inkling you have that all is not well is the still, small voice calling you back to repentance, reconciliation, and restoration. Will you set about rebuilding as soon as you can?

THE "INNOCENT" PARTY

When a letter I wrote to a man who chose divorce was published, I heard from a reader who said it was unduly harsh and did not seem to have any love in it. "I can't picture Jesus saying such a thing to anyone," he wrote. "It implies that Dick was bad and Sally was good."

Let's examine this for a minute. The harshness, I suppose, is inferred first because I said the news of the divorce was "like a kick in the stomach"—in other words, it hurt me personally. Any divorce ought to be bad news to a Christian because we know how God feels about it. This particular divorce was terrible news to me because I happen to love both Dick and Sally. If my letter to Dick seemed to my correspondent to have no love in it perhaps that was because he imagines that love and judgment are mutually exclusive. If you love people, you will never say anything that will make them uncomfortable.

I wonder how attentively he has read the Gospels. Jesus often made people uneasy. Sometimes he made them furious. I wonder, too, how attentively my correspondent has read the letters of Paul, Peter, and James. Those letters teach us clearly and strongly to call a thing what God calls it. If it's sin, call it sin. Deal with it as sin.

This goes for our own sins first, *of course*. We are judged by the Word. It is the straightedge that shows up our own crookedness. Let us confess our own sins, root them out, forsake them. Then, when we've done that (Jesus explained it vividly)—taken the "log" out of our own eye—we will be able to see well enough to take the "splinter" out of somebody else's. (Isn't it an act of kindness to take out a splinter for somebody?)

"Oh, come on, now—who do you think you are?" I hear someone saying. "What do you know about the situation between a husband and wife? You can't judge. Mind your own business!"

I said in my letter to Dick that there was much on both sides that I knew nothing about. I wrote to him solely about what I did know: he had made public vows, he had broken them. I hoped that there was still time to repent, to restore a relationship, to mend a shattered home and heal the appalling wounds of two little children.

But did I imply that Dick was bad and Sally was good? I did not. It is a very confused line of thought which says the guilt of one implies the innocence of the other. Let's assume that Sally was worse than Dick. He had promised to love and cherish her, for better or for worse. He broke that promise. That Dick sinned was clear enough and I said so. I did not say that Sally had not sinned. The person sinned against is not necessarily innocent. Far from it. Given the propensities of human nature, the very fact that one is sinned against dramatically enlarges the ordinary field of temptation to sin. I had no way of knowing how Sally might have sinned, but I supposed she did. I supposed that, being a woman, she is something like me. Full of pride, I would be dumbfounded, then hurt, devastated, furious, and vindictive. I would feel extremely sorry for myself and would spend a good deal of time and emotional energy thinking of ways to retaliate, as well as to condemn Dick and justify myself. In other words, I could not possibly be called an innocent party.

Those are things I would be likely to have done when Dick told me he was leaving. The man who wrote to me suggested a list of things Sally might have done before and after his decision. "I challenge you," he wrote, "to write another letter to Sally about how she demanded things done her way, was often nasty and sarcastic, often used 'the good of the children' to get her way. How she used every trick to get her man hooked and then did not follow through. How she finally convinced Dick the children were better off without him than to be a constant source of quarrels. How she sort of liked being a heroine and making Dick look bad. How she had to build up her ego by being not only the nurturer of the children but the breadwinner as well. How she in her self-rightousness is going to bring up the children away from the bad influence of their dad."

Sally may be guilty of all these sins and more. Dick's list of offenses may be even longer. I do not know either side of the sad story. I am sure if I heard Sally's side my sympathies would be with her. If Dick told me his side the very next day, my sympathies would promptly shift to him. I would conclude that both were right and both were wrong, there was a lot to be said on both sides, and we might as well throw up our hands and say, "Do your own thing. There's no way to work this out." Dick went to a psychologist who called himself a Christian (they tell me), who spent his time, not encouraging Dick to love Sally in obedience to God and thus to avoid divorce, but helping him "deal with his feelings" when the divorce happened.

I do not, I admit, know the story. But I know the One who knows it—all of it—and I know that *it is always possible to do what he tells us*.

The actress Katharine Hepburn had little patience for actors who surrendered to "the tortuous introspection of the Method,"

THE "INNOCENT" PARTY

Time says. "You do what the script tells you," she said. "Deliver the goods without comment. Live it—do it—or shut up. After all, the writer is what's important."

That goes for us Christians. There *is* a script. If there weren't, then we'd have to muddle through on our own, hoping by introspection and experiment to come up with something that might work. God hasn't left us to that method. He knew what we'd get into by sinning, and has made provision for us. Let's live it—do it—or shut up and quit pretending to follow Christ. The issue we are discussing here is not whether Dick had good reason for unloading his family, but whether he had an option, according to the Script. "We never discussed a script," said Hepburn, "we just did it. Naturally and unconsciously we joined into what I call a musical necessity." Easier, I suppose, in theater than in the confusion and pain of a real marriage, but there is a "musical necessity" for all of us. Even when we cannot solve our problems, we can please God. Even when one person disobeys him, the other can obey him. My husband Lars and I know this is true. Poor students though we are ("fools and slow of heart to believe") we're daily trying to do our lessons in the school of faith and obedience, finding the truth of the old gospel song, "There's no other way to be happy in Jesus."

There is a common assumption today that whatever we are and wherever we are is somehow fixed and inevitable, while it is the Ancient Word that must be bent. For example, a woman cheats a university by plagiarizing and is refused a diploma. She decides she has a right to the university's credentials even though she happens to be a cheater, so she sues. Another woman chooses abortion. It is fixed and inevitable, in her mind, that what might turn into a baby must be got rid of, never mind the possibility that it's murder. People protested the Abscam experiment because, after all, nobody can be expected to resist *that* much money. To be loving, caring, sharing, and daring in the Christian community too often means, for example, to tell Dick he's okay, he's got his

93

own life to live, and to tell Sally nobody can blame her for feeling sorry for herself.

"Blame"? The question here is who assigns blame? There is an Ancient Word, fixed, settled, which shall stand forever. The present situation is only grass which withers and flowers which fade. We must quit bending the Word to suit our situation. It is *we* who must be bent to that Word, *our* necks that must bow under the yoke. Love is no pleasing sentiment but a fiery law: *thou shalt love.* In Dick and Sally's predicament, I can only imagine how deeply that fire will have to burn if they decide to obey. I can imagine it, all right, for I know the sinfulness of my own heart and how much dross is there to be purified by the Refining Fire, how excruciating it is for me to submit to the Word that never permits the least indulgence of self-pity, self-vindication, self-aggrandizement, self-justification, or any other form of the self whatsoever.

A young woman called me the other day to describe what seemed an utterly insoluble marital problem. My heart was entirely with her. She lives with a man who seems to me and to many others "impossible." The things he asks her to do are unreasonable and absurd.

"He wants me to do so-and-so, but I'm not going to do it." I had little to say in reply, except that I would keep on praying for them.

"I guess you'd call that a stalemate, wouldn't you?" she said.

I guessed I would. There was a pause. Then she said, "But Elisabeth, you know, I have a strong feeling that it will remain a stalemate unless *I* do something. I think God is asking me to make the move, to submit to Jack. Do you think that would be right?"

"Yes."

"I don't think I can do it. I just can't do it. I keep hoping God will make it easy for me . . . but I guess he's not going to, huh?"

"Often in the Bible we find God bringing people to a place of decision—often an 'impossible' decision (think of the Israelites in the Old Testament, the man with the withered hand in the New)—and at that point it's up to them. The refusal to obey when the choice is clear is the end of blessing," I said. "Obedience leads to some unimagined solution."

I knew how fearsome the choice was in her case. God knew it too. But God is the one who takes responsibility for the results when the choice is made in obedience. This is always the thing we can count on. Human relations present "impossible" difficulties. Sin seems to tie us into hopeless knots and we seek desperate solutions: divorce, abortion, lawsuits. Of course, people understand. People sympathize. Some criticize, some judge as though they themselves would never be so tempted. This is wrong, and for me to say it is wrong is a *judgment*. But it is not my judgment. It is the judgment of the Bible. The Bible tells us it is wrong to judge—not wrong to use our critical faculties, but wrong to set ourselves up as righteous and immune to the sin we are judging. "Judge *righteous* judgment," Jesus said.

We have laid many traps for ourselves by forgetting how sinful we are and how badly we need the Script. We get into a mess and we declare ourselves bankrupt. Nobody can make any moral claims against us anymore. We are, spiritually speaking, out of business, closed. We're doing our thing, defying those who judge us, telling them it is always wrong to judge (which is in itself a judgment, but not one based on the Script).

My correspondent told me we should remember we've all broken vows, that Dick was doing the best he could and that I shouldn't make matters worse by making him feel bad, that I should love and care about him instead of criticizing so harshly. He said divorce was common in Bible times; it's better to separate than to live in hatred; and why don't we all just try to support the good and stop condemning the bad?

My correspondent was muddled. Trying to be humble and sensible and loving, I'm sure, but muddled nevertheless. Let's try to be clear. When sinful people live in the same world, and especially when they work in the same office or sleep in the same bed, they sin against each other. Troubles arise. Some of those troubles are very serious and not subject to easy solutions. God knows all about them, and knew about them long before they happened. He made provision for them. His Son bore all of them—all grief, all sorrow, all disease, all sin—for us. But why on earth (or in Heaven) should he have done that? Why "should" he? He shouldn't, but he did. Because of love. The love that is stronger than sin, stronger than death.

And here is the profound lesson for us in the midst of our troubles. To rescue us out of them, Christ relinquished his rights. Are we his followers? Then let's take a hard look at what we have a right to expect from others. What does Sally rightfully expect from Dick? Love. "Husbands, love your wives." What does Dick rightfully expect from Sally? Submission and respect. "Wives, be subject to your husbands as to the Lord," and "the woman must see to it that she pays her husband all respect" (Ephesians 5:25, 22, 23 NEB). What if the husband doesn't do what he's supposed to? What if the wife doesn't? Face up to it—in this world nobody gets what he is reasonably entitled to. There is the world's "solution" to this problem: fight. There is the Christian's: relinquish. God did not get what he had a right to expect—the love and obedience of the creature he had made. Instead he got rebellion and disobedience. Adam and Eve made a general mess of everything, and we carry on making new messes daily.

We have a Script. "Let your bearing towards one another arise out of your life in Christ Jesus. For the divine nature was his from the first, yet he did not think to snatch at equality with God but made himself nothing, assuming the nature of a slave" (Philippians 2:5, 6 NEB). What Christ gave up was not his divine nature (people are always worried about losing their "personhood"), but the glory that nature entitled him to. He was God by nature and he voluntarily became a slave, so that the Father would give back to him in boundless measure the glory he had given up.

What a Script! What a lesson! Christianity insists always on the *rights of others*. A Christian lays down his own life to obtain them. If he asks, Have *I* no rights? the answer is "The servant is not greater than his Lord."

Selah, Sally. Ponder that, Dick. And God help me (Elisabeth) when the next test comes. It probably won't be more than five minutes from now.

IS DIVORCE
THE ONLY WAY?

Every choice in life is made in some context. Not long ago I wrote a letter to a man named Dick who chose divorce. Then I wrote about Sally, the woman he turned loose, and about some of the choices she, the "victim" or the "innocent party" must make. Now I write to both of them—with trepidation, of course, aware that probably the last thing they want to hear about from me or anybody else is reconciliation. Hopelessness has perhaps set in by now, if not pure hatred, and they are convinced that everything has been tried and found wanting. The die is cast. The divorce is long since finished, and now they've got to get on with their separate lives.

The business of living a life for God is never finished, however, until we reach the gates of the City. ("Finished," did I say? But it is only then really begun!) I write to the man or woman in whose heart, even if that heart is broken or full of remorse and sin, still lies the longing to please God.

How can we do this? Well, let's not listen to any ungodly counsel. The man is called "blessed," which means happy, who walketh not in that kind of counsel (Psalms 1:1 Authorized

Version). The trouble with the ungodly is that they have no reference point but themselves, so they try everything that looks as though it might lead to a "solution." They leave out the one thing that really matters, the thing which, although not necessarily the direct route to solutions, is the only route to happiness. "Happy is the man who does not take the wicked for his guide, nor walk the road that sinners tread . . . . The law of the Lord is his delight" (Psalms 1:1, 2 NEB). That's what matters—the law of the Lord.

Not all who practice under the label "Christian" counselor are in the biblical sense godly. There is sometimes uncertainty as to the authority and relevance of "the law of the Lord," that is, of what the Bible says about human situations. "This is the end of the twentieth century," we are reminded. "There are no simple answers." I believe there are indeed some *simple* ones, but they are not *easy*. By that I mean that I can understand them—I cannot easily obey them. The road spoken of in that first psalm, the one sinners tread, is a wide one, smoothed by millions of feet. The road we must tread is narrow and rough, but we are not alone—the Holy Spirit has been "called alongside" to comfort, help, and teach us—and millions have walked the road of obedience before us.

If there is still a desire in the heart of either husband or wife for help, if there remains even the tiniest shred of forlorn hope that reconciliation is possible, might we ask first of all a question that precedes all other questions when godly counsel is sought. It is this: What is the context of our lives? There are two choices. We live our lives in the context of the world, which makes up its own rules as it goes along, or in the context of the Kingdom of God, in which the law is the Lord's.

What was the context of our conflict? Here we may run into difficulty. One or both partners may believe they did the will of God and that was what caused the conflict. Leave this one, then, and try the next: What did each of us do when the conflict arose? Was it dictated by concern for the Kingdom or God, or something else (personal happiness, perhaps)?

What is needed now to move into that heavenly Kingdom?

If both partners, humbly and honestly, answer that they want to live their lives in the context of the Kingdom, and are, humbly and honestly, prepared to pay the price exacted of those who live there, I believe with all my heart that there will be a "solution."

But suppose only one of them seeks God's will in the matter. It may be the one generally called the "innocent" party. He or she is being divorced by the other. Then again, the one claiming to seek God's will may be the one who filed the papers. He or she may have sought Christian counsel, prayed, tried to patch things up, and at last, in despair, turned to the law—that is, to divorce—as the only possible thing to do. *He* thinks of himself as the innocent one. There is yet another possibility—that the one who is seeking God's will is the one most acutely aware that he *is* at fault, that he is the *guilty* party.

What I have to say to this person, whichever he is, is not offered as a solution. God does not promise solutions to all our problems. The Gospel is not a guarantee of the healing of all diseases, the dissolving of all debts, the mending of all marriages, and the fulfilling of all desires *on this side of the Jordan*. The Gospel, as the good news of freedom from sin and self, is in fact also a guarantee of what Jesus called *tribulation*. You can't live as a Christian in a sinful world without tribulation. Jesus came to bring not peace but a sword. He described himself as a stone, rejected by the builders. "Any man who falls on that stone will be dashed to pieces; and if it falls on a man he will be crushed by it" (Luke 20:18 NEB). Too often we forget those stern words, or the prophecy of old Simeon when Jesus was a baby: "Many in Israel will stand or fall because of Him"(Luke 2:35 NEB).

What I have to say is infinitely more important than solutions. It is a matter of obedience. In other words, if you are the one deeply longing for help, there are answers—answers which will please God and enable you to do his will. Will they "work"? you ask. The answer is yes—in terms of the Kingdom. But be careful. The disciple cannot test the answers in terms of earthly success or satisfaction or solutions.

Obedience might in fact lead to reconciliation and thus to the miraculous repair of what seemed a hopeless mess. But then it might not lead to any such thing. Remember what Jesus promised to those who wanted to follow? "I have come to set fire to the earth . . . . Do you suppose that I came to establish peace on earth? No indeed, I have come to bring division" (Luke 12:49, 51, 52 NEB). "All will hate you for your allegiance to me. But not a hair of your head shall be lost" (Luke 21:17, 18 NEB).

What did he mean? He meant that sometimes there must be the choice between obedience and a solution—between his will and, for example, self-preservation. They are not always the same thing. As a matter of fact, in the Kingdom they often turn out to be quite opposite. "Whoever cares for his own safety is lost; but if a man will let himself be lost for my sake, that man is safe" (Luke 9:24 NEB). It's either/or. It's self-death and eternal life, or it's self-life and eternal death.

Divorce often seems the way not merely to happiness, but to simple survival and sanity. Not to divorce seems suicide. "This woman is ruining my entire career." "She's not a wife/he's not a husband." "This person is destroying my personhood." "Nobody can live with a woman like her."

It is clear that no direct action on your part will change another person. You can pray that God will change him, and you can let God change you (you may be the one who needs it more!).

"No," you say, "it's hopeless. Divorce is the only way. Not to divorce would be suicide." What a dilemma! A thing God hates on one hand, suicide on the other.

I must walk very softly here. I have never been in this fix. I cannot say "Our marriage was on the rocks and God worked a miracle for us." All I can say with confidence is that I have been in some other "fixes" in which obedience to God has appeared to be (humanly speaking) a terrible risk. At least once in my life it looked like "letting myself be lost." Suicide was not a word I used, because I was thinking in terms of Jesus' words quoted above, but it certainly was the word some people used regarding my decision.

Remember the martyr Stephen. It was witness that mattered, not self-preservation. Remember Shadrach, Meshach, and Abednego. It was witness that mattered, not self-preservation. I am not referring here to the popular use of the word *witness*—talking to somebody about his soul's salvation. I am speaking of a life laid down in obedience, whatever that obedience may entail. Such a life witnesses to love for God. One who loves him does what he says, cost what it may. Not a hair lost? No, not in terms of the Kingdom. But yes, in this world's terms, more than hair—the life itself—may be lost.

What, then, are the choices? I ask you gently and in the name of Christ, what do you really *want*? Is it Christ or happiness? Is it the will of the Father, or is it freedom from pain? Is it the Kingdom of Heaven or the kingdom of self?

If it is the Kingdom of Heaven you really want, then you can do only what fits the terms of that Kingdom. You will not be asking "Will this solve my problem?" or "What will I gain by this?" or "What are my rights?" You will be on your knees instead, saying "Thy kingdom come," which means "My kingdom go." You will be saying "Thy will be done," which means "My will be undone."

"So you're saying it's absolutely wrong for anybody to divorce anybody for any reason?" No. "Well, then, what are you saying? What am I supposed to do?"

So far I have been trying to encourage you to think as a Christian. We are all deeply infected by worldly patterns of thinking, and need constantly to bring our thoughts under

IS DIVORCE THE ONLY WAY?

Christ's authority. Pray for guidance. Clear up all that can be cleared up in your own heart and conscience, remembering always to act in the context of the Kingdom. The following chart may help to clarify your choices.

Which Context?

The Kingdom of Heaven	*The Kingdom of Self*
Thy will be done (which means my will be undone)	My will be done (which means Thy will be undone)
Losing myself and saving what matters far more	Saving myself and losing what matters far more
My aims: another's happiness and fulfillment; giving; glorifying God	my own happiness and fulfillment; getting; satisfying myself
My object: eternal gain	temporal gain
My right: that of John 10:18 to lay down my life	My right: to live life my way
My concern: obedience	solutions
The price: tribulation now; peace later; death to self; life forever	tribulation later, peace now; self-preservation; death forever

Christians are members of the Body of Christ. As such they do not act alone or in isolation, but always with reference to other members. For a clear, biblical treatment of the many complexities of the questions which are beyond the scope of this article, see Jay E. Adams: *Marriage, Divorce, and Remarriage* (Presbyterian and Reformed Publishing Co., Phillipsburgh, N.J.). Dr. Adams shows strongly the importance of the church's action in these matters. Discipline is the church's responsibility. Don't try to sort it all out alone. Go to the elders and deacons of a church where the Bible is believed to be authoritative, and submit yourself to their ruling.

It is very likely that the first task assigned you will be repentance. Whether you are the one suing for divorce, or the one sued, you will have sinned *in some way, at some time,* against your spouse and against God (I do not speak from experience here). Confess every sin you can think of—every nasty thought, every sinful word or deed, everything left undone that should have been done, every attitude of rebellion and resentment and bitterness and hate. Confess them to God. Perhaps you will next have to confess to your spouse if he or she is still around and willing to listen. Remember the question asked early in this discussion—what is needed now to move into that heavenly Kingdom? This is it: repentance. Turning around 180 degrees, and moving in the opposite direction. Taking a new route. Relinquishing the old.

After you have done that, you must forgive. You must forgive the other one even if he/she does not forgive you, and cares not at all to be forgiven. I do not say you must give him/her a list of offenses which you are now going to cross off. Read the list only to God and cross them off in his presence. The items which your spouse knows about, which you have accused him of, you will probably need to forgive him for, specifically, to his face. No matter what he or she has done (and "sides" don't matter here—there is sin on both) you must forgive.

Since unforgiveness roots itself down in hate, Satan has room for both feet in such a heart, with all the leeway action of such purchase. That word unforgiving! What a group of relatives it has, near and far! Jealousy, envy, bitterness, the cutting word, the polished shaft of sarcasm with the poisoned tip, the green eye, the acid saliva—what kinsfolk these!

S. D. Gordon: *Quiet Talks on Prayer*
p. 79, Revell

I have known what it is to lose a husband through death but not through divorce. When my first husband died, a newly divorced friend wrote, "Don't forget there are *much* worse ways to lose one!" I have no doubt about that. I am sure a much sorer wound results from rejection or unfaithfulness than from death. The healing of such a wound must be very deep, and, as with the healing of a physical wound, there may need to be both cutting and cleansing before there can be healing. The Word cuts. Taking heed to the Word cleanses. Then God (and only God) does the healing. He creates new life and new flesh. His forgiveness for us is as boundless and just as certain as it was for his disobedient people Israel, of whom he said, "I will bring them back to this place and let them dwell there undisturbed. They shall become my people and I will become their God" (Jeremiah 32:37, 38, NEB). It may be that the rest of that promise will be quite literally fulfilled as well: "I will give them one heart and one way of life so that they shall fear me at all times, for their own good and the good of their children after them" (verse 39).

Does it seem impossible? Then perhaps you're still thinking in the context of this world. Try the other context, the one in which all things become new and even the dead are raised.

IMAGES
OF HELL

Somehow or other North Dakota did not seem quite the place where my husband and I expected to find the sort of television program which shocked us. We were in a motel—not one of those that offers Home Box Office or other special shows for a fee, but a perfectly ordinary one. The program that stopped us in our tracks was, we discovered, a perfectly ordinary one that is shown all over the country, twenty-four hours a day. It hasn't gotten to the Boston area as far as I know, but it will. It is rock music—the screaming, thundering, pulsating, shrieking, ear-drubbing, earsplitting, ear-bludgeoning kind, played by groups with names like Cheap Trick, the Boomtown Rats, the Sex Pistols, Missing Persons, The Destroyers, and The Clash. Across the bottom of the screen ran a legend from time to time, giving the name of the soloist, the title of the "music," and the group performing. Song titles were such things as "Screaming for Vengeance," "Bad Boy Having a Party," "Children of the Grave," "Escalator of Life" ("I'm shoppin' the human mall" was a line from that one), "Combat Rock," "Maneater," and "Paranoid."

Songs, they're called. I had some idea that singing was supposed to touch the heart. What is the condition of the heart that is touched by titles like those? What was happening on the screen was at least as depressing. The music was being drama- tized by children. They were heavily made up, of course, doing their level best to act as sophisticated, blasé, and bored as adults must seem to them, but it was plain that most of them were teenagers, early teenagers. They were slinking around bars, slouching along brilliantly lighted city streets; toying with elegant wineglasses in high-toned restaurants, smoking with long, slim, shiny cigarette holders. They were gazing dully at the camera, looking up through lowered eyebrows or down through false eyelashes. They were writhing in horizontal positions, or girls were sashaying away from boys, casting over a raised shoulder the cruel come-on glance of the vamp. Boys were striding with thrust-forward pelvises toward the girls, breathing heavily through parted lips, hulking, swaying, scowling.

The camera went from these scenes to the rock groups sweating and screaming under the colored lights, dressed in rags, blue jeans, tights, sequins, undershirts, and in some cases nearly nothing. Hair was stringy, spinachy, wild—or "punk rock," dyed, partially shaved, stiff. They smashed, hammered, clob- bered those drums. They doubled up in agony over their guitars, striving, twisting, stamping, and jumping. Their faces were contorted with hatred or pain, at times jeering, insolent, defiant. Back the camera would go then to the slithering kids trying to "express themselves" or to play out the lyrics which were being yelled at top decibel by whoever was clutching the microphone. (How do their vocal cords stand it?)

But oh, the faces of those kids. I was riveted to the screen, aghast, horrified. There was a terrible fascination in the very absence of reality. How had they been programmed to erase from their fresh young faces every trace of personality, every least hint of humanity? They stared with unblinking blankness, lifeless, spiritless, cold. A strange and surreal alternative to the spastic seizures, paroxysms, and nauseated retchings of the "musicians."

This, then, is what rock music is all about. Images of Hell. That's all I could think of. Hell is the place where those whose motto is *My will be done* will finally and forever get what they want. Hell is agony and blankness and torture and the absence of all that humanity was originally destined to be. The glory has terminally departed. It is the heat of flames (not of passion—that will long since have burned out) and the appalling lifelessness of solid ice, an everlasting burning and an irreversible freezing.

Tyndale House's little paper, *The Church Around the World,* cited a study by Columbia University which helps to explain why we get what we get on TV:

- 50% of those controlling the media have "no religion"
- 8% attend church or synagogue weekly
- 86% attend seldom or never
- 84% believe government should have no laws regulating sex
- 55% believe extramarital affairs are not immoral
- 95% believe homosexuality is not wrong
- 85% believe homosexuals should be permitted to teach in public schools

I do not plan a campaign to squelch rock music. It is simply an accurate expression of the powers that are at work in our society:

> For the words that the mouth utters come from the overflowing of the heart. A good man produces good from the store of good within himself; and an evil man from evil within produces evil. . . . Out of your own mouth you will be acquitted; out of your own mouth you will be condemned.

Matthew 12:35, 36 NEB

108

From racket, din, cacophony, and pandemonium ("all demons"), Good Lord, deliver us. Give us the strength that comes from quietness; your gentleness, Lord, your peace. And one more thing, Lord—put a new song in our mouths, even praise to our God.

WHEN I WAS
BEING MADE
IN SECRET

As I drove into the yard a boy of nine raced across the lawn with his new golden retriever puppy on a training lead.

"Aunt Betty! This is Bucky! We just got him!" Within the next few minutes, I heard all about Bucky and about Charles's new collections of stamps, baseball cards, and toy cars (among them a police car, a space vehicle, a green hatchback, a Volkswagen with oversize tires, and a model of "Le Car"), as well as about his golf lessons ("I got a set of clubs, too!"), tennis lessons ("Look at my new racquet!"), the Christmas cards he is selling in order to win prizes, and about sleeping on the screened porch in a sleeping bag.

Nothing extraordinary or astonishing about this nine-year-old. He's lively, he has a very wide grin, he wears ragged cutoffs, and he even chopped up his shirt with scissors (collar and sleeves were too hot, he explained). His blond hair sticks out in funny places, and his striped tennis shoes seem as clumsily huge as Mickey Mouse's always did.

But yesterday when I visited this charming nephew of mine I thought of some people I saw last month when I went to a hospital in Mississippi to visit my new granddaughter Elisabeth. I peered eagerly through the nursery window along with all the other grandmothers and the smug fathers. "Ours" was shown to us by the nurse, a beautiful tiny thing clenching her perfect fists. I gazed as enthralled as though I had never seen a newborn child, as though Elisabeth were the first of her kind ever to appear to mystify and bewitch and melt the soul of a grandmother.

It was at the back of the nursery that I saw the people who affected me very differently but also very deeply. They were extremely small. A nurse thrust her hands into built-in rubber gloves in the side of an incubator and ever so gently lifted a little creature that looked infinitely more fragile and helpless than our baby, a "preemie" of perhaps two and a half pounds. He was one of several in incubators, and as I watched them lying there, eyes bandaged against the heat lamp, moving and breathing in their plastic boxes, I thought of Charles, who was just such a baby nine years ago. Born three months early, he was not expected to make it through the first night.

Earnestly prayed for by his parents and many others, cared for continuously by many hands as gentle as those of the nurse I watched in Mississippi, he survived.

Not long ago I saw a picture which will remain ineradicable in my mind: a black plastic garbage bag which contained what was left of the morning's work in one city hospital—four or five babies, some of them the size of Charles when he was born, some of them larger. They were rejects.

Who is it that makes the "selections"? Who may determine which tiny person is acceptable and may be permitted to be born (and if necessary, hovered over, cradled in a sterile temperature-controlled incubator to assist his survival), and which is unacceptable and may be treated as a cancer or a gangrenous growth and surgically or chemically removed? What perverted vision of "life enhancement" warrants such a choice?

Gloria Steinem appeared on television recently to speak about what she calls "pro-choice." What she did not say, what no proponent of abortion ever says, is that the choice they defend is the choice to kill people. Babies are people, but the U.S. Supreme Court has decreed that certain people, if they are young enough and helpless enough, may be killed.

Another choice which the courts and modern liberality and morality permit us to make is the choice of a tasteful vocabulary. To begin with, the rejects I saw in the plastic bag are not babies, they are not people, they are, if small enough and unrecognizable enough, merely "tissue" or, as ethicist Charles Curran puts it, "the matter involved in the research." If undeniably identifiable, they are but the "products of conception." Well, so is Charles. So am I.

Words most assiduously to be avoided are "kill" and "murder." They were also avoided by the physicians who supervised the "selections" in Nazi concentration camps. Heirs to Europe's proudest medical traditions, they resorted to complicated mental gymnastics to provide moral and scientific legitimacy for Hitler's crazed racial and biological notions. In a world forty years advanced from those barbarities we speak of freedom, of the liberation of women, of the right over our own bodies— viewing ourselves as emancipated and enlightened while we sink into ever more diabolical (though always finely calculated and carefully rationalized) modes of self-worship and idolatry.

When anyone has the indelicacy to call a spade a spade (i.e., an abortion a murder) he is accused (as in *Time*, July 30, 1979) of "hateful propaganda, harassment, disregard of other people's civil rights . . . an attempt to force [his] own perception of morality on everyone else." It was Uta Landy, executive director of the National Abortion Federation in New York, who wrote that.

Shall we, like those idealists in Germany, in order to evade the real horror, invoke such forms of self-delusion and insist on innocuous and deceptive terms like "procedure" or "loss" instead of "killing," or "tissue" for "child"? While we pharisaically deplore Malaysia's management of the pitiful "boat people" (the Home Affairs Minister, Ghazali bin Shafie, said, "The Vietnamese keep throwing rubbish into our gardens"), we rationalize and legalize—we even feel it our duty to facilitate and finance—the disposal of tens of thousands of—what shall we call them if not *people*?

I could not miss the ironies of *The New Yorker*'s editorializing about Malaysia. Not many months ago it threw up its hands in horror at those who would oppose "the right to choose" abortion. Now it points out that it is the policy of our government to favor human rights around the world, yet "one of earth's peoples is being set adrift on the high seas, and in the whole wide world there is no dependable place of refuge."

Let us who claim to accept moral responsibility for refugees and the world's rejects remember that another of earth's peoples is being "selected," shall we say, for annihilation. We are accused of insensitivity if we mention the black plastic garbage bags or saline burning or the intrauterine dismemberment of gestating human beings, but in the whole wide world is there for them "no dependable place of refuge"?

Let us consider these things in quietness before God who sees them all. "O Lord, thou hast searched me and known me . . . my frame was not hidden from thee when I was being made in secret . . . . Thy eyes beheld my unformed substance; in thy book were written, every one of them, the days that were formed for me, when as yet there was none of them . . . . See if there be any wicked way in me, and lead me in the way everlasting."

LONDON DIARY

Maundy Thursday   TWA out of Boston at 8:30 P.M. Huge plane, a 1011, every seat full—at least a third of them, it seems, with kids on vacation. (If they go to England for spring vacation when they're in the ninth grade, what do they do in the tenth?)

I am in row 27 next to a woman who is traveling with the two women in front of us. Steward pauses in aisle: "Excuse me, ladies, are you traveling together?" he asks me. "No." He studies the paper in his hand. "Well, you see, I need these seats." My hopes soar. Once before in my life I've heard this and been moved up to first class. "I'll be happy to change," I tell him. My seatmate explains that she is traveling with the others. "Must you travel together?" he asks, still studying his seating chart. "Yes." Long pause. "Well, then, I'll take the three of you." Off they go to first class, elated. I, deflated, stay in tourist class.

Dinner served at 11:00 P.M. I doze off when the movie begins. Shortly after midnight, Eastern Standard Time, sky turns orange. At 1 they bring breakfast and at 2 we are at Heathrow Airport.

Good Friday   I breeze through passage marked "Nothing to Declare." Mary, former missionary colleague from Ecuador, bursts from crowd, runs toward me grinning. Friend with car (which we cannot find for some time—he forgets which level he parked it on) drives us to Mary's flat, stopping in Kew Gardens. "Come down to Kew in lilac time . . . it isn't far from London." But it is too early for lilacs. Tulips and daffodils in abundance. Lovely freshness, greenness of new spring grass, budding trees. Bicycles, baby carriages, strollers. People on benches, being blessed by sun. Hideous scream of 747s overhead, directly on landing pattern for Heathrow. (It is nice to be a privileged person inside one. Now I am an annoyed person under one.)

Mary's flat in East Dulwich (pronounced Dullage) very tiny. In row of houses called "terraces," of which England has millions. Every house has two stories, two chimneys, four chimney pots. Bay window on each floor, brightly painted trim (liver green, electric blue, lavender are favorites), four-foot square "garden" in front with hedge and/or wall and gate. Tiny cars parked in street. Flat has living room "lounge,"single bedroom, bath, and diminutive kitchen. Tiny stove, tiny refrigerator, tiny sink. To an English housewife, surely, everything in my kitchen would be huge—unnecessarily, perhaps outrageously, huge. In lounge are seven chairs, three small tables, bookcases, two electric heaters, two afghans, two candlesticks, two Ecuadorian paintings, two wood carvings, thirteen Easter cards taped to back of door.

Jet lag. Afternoon nap. Mary gives me bedroom, sleeps on floor of lounge. Bach's *St. Matthew Passion*, sung from Lincoln Cathedral, is on the "telly" when I awake. Followed by Stainer's *Crucifixion*.

Saturday   Red double-decker bus to Tottenham Court Road. Lecture on Elgin (the *g* is hard) Marbles at British Museum. We see the Marbles—the frieze removed from the Parthenon by Lord Elgin in order to preserve it. Sublime, almost alive. 192 men on horseback. Men mounted on horses in Greek sculpture represent heroes. Herodotus, the lecturer tells us, reported 192 men killed in the Battle of Marathon.

Rosetta Stone. Mummy from 3000 B.C., body in fetal position, hair still intact. Library closed. E. M. Forster's childhood letters on display.

Easter Vigil at All Saints, Margaret Street. Total darkness, fire kindled in courtyard, candles in hands of all worshippers, music, litany, then darkness again. Sudden burst of light and organ music, the ringing of many bells. *He is Risen!*

Easter Sunday   Westminster Abbey, founded by Edward the Confessor in 1065, originally a Benedictine monastery with an enclosed choir in which the monks sang offices. We sit in choir, close to boy singers, their music and discipline nearly perfect. Hymn from Medieval Latin with seventeenth-century German melody: "Light's glittering morn bedecks the sky; Heaven thunders forth its victor-cry: Alleluia!" A black man opposite me sings every word from memory, his face radiant.

The prayers: "To Thee we give high praise and hearty thanks . . . above all for Thine inestimable love in giving Thine only Son, our Saviour Jesus Christ . . . He made a full, perfect, and sufficient sacrifice for the sins of the whole world. . . ." For nine hundred years of sinners who met in this one place—kings, queens, monks, tailors, candlestickmakers, tourists. Prayers and hymns ascend from all of them through these arches and clerestories, unknown to one another, fully known to God, fully loved. Wesley's hymn, "Vain the stone, the watch, the seal, Christ hath burst the gates of hell!" Sermon by the dean of the abbey: "The splendor of Easter is born out of the dereliction of the Cross."

Tombs, sarcophagi, memorial tablets—"In memory of the people who served in the Sudan," "In memory of twenty-six monks who died in the Black Death, 1342." David Livingstone, "brought by faithful hands over land and sea." Tablets commemorating a plumber and a musician who served the abbey. Bells ring from the steeples, Big Ben chimes as we leave.

Victoria Embankment Gardens. Daffodils, daffodils, daffodils. Blackbirds singing. Sunshine. Statue of William Tyndale, 1484–1536. He prayed before his martyrdom, "Lord, open the King of England's eyes." A year later, says the inscription, a Bible was placed in every church by the king's command. All London—all Europe and India, in fact—seem to be on the embankment. Sunday papers, queues for the tour boats, iced lollies, cameras. At St. Paul's a notice: "Please do not carry ice creams into the cathedral." We obey.

Monday To Waltham Abbey, founded by King Harold in 1066. Waltham Cross, erected at one of the stations where King Edward halted in his journey to bring the body of his queen Eleanor from the north to London. Tea with Mary's friend, Gae, in her old country house. Hot cross buns, cake. Gae's nephew, Mark, three years old, in cultured English accent, asks, "May I show you the lawn mowah?" To the garden shed. "This one is the fly (i.e., rotary) mowah. It spreads the grass all over the place! And this one is the blade mowah." Someone tells Mark that I have a grandson, Walter. "Has his daddy got a fly mowah?" he asks at once.

Tuesday I speak at Peckham Road Gospel Hall. Tea and cakes beforehand. ("Gracious living does take time," my sister-in-law once remarked.) Old ladies in brimless, cushionlike hats, winter coats. One of them sees a picture of my daughter Valerie: "She looks an absolute poppet!" Many West Indians in audience. A lady whispers to me afterwards, "You are the first woman my husband has ever listened to!"

Wednesday I speak at St. Patrick's Church, Wallington. The canon takes me home for dinner. Ham, creamed (i.e., mashed) potatoes, roast potatoes, peas, beans, trifle. Lady at table says, "But of course Americans have many domestic servants!" In my talk at the church I mention Edith Cherry's hymn, "We Rest on Thee, Our Shield and Our Defender," speaking of how five missionaries in Ecuador sang it and then were speared to death. Our faith must embrace this, as did the faith of John the Baptist who lost his head and of Stephen who was stoned to death. Man says to me later, "That hymn will never be the same to me again." People who want autographs queue very politely. Another difference from Americans.

Thursday   Taxi, bus, train to Edenbridge. Taxi driver, asked how he'd like a woman prime minister, says, "Ah've got one woman over me now—and a good one, mind, Ah'm not complainin'—but I don't want another one!" Bus driver: "That's right, ducks, up you go!" Trainman: "Come along, love!" Station buffet offers pork pie, steak-and-kidney pie, sausage rolls, chocolate biscuits, coffee, tea, bovril, mineral water. No hot dogs, milk shakes, Fritos. From the train we see small houses, small gardens, small cars, small people, small shops. English economy. No wonder. It's a small island. No wonder Americans seem crass and extravagant. In one garden we see espaliered fruit trees (trained to grow flat on a trellis), a wonderful economy of space.

Friday   Coach from Marylebone Station to Derbyshire, where I am to speak at a conference of the South American Missionary Society. (I learn that a bus is red, and double-decker. A coach is what Americans would call a bus, usually chartered.) Women clutching umbrellas, shopping bags (*all* English women, I think, have shopping bags), thermos "flasks," sandwiches, chattering happily. Men with briefcases, sweaters underneath suitcoats, earnestly discuss mission strategy. An Australian woman across the aisle is the only one wearing makeup. English countryside—hedgerows, green pastures, daffodils (they seem to grow wild), rooks' nests in bare trees. Man flies a red kite that has a blue tail. Clean new lambs with black faces and black legs caper around placid weatherstained ewes. "Little Lamb, God bless thee!"

Lorries, which outnumber cars on the motorway, are labeled "Bird's Custard," "Removals and Haulage," "Walker's Potato Crisps," "King's Road Tyres."

Swanwick (pronounced Swanick), a once lovely country house turned into a conference center. Wallpaper in my room: yellow, green, orange flowers, each eighteen inches in diameter. Carpet: red and black. Bedspread: brown. Curtains: purple and brown. Hallway: green and purple striped wallpaper, red and blue striped carpet, turquoise woodwork, lavender doors. Outdoors, loveliness everywhere. Formal gardens, pastures with cows, pond, rolling meadows, blackbirds. Daffodils, of course.

Saturday   Meetings in morning. A Latin American evangelist, a bishop from Chile, an ex-missionary from Ecuador. Afternoon: drive to Matlock where we have a "cream tea"—tea, scones, thick "clotted" cream, strawberry jam.

Sunday   Archbishop Donald Coggan preaches a brief and moving sermon from John 20: "He came . . . stood . . . spoke . . . showed . . . breathed. So He comes to us, frightened at the unknown. . . ." At lunch Major Somebody talks to me about how to minister to widows. A young man speaks of how his own life was changed—he became a missionary with SAMS—because of the testimony of Jim Elliot. I am driven to London by a Baptist minister who attended conference. Stay with a friend in elegant flat in Kensington. Fifteen-foot ceilings, beautiful mouldings, antique furniture, fabrics all designed by my friend Leonie herself.

Monday   Shopping at Harrod's department store. I buy small leather books, Beatrix Potter table mats for friends. In the Food Hall hundreds of sausages, hams, cheeses suspended from lofty ceiling. Great slabs of smoked salmon. Cans of ox tongues. In the garden furniture department, real fruit on the tables, a real tree bearing limes. Could this be anywhere but in England, anywhere else than Harrod's? Lunch at Simpson's—roast beef and Yorkshire pudding. Good-bye to Mary and Gae at air terminal. Gae says Mark has informed everyone this week that Waltah's daddy has a fly mowah.

Leave London on TWA, 5:00 P.M., Daylight Time. Reach U.S. 6:30 P.M., Eastern Standard Time, after seven hours' flight.

I go over my notes. Only a travelogue. A few highlights from many things that seemed to happen in an instant of time. The distance is hard to grasp, having been swallowed up with such speed—rushing into dawn one night, rushing back toward the sunset so fast it hadn't time to fade but hovered stationary on the horizon for seven hours.

Strangely, the vignettes that stay with me were not in the diary notes. A "punch-up" on the sidewalk below Mary's window as we sat at tea. Two women screaming obscenities (some of them new to me), kicking each other in the face, pulling hair, rolling on the street. The desperation of their empty lives tore at my imagination.

The tall sorrowful woman in purple in Westminster Abbey. A purple crocheted hat with ribbons, two long gray pigtails, a flowing purple silk scarf, long purple skirt, purple shoes. She stood gazing at something high above her.

The taxi driver who refused to take us home late, following the vigil. "Well, thanks anyway," Mary called. "Have a Happy Easter!"

"Oh, I could never have that, love," he said. "My wife's just got cancer."

Lord, by the stripes which wounded Thee
From death's dread sting Thy servants free
That we may live and sing to Thee, Alleluia!

HOW TO
SELL
YOURSELF

A couple of hundred secretaries attended a seminar in Syracuse a few months ago. Because I happened to be in the hotel that day, I did a little eavesdropping.

The speaker was a snappily dressed, fast-talking Yuppie who dished out a lot of expensive advice about how to sell yourself in the business world. By the way you dress, she explained, you can put across a message of power (suits, ladies, not soft sweaters; skirts, not slacks; pumps, not sandals).

The way you wear your hair tells the boss more than your resume did. Hair over the forehead tells him (yes, the lecturer did actually refer to the boss as "him" most of the time) you're shy, coy, or afraid of something; long, loose stuff says you haven't grown up. And you *know* what fluffed-out hair proclaims the minute you walk into the office: fluffbrain!

What you eat for lunch and how you arrange your desk lets people know who's in charge. No creamed dishes, no desserts; no teddy bears or cutesy mottoes on the desk. Feel good about yourself—slim, trim, lots of vim. Be assertive. Be confident. Walk into the head office in your elegant Joseph A. Bank suit—dark (of course) impeccably (of course) tailored (of course). Stand tall. Head up. Smile. Give him the kind of handshake that lets him know it could have been a knuckle-cruncher—he'll get the message: *power*. You're in charge.

Beneath the Surface

In *Tree of Life* magazine Peter Reinhart writes:

The spirit of this age is one of personal power; the spirit of Christ is one of humility. The spirit of this age is one of ambitious accomplishment; the spirit of Christ is one of poverty. The spirit of this age is one of self-determination; the spirit of Christ is one of abandonment to Divine Providence.

He goes on to suggest a new kind of seminar: training in the assertion of *virtues*—humility, for example, spiritual poverty, purity of heart, chastity of mind. Instead of self-reliance he sees reliance on Christ as the source of empowerment and liberation.

So do I. To be Christ's slave is perfect freedom.

Will this idea sell? Will it work? Can we really get what we want this way? The third question is the crucial one for Christians. Answer it, and you already have the answer to the first two.

If what you want is what the world wants, nobody will be able to sell Reinhart's seminar to you. It isn't going to work.

But if you've made up your mind to have what the world despises—the things that last forever—and if Jesus Christ is Lord of your life, the whole picture, even in the dog-eat-dog world of competition and big money and big success, will be different.

What distinguishes the Christian from others in that world? I admit the validity of some of the Yuppie's advice, silly as it sounds. The medium, alas, *is* to a certain extent the message. A Christian must be at least as careful, sensible, and serious about doing the job properly as anybody else. He must also dress and act carefully, sensibly, seriously. Man looks on the outward appearance because it's the only thing man can look on. God alone can look on the heart.

What's in the heart reveals itself sooner or later. You may get the job on the basis of first appearance. You'll keep it on the basis of how you perform day by day. Many perform well because they're after money and power—but there's nearly always room for a little fudging here and there, a lot of elbowing and shoving and downright trampling of whoever's in your way, not to mention high-level crimes that people get away with.

The Christian in the office or factory or construction job operates from a wholly different motive: "service rendered to Christ himself, not with the idea of currying favor with men, but as the servants of Christ conscientiously doing what you believe to be the will of God for you" (Ephesians 6:5, 6 PHILLIPS).

How High, How Mighty?

I would hope that the Christian businessman or woman, whether lowest on the corporate totem pole or the chief executive officer, would be distinguished from the rest not only by conscientious work but also by graciousness, by simple kindness, by an unassuming manliness or a modest womanliness, and above all by a readiness to serve. There's nothing intrinsically wrong with ambition—Jesus often appealed to it—but the nature of those ambitions makes a huge difference: "He that would be chief among you must be servant of all," even if that means serving coffee instead of serving on the committee you were itching to join.

A Christian is the sort of person who can be asked to do whatever needs to be done without retorting, "That's not *my* job." Somebody is bound to remind me that you can get in trouble with the unions this way. Well, you know what I mean.

ON ASKING GOD WHY

Christians are *available*. Christians aren't too high and mighty to do the nasty little task nobody else will do. Christians can be counted on, imposed on, sometimes walked all over. Why not? Their Master was.

I think of my friend Betty Greene, a pilot (called an aviator in her early days) who ferried bombers during World War II and helped found Mission Aviation Fellowship. "I made up my mind," she told me, "that if I was to make it in a man's world, I would have to be a lady." A more ladylike lady I have never known. She knows when to keep her mouth shut. She's modest. She's the very soul of graciousness. She isn't trying to prove anything. Nate Saint, an early colleague of hers, once told me he had had no use for women pilots until he met Betty. She shook up his categories.

Christians ought to be always shaking up people's categories. I guess one of the things the world finds most infuriating about much-maligned Jerry Falwell is his unflappable graciousness, his refusal to retreat behind spurious logic. They'd like to call him a rednecked bigot, but he doesn't fit the category. His worst offense is that he's so often right. He speaks the truth—that's bad enough—and he speaks it in love. That's unforgivable.

"The very spring of our actions," said the apostle Paul, "is the love of Christ." That goes for all of us who claim the name *Christian*. It is the energizing principle of whatever we do—from praying and serving the church to laundry and lawn mowing and the jobs we get paid for. Charity is the word.

Charity? In the late twentieth century? Yes. If in home, school, and workplace the rule of each Christian's life were MY LIFE FOR YOURS ("in honor preferring one another") it would make a very great difference.

The Christian's distinctive mark is love. It was what set the Lord Jesus apart from all others. It was, in the end, what got him crucified. If we follow him in the marketplace, many of the self-promotion methods others use will be out of the question to us.

Won't we run the risks of being ignored, stepped on at times, passed over for a promotion? Yes, those and a good many others. But what price are we willing to pay for obedience? The faithful, unconcerned about self-actualization, will find along the pathway of self-denial the blossoms of fulfillment. We have our Lord's paradoxical promise in Luke 17:33: "Whoever tries to preserve his life will lose it, and the man who is prepared to lose his life will preserve it."

MEETING
GOD ALONE

A very tall man, wrapped in a steamer rug, kneeling alone by a chair. When I think of my father, who died in 1963, this is often the first image that comes to mind. It was the habit of his life to rise early in the morning—usually between 4:30 and 5:00 A.M.—to study his Bible and to pray.

We did not often see him during that solitary hour (he purposed to make it solitary), but we were used to seeing him on his knees. He had family prayers every morning after breakfast. We began with a hymn; then he read from the Bible to us; and we all knelt to pray. As we grew older, we were encouraged to pray alone as well.

Few people know what to do with solitude when it is forced upon them; even fewer arrange for solitude regularly. This is not to suggest that we should neglect meeting with other believers for prayer (Hebrews 10:25), but the foundation of our devotional life is our own private relationship with God.

My father, an honest and humble disciple of the Lord Jesus, wanted to follow his example: "Very early in the morning . . . Jesus got up, left the house and went off to a solitary place, where he prayed" (Mark 1:35).

Christians may (and ought to) pray anytime and anywhere, but we cannot well do without a special time and place to be alone with God. Most of us find that early morning is not an easy time to pray. I wonder if there is an *easy* time.

The simple fact is that early morning is probably the *only* time when we can be fairly sure of not being interrupted. Where can we go? Into "your closet," was what the Lord said in Matthew 6:6, meaning any place apart from the eyes and the ears of others. Jesus went to the hills, to the wilderness, to a garden; the apostles to the seashore or to an upper room; Peter to a housetop.

We may need to find a literal closet or a bathroom or a parked car. We may walk outdoors and pray. But we must *arrange* to pray, to be alone with God sometime every day, to talk to him and to listen to what he wants to say to us.

The Bible is God's message to everybody. We deceive ourselves if we claim to want to hear his voice but neglect the primary channel through which it comes. We must read his Word. We must obey it. We must live it, which means rereading it throughout our lives. I think my father read it more than forty times.

When we have heard God speak, what then shall we say to God? In an emergency or when we suddenly need help, the words come easily: "Oh, God!" or "Lord, help me!" During our quiet time, however, it is a good thing to remember that we are here not to pester God but to adore him.

All creation praises him all the time—the winds, the tides, the oceans, the rivers, move in obedience; the song sparrow and the wonderful burrowing wombat, the molecules in their cells, the stars in their courses, the singing whales and the burning seraphim do without protest or slovenliness exactly what their Maker intended, and thus praise him.

We read that our Heavenly Father actually looks for people who will worship him in spirit and in reality. Imagine! God is *looking for* worshippers. Will he always have to go to a church to find them, or might there be one here and there in an ordinary house, kneeling alone by a chair, simply adoring him?

How do we adore him? Adoration is not merely unselfish. It doesn't even take into consideration that the self exists. It is utterly consumed with the object adored.

Once in a while, a human face registers adoration. The groom in a wedding may seem to worship the approaching bride, but usually he has a few thoughts for himself—how does he look in this absurd ruffled shirt that she asked him to wear, what should he do with his hands at this moment, what if he messes up the vows?

I have seen adoration more than once on faces in a crowd surrounding a celebrity, but only when they were unaware of the television cameras, and only when there was not the remotest possibility that the celebrity would notice them. For a few seconds, they forgot themselves altogether.

When I stumble out of bed in the morning, put on a robe, and go into my study, words do not spring spontaneously to my lips—other than words like, "Lord, here I am again to talk to you. It's cold. I'm not feeling terribly spiritual. . . ." Who can go on and on like that morning after morning, and who can bear to listen to it day after day?

I need help in order to worship God. Nothing helps me more than the Psalms. Here we find human cries—of praise, adoration, anguish, complaint, petition. There is an immediacy, an authenticity, about those cries. They speak for me to God—that is, they say what I often want to say, but for which I cannot find words.

Surely the Holy Spirit preserved those Psalms in order that we might have paradigms of prayer and of our individual dealings with God. It is immensely comforting to find that even David, the great king, wailed about his loneliness, his enemies, his pains, his sorrows, and his fears. But then he turned from them to God in paeans of praise.

He found expression for praise far beyond my poor powers, so I use his and am lifted out of myself, up into heights of adoration, even though I'm still the same ordinary woman alone in the same little room.

Another source of assistance for me has been the great hymns of the Church, such as "Praise, My Soul, the King of Heaven," "New Every Morning Is the Love," "Great Is Thy Faithfulness," "Glorious Things of Thee Are Spoken," and "O Worship the King." The third stanza of that last one delights me. It must delight God when I sing it to him:

> *Thy bountiful care, what tongue can recite?*
> *It breathes in the air, it shines in the light;*
> *It streams from the hills, it descends to the plain,*
> *And sweetly distills in the dew and the rain.*

That's praise. By putting into words things on earth for which we thank him, we are training ourselves to be ever more aware of such things as we live our lives. It is easy otherwise to be oblivious of the thousand evidences of his care. Have you thought of thanking God for light and air, because in them his care breathes and shines?

Hymns often combine praise and petition, which are appropriate for that time alone with God. The beautiful morning hymn "Awake, My Soul, and With the Sun" has these stanzas:

> *All praise to Thee, who safe hast kept,*
> *And hast refreshed me while I slept.*
> *Grant, Lord, when I from death shall wake,*
> *I may of endless light partake.*
> *Direct, control, suggest, this day,*
> *All I design, or do, or say;*
> *That all my powers, with all their might,*
> *In Thy sole glory may unite.*

Adoration should be followed by confession. Sometimes it happens that I can think of nothing that needs confessing. This is usually a sign that I'm not paying attention. I need to read the Bible. If I read it with prayer that the Holy Spirit will open my eyes to this need, I soon remember things done that ought not to have been done and things undone that ought to have been done.

Sometimes I follow confession of sin with confession of ʿaith—that is, with a declaration of what I believe. Any one of the creeds helps here, or these simple words: "Christ has died; Christ is risen; Christ will come again. Lord, I believe; help my unbelief."

Then comes intercession, the hardest work in the world—the giving of one's self, time, strength, energy, and attention to the needs of others in a way that no one but God sees, no one but God will do anything about, and no one but God will ever reward you for.

Do you know what to pray for people whom you haven't heard from in a long time? I don't. So I often use the prayers of the New Testament, so all-encompassing, so directed toward things of true and eternal importance, such as Paul's for the Christians in Ephesus: ". . . I pray that you, rooted and founded in love yourselves, may be able to grasp . . . how wide and long and deep and high is the love of Christ" (Ephesians 3:17, 18). Or I use his prayer for the Colossians, "We pray that you will be strengthened from God's boundless resources, so that you will find yourselves able to pass through any experience and endure it with joy" (Colossians 1:11). I have included many New Testament prayers in a small booklet entitled *And When You Pray* (Good News Publishers).

My own devotional life is very far from being Exhibit A of what it should be. I have tried, throughout most of my life, to maintain a quiet time with God, with many lapses and failures. Occasionally, but only occasionally, it is impossible. Our Heavenly Father knows all about those occasions. He understands perfectly why mothers with small children bring them along when they talk to him.

Nearly always it is possible for most of us, with effort and planning and the will to do his will, to set aside time for God alone. I am sure I have lost out spiritually when I have missed that time. And I can say with the psalmist, "I have found more joy along the path of thy instruction than in any kind of wealth" (Psalms 119:14).

THE SONG
OF THE
ANIMALS

The sea gulls who daily fly past our house have a regular pattern: east to the rock called Norman's Woe in the morning, west to Kettle Island in the evening, with the setting sun rouging their feathers to glowing pink. Sometimes, in a strong wind, they sail up and over our house, but they do not land nearer than the sea-washed rocks. One day I was surprised to find a lone gull sitting on our deck. There was something odd about the way he sat, and the shape of his head. Moving to the window I saw that he had the plastic rings from a six-pack of drinks clamped in his bill and circling his neck. He sat very quietly, a little hunched, his head tipped inquiringly. He was caught in the rings, unable to close his beak. Was he perhaps, by daring to perch on our deck, asking for help? Slowly I opened the door and tiptoed toward him. His fierce bright eyes followed me unblinking, but he did not move. When, incredulous, I nearly touched him, off he flew.

Captive to one of the complicated "blessings" of civilization that sea gulls were never meant to cope with, my gull will have starved to death by now.

That ninety seconds or so on our deck brought to focus once

more a phrase I turn over and over in my mind: the redemption of creation.

"Redemption? But animals have no *souls*!" someone objects. Have they not? My Bible tells me of a great hope shared not only by angels and men and women, but "all things, whether in heaven or on earth" (Colossians 1:20); it tells me that *all* is to be "brought to unity in Christ" (Ephesians 1:10). What can this mean if not that in some way unimaginable to us now the suffering sea gull, along with all feathered, furred, scaled, and carapaced creatures, will be redeemed? "The universe itself is to be freed from the shackles of mortality" (Romans 8:19). Will not our ears someday hear the Song of the Animals? I think so. I pin my hopes on the vision of John: "Then I heard every created thing in heaven and on earth and under the earth and in the sea, all that is in them, crying, Praise and honor and glory and might to him who sits on the throne and to the Lamb for ever and ever" (Revelation 5:13).

WE'VE COME A LONG WAY—
OR HAVE WE?

Nowadays Christian women seem to be operating on the premise that they're perfectly free to do anything they like, including work outside the home. Whether they're young, middle-aged, or old, married or single, with children or without, droves of Christian women are now career-minded.

Isn't that okay? I'm not sure it is. Francis Schaeffer, shortly before he died, said, "Tell me what the world is saying now, and I'll tell you what the Church will be saying seven years from now." Careerism is one of the great cries of the feminist movement, and Christian women seem to be trotting along quite willingly, though perhaps five or seven years behind the secularists, tickled pink that "we've come a long way, baby."

Well, we certainly have. But is it in the right direction? Have Christian women's seminars, Christian books (and, dare I suggest it, Christian women's magazines), encouraged us, by the tacit acceptance of notions not carefully examined, to move in a direction which does not lead to freedom at all?

It's interesting to note a growing swell of disillusionment among women of the world. They're beginning to discover that the "fulfillment" they had sought in the business or professional world hasn't proved to be all that fulfilling. For many of them it's more like a sucked-out lemon.

Not long ago on the "Today Show" Jane Pauley hosted a TV special on working women. She's one herself, and I have a hunch she was wondering if other women had any unconfessed misgivings about the joys of a career. Is a career really stimulating? Is it really more "creative" than mothering or homemaking? Is it satisfying? Is it fun? Has it brought the fulfillment it promised? Her show was not a parade of happy faces. Women actually looked straight into the cameras and admitted they'd been had. They were willing to change their whole life-style, make sacrifices, do whatever was necessary, to get out of the work world. Several hard-driving executive types said they were going home to take care of their children. One newspaper columnist described the results of the new forms of child rearing as "emotional carnage."

Two psychologists, one from Yale, one from Harvard, have echoed these career women's misgivings, stating that what we are doing to our children now may be the equivalent of "psychological thalidomide." It's sobering to me to think that we may be maiming our children by depriving them of normal home life.

"You've got to be kidding," I hear someone say. "You aren't going to tell me that women with children aren't supposed to be working?" I'd be crazy to try to tell anybody that unless I had some authority more convincing than my personal bias. I think I have. It's a clear and simple list of things godly women—all of them—are meant to do, and it's found in Paul's instructions to a young pastor (Titus 2:3-5):

> Likewise, teach the older women to be reverent in the way they live, not to be slanderers or addicted to much wine, but to teach what is good. Then they can train the younger women to love their husbands and children, to be self-controlled and pure, to be busy

at home, to be kind, and to be subject to their husbands, so that no one will malign the word of God.

Might there be a pattern in these verses that we've ignored? I've met women lately who had jumped on the careerism bandwagon but have now discovered the Bible's pattern (more of it can be found in 1 Timothy 5). Realizing that the life-style they've been pursuing doesn't fit the biblical pattern, they are making drastic changes. For some of them the cost has been high, but not too high for the liberation that comes with honest obedience.

I'm one of those older women Paul refers to. If I'm a Christian, I am bound by what Scripture tells me to do (there's no Christianity without obedience). By every means open to me, I am to "teach," that is, to set an example, to be a model for younger women—by reverence; by self-control; by being a loving wife and mother; pure; kind; working *at home;* respecting the authority of my husband; prayerful; worshipful; hospitable; willing to do humble and dirty jobs; taking "every opportunity of doing good" (1 Timothy 5:10 NEB).

That's a tall order. Who of us is sufficient for these things? None of us, of course, without a large portion of the grace of God every minute of every day. But if we will trust him for that grace, we must be sure our wills are lined up with his and our lives ordered according to his pattern.

There are many "buts" in our minds whenever we face truthfully any of God's clear directives. I am well aware of the thousands of women without men who must find some way to support themselves and their children. The Lord who gave us his pattern also knows intimately every situation: "Your Heavenly Father knows that you need these things." Might he have another way than the one which seems inevitable? Might there be a way to work at home? How serious are we about following him? Whoever is willing to obey will be shown the way.

THE CHRISTIAN'S SAFETY

One afternoon more than twenty years ago I was sitting in a hammock in eastern Ecuador. On the floor of my thatched house sat Minkayi, an Auca Indian, telling a story into the plastic microphone of a battery-powered tape recorder:

"One morning I had gone a short distance in my canoe when I heard the knocking of another man's canoe pole. It was Dabu. 'Are you going home?' I asked him. 'Yes,' he said. 'Naenkiwi says those foreigners are cannibals.' Later I found Gikita in his house. He said he was going to get some spears. My spears were not far away.

"Soon I found Gikita and Dyuwi putting red dye on their spears, getting them ready. 'Naenkiwi says those foreigners are going to eat us,' they told me. I still had not dyed my spears, but when afternoon came they had all dyed theirs and I was just sitting there. Finally I told my mother to go down and bring my spears up so I could dye them. 'Just bring a few,' I said, and off she went. I asked Naenkiwi how many spears he had. 'Two hard ones and two lightweight ones,' he said."

Rummaging in the old footlocker in the basement years later I found my transcript of Minkayi's story. Six pages long, it was a minutely detailed account of how six Indian men ambushed five Americans one hot Sunday afternoon on a sandspit of the Curaray River.

Minkayi got quite excited telling the story. He described the journey to the beach, up hills, across rivers, through an old clearing where he had once seen a jaguar, finally reaching the place where they knew a small plane had landed. He told how one foreigner was walking up and down the beach, calling and calling. "Come!" he was saying. "Come in a friendly way, come without harm!"

Then, with vivid sound effects which I had transcribed phonetically, Minkayi told of the sudden rush with spears, accompanied by Auca war cries, and of the sounds the spears made hitting their targets. He did not spare the details of the long struggle, the suffering, and the Indians' final victory.

As I read the words, memory brought into sharp focus the cheerful, friendly man holding the microphone. Minkayi knew, of course, that one of the supposed cannibals had been my husband. When he had finished his tale, he picked up Jim's picture from the top of the kerosene boxes that served for my bookcase.

"Look at him smiling at us!" he said. "If we had known him as we know you, he'd be sitting here smiling with us this morning. A cannibal! We thought he was a cannibal!" I remembered how his face broke into a grin.

God is God. That was the stunning lesson of that most stunning event in my life. Jim's death required me to deny God or believe him, to trust him or renounce him. The lesson is the same for all of us. The contexts differ.

There was nothing new to Minkayi about killing people. He and the others had done it any number of times. If you think you are going to be eaten, you protect yourself somehow. It probably looked like a duty. I thought of Jesus' words when he was about to leave his disciples: "The time is coming when anyone who kills you will suppose that he is performing a religious duty. They will do these things because they do not know either the Father or me. I have told you all this so that when the time comes for it to happen you may remember my warning" (John 16:3).

"The time is coming. . . . Remember my warning." How safe are we? The five men had been missionaries, not cannibals. They had gone into Auca territory to take the Gospel there, not to eat Indians. They loved God. They trusted him. They had prayed for protection, guidance, and success, and they had put their faith in him as shield and defender. As we, their wives, prayed with them over every step of the preparations for this venture, we thought surely God would protect and guide and give success. But it was the Indians who had the success. They won.

What then is faith? What in heaven's name do we mean when we say, "In God we trust"?

Dr. James I. Packer, in his book *God's Words*, says "The *popular* idea of faith is of a certain obstinate optimism: the hope, tenaciously held in face of trouble, that the universe is fundamentally friendly and things may get better."

I would have had to be an optimist of the most incorrigible obstinacy to have held on to that sort of faith in the dark times of my own life. It has been another faith that has sustained me—faith in the God of the Bible, a God, as someone once put it, not small enough to be understood but big enough to be worshipped.

I grew up with the Bible. I learned what faith is through the example of my parents and many other godly people. I went to Sunday school, church, missionary conferences, a Christian high school and college, and a Bible school. I yielded heart and life to Christ at an early age.

But when I arrived in Ecuador as a missionary, well prepared, I felt, for whatever lay ahead, my expectations were far from spiritually mature. Like Peter, I was still thinking as men think, not as God thinks. Peter recoiled in horror when his master explained what was to happen to Jesus when he got to Jerusalem. "Heaven forbid!" was Peter's response. "Nothing like that must happen to you!" Jesus turned to him with a devastating rebuke, identifying his disciple with Satan, because he stood in the way of obedience to the Father.

As I began mission work, I expected God to operate my way. "Heaven forbid that anything unfavorable should interrupt my work!" I expected him to do what I asked, not realizing what it means to pray, "Hallowed be thy name, thy kingdom come, thy will be done." I wanted God to explain himself to me when my expectations were turned upside down.

God knew that what I really needed was not explanations but sanctification, *purifying*. My notions about myself, my work, and my God needed to be put through the fire. My heart needed deep and painful scouring. "Blessed are the pure in heart, for they shall see God."

As I studied the Bible and tried to obey it, I gradually saw that the God who is in charge has allowed all kinds of things to happen in the world that we would rather he had left out. Oh, we want our freedom, of course. Free will is a gift we would not wish to do without. Yet we wonder why God does not intervene in the exercise of *other* people's free will. Why are *they* allowed to cause wars and misuse resources and make others suffer? Why are poverty, government corruption, tyranny, and injustice permitted to go on and on? Of course it is never our choices that are at stake here; it is other people's. We do not want God to curtail our freedom; we only want him to restrain others'.

My questions were not answered, but I wanted to "see" God, to know him. So I kept on reading the Book, kept trying to apply it to my life, kept bringing my own thinking and conduct under its authority, seeking God's meaning in every event that touched me, including Jim's death and other crises. As God had promised, his Word proved true. He instructed me. He kept me. He held me. He showed me all I *needed* to know for life and godliness, although he did not unfold all I *wanted* to know for understanding.

After Jesus had rebuked Peter for not thinking as God thinks, he went on to point out exactly what the cost of discipleship would be: the end of self, the acceptance of a cross, and unconditional obedience. "Whoever cares for his own safety is lost," he said (Matthew 16:25).

Does this mean there is no safety for us? Is there no sure protection for the godly? Note what Jesus said about Elijah: "They worked their will upon him, and in the same way the Son of Man is to suffer at their hands" (Matthew 17:12).

Evil men have often been permitted to do what they please. We must understand that divine permission is given for evil to work. To know the God of the Bible is to see that he who could have made automatons of all of us made instead free creatures with power and permission to defy him.

There is a limit, of course. Let us not forget this. The Tower of Babel was stopped. God has set limits on what man is allowed to do, but one day he put himself into men's hands. Jesus had sat in the temple teaching and nobody touched him, but the time came when the same people who had listened to him barged into Gethsemane with swords and cudgels. Jesus did not flee. He walked straight up to them. He was unconcerned about physical safety. His only safety was the will of the Father. "This is your moment," he said, "the hour when darkness reigns" (Luke 22:53).

Why did God make room for that moment? Why should there ever be an hour when darkness is free to rule?

When Jesus refused to answer Pilate the next morning, Pilate said, "Surely you know that I have authority to release you and I have authority to crucify you." Jesus' reply embraces the mystery of evil: "You would have no authority at all over me if it had not been granted you from above" (John 19:10, 11).

Every man and woman who chooses to trust and obey God will find his faith attacked and his life invaded by the power of evil. There is no more escape for us than there was for the Son of Man. The way Jesus walked is the way we must walk. Again and again we will find ourselves looking to heaven in bewilderment and asking the old question *why*.

In Jesus' last intimate discourse with his disciples before going to the cross, he seems to have drawn back a corner of the curtain for a moment to give them a glimpse of a profound truth that was still very far beyond them yet had tremendous implications for them, as well as for us. These were his words: "The prince of this world approaches. He has no rights over me; but the world must be shown that I love the Father and do exactly as he commands" (John 14:30, 31). It is not an explanation of the mystery. It is a simple statement of fact and of duty: This is what will happen; therefore this is what I must do. Evil will come, but I must obey. The world must be shown.

The world's prince has power. That power does not nullify the will of the Father (it is still in effect), or defeat the obedience of the Son (he will go straight into the jaws of death). Nevertheless, the will of the Father, plus the obedience of the Son, plus the power of evil equalled the Crucifixion. *The world must be shown.* Through that hideous punishment the world would be shown two things: the Son's love and his absolute obedience.

The lesson is thus set for Christ's followers: If we believe that God is God, our faith is not a deduction from the facts around us. It is not an instinct. It is not inferred from the happy way things work. Faith is a gift from God, and we must respond to him with a decision: The God of the universe has spoken, we believe what he says, and we will obey. We must make a decision that we will hold in the face of all opposition and apparent contradiction.

The powers of hell can never prevail against the soul that takes its stand on God and on his Word. This kind of faith overcomes the world. The world of today must be shown. We (you and I) must show them what Jesus showed the world on that dark day so long ago—that we love the Father and will do what he says.

What was it about the film *Chariots of Fire* that struck so many people? I believe it was the young man's clear commitment—uncompromising, unapologetic. We do not know much about that type of commitment nowadays. Here was a man determined to obey God, and nothing could shake that—not the Prince of Wales, the prospect of an Olympic medal, or world fame.

The one thing this young man cared passionately about was what Jesus cared about. That was what took five men into a place they well knew was dangerous. In each case a decision had been made long before which covered all subsequent decisions. These men trusted and were not afraid. They had found the only place of safety in all of earth or heaven, the Lord God himself.

"In the Lord I have found my refuge; why do you say to me, 'Flee to the mountains like a bird; see how the wicked string their bows and fit the arrow to the string, to shoot down honest men out of the darkness'?" (Psalms 11:1, 2).

"Whoever cares for his own safety is lost; but if a man will let himself be lost for my sake, he will find his true self" (Matthew 16:25).

Letting go of what the world calls safety and surrendering to the Lord is our insurance of fulfillment. Christ knew his Father and offered himself unreservedly into his hands. If we let ourselves be lost for his sake, trusting the same God as Lord of all, we shall find safety where Christ found his, in the bosom of the Father.

TENDERNESS

There isn't a man or woman anywhere, I am convinced, who does not long for tenderness.

When I was in college, a girl who lived on my floor in the dormitory was pursued by a number of ardent young men on the campus. When the floor phone rang, we assumed it was for her. She was the kind who "could have anybody," it seemed, and treated most of them with casual carelessness. But one young man in particular would not be discouraged in his efforts to win her, even though she kept him at arm's length and declined some of his invitations. She made light of his attentions, as she did of many others', but was given pause one day when a bouquet arrived.

Like any woman, she eagerly snatched the card from its tiny envelope. Although one is supposed to be able to "say it with flowers," we all want plain English, too.

On the card were two words: *Tenderly, Bill.*

I think it did her in. She was a buoyant, outgoing, attractive, sometimes flippant girl, but that word pierced the armor. When she showed it to me, it gave me a whole new vision, through a single powerful word, of what that man was made of. He was not handsome by any means. He was rather ordinary, in fact. But suddenly I saw him as strong and unusually desirable. I had not known that tenderness was an absolutely essential ingredient in a man, but I knew it at once, when I saw the card, and mentally added it to the list of qualifications I would need if I ever found a husband.

PARABLE IN A
CAR WASH

My eighteen-month-old grandson Walter, his father, and I were out for a drive when his father decided it was time to have the car washed. Those automatic car washes can be a bit scary on the first run-through, even for an adult.

I watched Walter's face as the car was drawn into the dark tunnel. The water suddenly began to roar down over all four sides of the car, and his big blue eyes got bigger—but went immediately from the windows to the face of his father.

He was too small to understand what it was all about, and he'd had no explanation beforehand. What he did know was that Daddy would take care of him. Then the giant brushes began to close in around us, whirling and sloshing and making a tremendous racket. It grew even darker inside the car.

The boy had no way of knowing whether we'd get out of this alive. His eyes darted again from the brushes to the face of his father. I could see he was afraid, but he didn't cry.

Then the rubber wheel came banging down on the windshield, and hot air began to blast us. It must have seemed to the child that this tunnel had no end. What further terrors awaited us? He clung to only one thing; he knew his father. His father had never given him any reason not to trust him, but still. . . .

When the car finally broke out into sunshine, the little boy's face broke into a big smile. Everything was okay; Daddy knew what he was doing after all.

Like Walter, I have been through some dark tunnels. Although they were frightening, in the end I've found my Heavenly Father always knows the way out.

Thirty years ago I was standing beside a shortwave radio in a house on the Atun Yacu, one of the principal headwaters of the Amazon, when I learned that my husband, Jim Elliot, was one of the five missionaries missing. They had gone into the territory of the Auca Indians, a people who had never heard even the name of Jesus Christ. What did I do? I suppose I said out loud, "O Lord!"

And he answered me. Not with an audible voice (I've never heard him speak that way in my life). But God brought to mind an ancient promise from the Book of Isaiah: "I have called you by name, you are mine. When you pass through the waters, I will be with you, and through the rivers, they will not overwhelm you. When you walk through the fire, you will not be burned. . . . For I am the Lord your God" (Isaiah 43:1, 2).

I am the Lord your God. Think of it! The One who engineered this incredible universe with such exquisite precision that astronomers can predict exactly where and when Halley's comet will appear—this God is my Lord.

Evelyn Underhill said, "If God were small enough to be understood, He would not be big enough to be worshiped."

Can we imagine that God, who is concerned with so many stupendous things, can possibly be concerned about us? We do imagine it. We hope he is. That is why we turn to him in desperation and cry out, as I did, "O Lord!" Where else can we possibly turn when we have come to the end of our resources?

Does God love us? Karl Barth, the great theologian, was once asked if he could condense all the theology he had ever written into one simple sentence.

"Yes," he said. "I can. 'Jesus loves me, this I know, for the Bible tells me so.' "

Think about the account of the Crucifixion in Mark 15. Jesus was fastened to a cross. It was a man-made cross, and man-made nails were hammered through his hands—the hands that had formed the galaxies. Wicked men put him up there. Then they flung at him a bold and insolent challenge: "If you're the Son of God, come down! Then we'll believe."

Did he come down? No. He stayed there. He could have summoned an army of angels to rescue him, but he stayed there. Why? Because he loved us with a love that gives everything.

Because of the love of the father for us, he gave his son. Because of the love of the son for his father, he was willing to die, "so that by God's gracious will, in tasting death, he should stand for us all" (Hebrews 2:9).

When I heard Jim was missing, my first response was "O Lord!" God answered by giving me a promise: "When you pass through the waters, I will be with you."

Was that enough for me? Was that all I wanted? No, I wanted Jim back alive. I didn't want to go through that deep river, that dark tunnel. Five days later I got another radio message: Jim was dead. All five of the men were dead.

God hadn't worked any magic. He is not a talisman, a magic charm to carry in our pocket and stroke to get whatever we want. He could have sent a rescue squad of angels to save Jim and the others, but he didn't. Why not? Didn't he love us?

Fourteen years later God brought another man into my life. I thought it was a miracle I'd gotten married the first time! Now, once again, I was a wife.

However, Addison Leitch and I had not yet reached our fourth anniversary when we learned he had cancer. *O Lord,* I thought, *another dark tunnel.* The medical verdict was grim, but we prayed for healing. We did not know positively what the outcome would be, but like little Walter, we knew our Father. We had to keep turning our eyes from the frightening things to him, knowing him to be utterly faithful.

Whatever dark tunnel we may be called upon to travel through, God has been there. Whatever deep waters seem about to drown us, he has traversed. Faith is not merely "feeling good about God" but a conscious choice, even in the utter absence of feelings or external encouragements, to obey his Word when he says, "Trust Me." This choice has nothing to do with mood but is a deliberate act of laying hold on the character of God whom circumstances never change.

Does he love us? *No, no, no* is what our circumstances seem to say. We cannot deduce the fact of his unchanging love from the evidence we see around us. Things are a mess. Yet to turn our eyes back to the Cross of Calvary is to see the irrefutable proof that has stood all the tests of the ages: "It is by this that we know what love is: that Christ laid down his life for us" (John 3:16 NEB).

We are all little Walters to God. He knows the necessity of the "car wash," the dark passages of every human life, but *he* is in the car! The outcome will be most glorious.

TWO MARRIAGEABLE PEOPLE

What Holly thought would be an ordinary Sunday evening turned into an enchanted evening. She met Scott.

"I'd seen him around church a few times, but it's a big church and we had never spoken. During the social hour following the service we got into conversation. He offered to drive me home, and—well, you know the story. He started calling me, we'd talk for hours on the phone. He decided to join the singles group, hung around afterward and we'd talk, and finally he actually asked me out. Sometimes he picked up the tab, but usually I paid my own way. I didn't want to feel obligated to him.

"Once when we had dinner together he prayed," Holly confided to me, "thanking God for our friendship and for the fact that the singles group could witness a man and a woman who could be good friends without falling in love."

Without falling in love. Uh-huh. I've heard that story from both men and women, perhaps hundreds of times.

Who did Scott think he was kidding? Had it not crossed his mind that *one* of them might fall? One of the two always does. Poor Holly had fallen flat. She was in her early twenties and attractive, yet she told me she "had a problem." She did—her heart was on hold.

When one's heart is on hold, you do what Holly did—a lot of praying and crying and hoping for the telephone to ring. Scott kept her hopes up. He invited her to a big family wedding, even to the reception meant only for family and close friends. Surely he must be getting on toward serious. Would he put words to his feelings? Well, almost. He talked about marriage, telling Holly he often dreamed of having a wife and how he hoped to find one. He told her how much he wanted children, offering her his ideas on raising them. The time came when Holly could stand it no longer.

They were eating pizza by the fire in her living room. Scott always accepted her invitations. Once or twice he had brought flowers or a bottle of wine.

Tonight he was enjoying the pizza, chattering away about a game he'd been to. But Holly's mind wasn't on the game.

"Scott," she said hesitantly, "we need to talk about something."

"Yeah?"

"I mean—like, we've been, you know, *friends* long enough."

The man was startled. He took a huge bite of pizza and said nothing.

"This is really hard for me to say, but, Scott, if you don't have any intentions of, well, a real relationship, I can't spend any more time alone with you. I've felt so comfortable with you. I can be myself, you know? My real self, I mean. I've told you a lot of—well, of my *heart*. But if it doesn't—if you aren't, you know. . . ." Her voice trailed off.

The silence was thundering. Holly looked at Scott. Scott looked at the fire. After another bite and another gulp he said he couldn't see himself married to her. The truth was, of course, that for months Holly had been seeing herself married to him. To her, a "real relationship" meant engagement, although she didn't use that word. In fact, she told me, she had never voiced any desire whatsoever to be married to him. Hadn't she? Scott might be a little obtuse, but he knew what a "real relationship" had to mean. He thought he was forestalling any such complication by telling Holly about his hopes. Didn't she catch on that *she* wasn't what he was looking for?

So here are two marriageable people who would like to be married, though not in both cases to each other. What's wrong? Both the why and the how, it seems to me, are wrong.

Note that Scott took no risks, as far as he knew. Talked to a girl after church, drove her home—pretty innocuous, spur-of-the-moment gestures. Nobody would make anything out of that. She was nice and let him talk about what interested him. So he started going to the singles group, talked to a few others, phoned Holly now and then, went to dinner and let her pay her half (didn't want her to "think anything," didn't want to put her down by turning down her offer to pay). Then, because once or twice he thought maybe he caught a little glimmer in her eyes, he put across an important message—in a *prayer*. She couldn't suspect any nefarious designs here, could she? When he took her to the family wedding she should have known she was just a sister to him.

She didn't. It was quite out of the question for her *not* to think of marriage. Any smallest sign of a man's interest was a big thing. She tried to deny it, tried to tell herself not to "think anything," but she couldn't refrain.

The man didn't mean to put her heart on hold. How did it happen? Had he wronged her? Was he being dishonest, unfair? What was he supposed to do—take 'em *all* out, give 'em equal time? He was no Casanova, just an ordinary guy. He meant well. He'd tried to play it cool. *The trouble is you can't play it cool with a powder keg.*

I wonder if it isn't time for Christian young people to discard the currently accepted methods of mate-finding, which haven't scored higher in marital success than the ancient matchmaker method. I offer the following as humble suggestions for the *why* and the *how* of finding a mate. They don't constitute the Law of Sinai, but I ask you to think soberly, even to pray, about them.

You men are the ones on whom God originally laid the burden of responsibility as head, initiator, provider. *Why* do you want to marry? If Scott had given sufficient thought and prayer to that one, perhaps he would not have been the bull in the china shop of Holly's heart. God ordained marriage. God provided the equipment needed for reproduction. But it is not his plan for every man to marry. How about getting down to business, when you reach the age of responsibility, and specifically asking God whether marriage is, in fact, a part of his plan for you? In order to listen to him without distraction you will need to:

1. Stop everything—intimacy, dating, any "special relationship."
2. Be silent before God. Lay your life before him, willing to accept the path he shows you. If you get no answer, do nothing in that direction now. *Wait.*
3. If it seems the answer is yes, go to a spiritual mother or father (someone older in the faith than you are, someone with wisdom and common sense who knows how to pray) and ask them to pray with you and for you about a wife. Listen to their counsel. If they know somebody they think suitable, take them seriously.
4. Study the story of Abraham's servant who was sent to find a wife for Isaac (Genesis 24). He went to the logical place where he might find women. He prayed silently, watched quietly. The story is rich in lessons. Find them.
5. Keep your eyes open—in your own "garden." You don't have to survey all the roses before you pick *the* one for your bud vase. When you spot the sort of woman you think you're looking for, watch her from a respectful distance. Much can be learned without conversation, let alone "relationship." Ask about her of others who know her and whom you can trust to keep their mouths shut. Does she give evidence of being a godly woman? A womanly one? Expect God to lead. "Let the one to whom *I* shall

say . . . let her be the one whom *thou* hast appointed'' (Genesis 24:14 RSV).

6 Proceed with extreme caution, praying over every move. By this I do not mean mumbling prayers while you're charging across the church campus to ask her for a date. I mean giving yourself whatever it takes, whether weeks or years, to take his yoke and learn of him. It is "*good* for a man that he bear the yoke in his youth.''

7 Talk to her in a casual setting. You will be able to discover if she is a woman of serious purpose. Do not mention "relationships,'' marriage, feelings.

8. Give yourself time to think. Go back to your spiritual mother or father. (In our family, our own parents were our spiritual parents as well, and they prayed for four specific people to marry four of their children. It happened.)

I'm not going to outline the chronology of dating. I would only suggest that you start small—a simple lunch somewhere rather than a gala dinner. *You* pick up the tab. Treat her like a lady, act like a gentleman. (See my book *The Mark of a Man* for more guidelines.)

If you find yourself falling for a girl who offers you only casual friendship, or worse, the cold shoulder, first get it settled with God that she is the one to pursue. Even if a woman tells a man to "get lost" but he knows in his heart she's the right one, he can still wait and pray for God's timing. I know of many married couples whose courtship began this way.

The time will come when your conversations have revealed, without direct inquiry, whether this woman would be prepared to accept your destiny and your headship; whether she is maternal, a homeworker—in short, whether she is what you've been praying for.

It is a great mistake to put too much stock in physical beauty or in thrills and chills. Neither has anything to do with a sound foundation for a marriage. Remember that the love of 1 Corinthians 13 is action, not a glandular condition. The love that makes a marriage is basically a deep respect and an unselfish kindness. That's pleasant to live with.

Now a few words, and only a few, for you women. I know—oh, how well I know—your position. Because we are women we are made to be responders, not initiators (see *Let Me Be a Woman*). This means that the burden of responsibility of seeking and wooing a mate does not belong to us. To us belongs the waiting.

This does not mean inactivity. It means first of all a positive, active placing of our trust in him who loves us, does all things well, and promises to crown us with everlasting joy. It means next a continued obedience in whatever God has given us to do today, without allowing our longing to "slay the appetite of our living," as Jim Elliot once wrote to me, long before God gave us the green light to marry. It means just what Paul meant when he wrote from prison to the Philippian Christians, "Don't worry over anything whatever; tell God every detail of your needs in earnest and thankful prayer, and the peace of God, which transcends human understanding, will keep constant guard over your hearts and minds as they rest in Christ Jesus."

Often the awkward scenario depicted in Holly and Scott's story is more the woman's fault than the man's. That is because women generally allow too many liberties, make themselves too available, and press for explanations when they should remain quiet. It is foolhardy to stick your neck out that way. When *your* heart is on hold, it's best quietly to decline any further invitations rather than to try to "preserve the friendship." It can't be done. Better to simply back off.

If our supreme goal is to follow Christ, the rule of our lives will be *my life for yours*. We will be directing our energies far more toward the will of God and the service of others than to our own heart's longings. And that, believe me, is the best possible training course for marriage.

PICK UP
THE BROOM!

Four more days until she would be seventeen. It would be her father's birthday, too, but there would be no celebration this year. It was the depth of the Great Depression and her father was dying. The children knelt around his bed while their mother prayed, but the girl wondered whether anyone was listening. Was God near enough to hear a prayer? Did he take any notice of their situation?

On the day of the funeral it rained. Only the mother's friends came—the father's didn't bother. The girl, who was working as a maid, had to borrow a dress for the occasion. When they returned to the empty house the sense of desolation was nearly overwhelming. But the widow, who had been silent for three days, went into the kitchen, picked up her broom, and began to sweep.

"I cannot explain how that action and that soft *whisk-whisk* sound gave me courage to go on," the girl wrote many years later. "My mother was now the head of the house, and we followed. We did not sit down and ask 'What next? What will we do?' Our home was mortgaged and my father's lawyer stole her property. She walked out of his office a penniless widow with seven children, ages eight to eighteen. Later someone asked my mother how she had stood it. The answer was simple: 'I prayed.' "

The combination of prayer and faithful carrying out of duty has been balm to many, when all hope has seemed to dissolve. The Word of the Lord came to Ezekiel: "I am taking from you at one blow the dearest thing you have, but you must not wail or weep or give way to tears. Keep in heart; be quiet, and make no mourning for the dead" (Ezekiel 24:15–17 NEB). God denied Ezekiel the usual expressions of mourning and told him he was not to "eat the bread of despair." Ezekiel's response was, in effect, *Yes, Lord.* "I spoke to the people in the morning," Ezekiel said, "and that very evening my wife died. Next morning I did as I was told." Obedience was his consolation.

So the psalmist also found it: "Happy are they who obey his instruction. . . . In thy statutes I find continual delight. . . . I will run the course set out in thy commandments, for they gladden my heart" (Psalms 119:2, 16, 32 NEB). Happiness, delight, gladness—where can they come from when the world has fallen in?

A study of this psalm reveals the psalmist's firsthand knowledge of nearly every sort of human woe. For each he finds the same comfort: the Word of the Lord, variously called "commandments," "instruction," "counsel," "law," "statutes," "truth."

He understood the sense of alienation all of us experience: "I am but a stranger here on earth." He knew unfulfilled desire: "My heart pines with longing." He had been "put down": "Set me free from scorn and insult . . . the powers that be sit scheming together against me." He knew all about the sense of utter desolation: "I lie prone in the dust . . . I cannot rest for misery." He had been persecuted: "Bands of evil men close round me. . . . Proud men blacken my name with lies."

The one who wrote this psalm had plenty of reason, humanly speaking, to feel very sorry for himself. But it is not self-pity that prompts him to list his troubles. It is rather a candid assessment, in the presence of the Lord, of the truth of his situation, each item on his list followed by prayer for the particular help needed, or by a renewed affirmation of trust in the Word of his God.

The one who is called "a Roaring Lion" (1 Peter 5:8) knows well that his prey will be much easier to catch when weakened by sorrow or trouble of any kind. The woman with the broom shamed that lion. She did not "faint in the day of adversity," collapse in a heap, or wallow in a slough of self-pity. She knew where to find the strength to carry on. She went there at once and received the power which, as the apostle Paul discovered, "comes to its full strength in weakness."

In the same way I have been rescued from the lion's claws when everything in me said *"You can't take this."* I woke one morning in a tiny temporary leaf shelter in Ecuador's jungle to find rain falling in solid sheets. The river had risen dangerously. The thought of trying to pack up in the downpour, get into a dugout canoe with my little daughter, and be poled up another river all day long to a remote clearing was too bleak. I was lonely, desolate, trapped. But that "Amazing Grace" that had brought me safe thus far reminded me of what I should do. I looked up to the Lord. "Lo, I am with you all the days" came the word. *All* the days, no matter what the weather, or how total the isolation. I took heart and, like the woman with the broom, did the next thing, which was to pack up and get myself and Valerie into the canoe. I think it rained all day, but it didn't matter, for the weather in my soul had cleared up.

A wonderful thing happens when we turn to the Lord and "pick up the broom." We find, as the psalmist found, that "this day, as ever, thy decrees stand fast; for all things serve thee" (Psalms 119:91 NEB).

A JUNGLE GRAVE

Kimu's bare feet were planted firmly on the floor of the dugout canoe in front of me, as if the balls of the feet were bolted. His heels rose and fell as he raised his arms and plunged the pole to the bottom of the shallow river, rhythmically, steadily. Many times I had been fascinated by the strength and stability of Indian feet, standing in canoes, moving over trails, hanging from hammocks in the firelight. They were thick, square-toed, making the pale narrow feet of the white man, with the toes bent and crushed by years of confinement in shoes, seem pathetically deformed by comparison.

The canoe tipped and jerked at times with the motion of the poling or the river's current rushing against a fallen log. But Kimu's balance was perfect. The pole plunged, swung out, dripped softly, plunged. Kimu's shoulder muscles shifted effortlessly and his powerful thighs became taut as he pulled the canoe forward.

We were traveling the Añangu River in eastern Ecuador. I was watching, without very much hope, for signs of wildlife in the reeds along the shores. The light knocking and scraping of canoe poles, the voices of the men as they shouted taunts at the parrots that flew over or made ribald jokes to one another, warned most creatures of our approach. Besides this, my eyes were not trained as an Indian's eyes are to see things in the jungle. On a previous occasion the Indians had tried to point out to me an alligator which, they said, lay directly beneath my gaze on the river bottom. The water was not more than five feet deep and seemed perfectly clear. The Indians stopped the canoe, pointed with their poles. "There, señora! Right there." I saw nothing. Then with an astonishingly slow and deliberate jab, one of the men impaled the alligator on the end of his fish spear and brought it to the surface.

Another time my guides yelled, "There goes a boa!" I looked quickly where they pointed but did not see so much as the movement of a leaf where it had disappeared. It was as big as a man's thigh, they said.

Now this morning we saw only birds and the tracks of tapir and peccary. The forest moved slowly by on either side of the narrow river. The water was shallow in most places, with a bright sandy floor, and the Indians saw fish now and then, but even these escaped me. At the bends of the river the water deepened into lucid green pools beneath rock walls which were hung with mosses and orchids. Here we heard the sudden strong purr of hummingbirds' wings.

The morning was still and sunny. Except for the mild discomfort of my seating arrangement—two sticks wedged across the canoe—I felt almost a sense of beatitude. There was not a single human habitation on the entire length of this jungle river, and its primeval peace entered into me. The awareness that we were the only human beings anywhere around made me reluctant to violate the silence, even when I saw a bird or animal track I wanted to ask about.

We soon reached the mouth of the Añangu and moved on into the Curaray, a wider, more sluggish stream. I thought of the first time I had seen this river. It was over five years ago, from thousands of feet up in the air. Four other widows and I were being flown by the U.S. Air Rescue Service over the scene where Kimu and four fellow tribesmen had killed our husbands a few days before. We had knelt on the floor of the C-47, straining our eyes through the tiny windows toward the billowing forest below. There was nothing to see, really. The immense vista of jungle was unrelieved except for this winding river with its white stretches of beach. When the plane began to circle we knew which beach it had been. It was just like the others, except that we could discern the remains of a little airplane on the sand. We flew back to the air base, and I remember asking myself what I suppose thousands who are newly bereaved must ask: How is it that the sun shines today? It is as bright and cheerful as it was last week, when they were all alive.

Now, traveling down this same river by canoe, it looked as it had looked from the air, like countless other rivers in the Amazon rain forest. I had been up and down it a dozen times in the past three years but had never been as far as the beach we had seen from the plane. We were going now to visit that beach.

We had left home—a small jungle clearing with eight thatched houses—just after dawn and hiked over the trail to where the canoes lay tied. An hour's walk from home I suddenly thought of matches. I had become so accustomed to depend on the Indians for all that we would need on the trail that I seldom packed more than blanket and clothes for myself and my daughter Valerie. The Indians hunted and fished, cooked the food, and we all ate together; they built shelters for us all to sleep in. But inevitably the Indians were beginning to count on some civilized conveniences, and suppose this time they had expected me to bring the matches? I asked if they had any. No—hadn't I brought any? When I admitted that I hadn't they laughed. Kimu slung down his carrying net beside the trail. "Let me go get some," he said. This seemed a big thing to ask, but it was nothing to him. Back over the trail he went for what had been an hour's walk for us, another hour to retrace his steps. We went on, expecting to wait for him at the river, but just as we reached it, exactly one hour after he had left us, he stepped out of the trees behind us, smiling his benign smile. He said nothing. I couldn't say anything either, for his language has no words for thank you or sorry.

In the canoe was Benito, a member of the Quichua tribe, who live nearest to the Aucas. He would have killed Kimu on sight a few years before. Now he stood on the flat tail of the canoe, poling, shouting to Kimu in Kimu's language. Benito's wife Gimari, an Auca woman, sat behind the food and blankets which were piled on a bamboo platform in the center of the craft. She had been one of three Auca Indians who made a friendly visit to the camp where my husband Jim and his four friends were, two days before they died. She had said she would show me just where she had first glimpsed the foreigners through the trees.

I was not sure there would be any beach left. Jungle rivers change with every heavy rain. The sand shifts, logs are carried downstream and lodged in new positions each time, piling up debris and making new islands. The channels swerve from one side to the other, banks cave in. Yet nothing really changes. No bridges span them, no dams choke them—except the little split-bamboo and rock dams which Indians build in order to poison the water for a day's fishing. We passed several campsites where Quichuas had left flimsy reed shelters on these expeditions. They would be washed away in the next swelling. We had slept in such shelters many times and had nearly been washed away ourselves once when the river flooded at midnight. Valerie, now six years old, looked longingly at these cute little houses as we passed and wondered why we couldn't stop and spend the night in one of them. I explained that we would be stopping when it was time to sleep. But we wanted to get farther downriver this afternoon.

About midmorning the polers were thirsty. They beached the

canoe and Gimari broke open a leaf packet of *chicha,* as it is called in Spanish. In this case it was a mass of cooked manioc root, masticated and slightly fermented, which Gimari squeezed by the fistful into a gourd of water and offered to each of the men first, and then to us. Val drank in great greedy gulps, the lumps and strings in the milky fluid bothering her not at all. I had learned to appreciate the refreshment if not the consistency of this highly nourishing food and was only too glad to be spared the endless fuss of the American-style picnic. There is no packing and unpacking of utensils, no dishwashing, no time wasted. It does not take long to see the common sense of the Indian way.

When everyone had taken on sufficient fuel we climbed back into the canoe and sailed on.

Distances on the rivers are measured by curves. Indians' landmarks are species of trees, deep places in the water, or places where so-and-so was speared or where they just missed the herd of wild hogs on the trip before last. I gave up long ago trying to follow their descriptions of locations. One curve is like the next one to me; even the trees have little to distinguish them, being so nearly obliterated by masses of lianas and air plants. Every twenty minutes or so we rounded a new curve—a strip of sand on the right, a wall of forest on the left; then a strip of sand on the left, a wall on the right. Curve after curve, the river doubling back on itself so as nearly to cut through the narrow neck of land which formed the curve in some places.

At about two o'clock we saw ahead of us a long straight stretch of water, with a long straight stretch of sand at the right. The Indians gently slid the canoe onto the upper point of this beach, threw down their poles, and jumped out. No one said anything, but I deduced that this must be the place.

"This?" I asked.

"This," they said. They started walking down the beach. I followed. This was where Jim had died. He was buried some-where here. Hundreds of times I had tried to reconstruct in my imagination the scene which took place here. I had seen the colored slides and movie film which the men had made here. I had read their diaries of events which led up to their deaths. The five Auca Indians who had killed them were now my friends, and they had told me quite candidly all that happened.

My thoughts were immediately distracted by a jaguar. I could hardly believe it. He shot from a pile of immense logs which lay along the sand and bounded with long, slow leaps toward the forest, looking over his shoulder at us. It was the first one I had ever seen in the jungle. I was stupefied. None of the others saw it, and I could think of neither the Quichua nor the Auca word for jaguar and could only shout, "What is it?" Finally the Indians saw it too and raced after it. No one had a gun, or even a blowgun, and it was too far away from Kimu to throw his spear. Of course it disappeared long before we reached the place where it had lain, probably asleep, under the huge logs. We examined the footprints. I remembered then a phrase from a little note Jim had written to me from the tree house at this beach, flown out to me a few days before he died. "Saw lots of puma tracks this morning—some as big as a woman's hand." There they were. (The Quichua word *puma* means any kind of jungle cat.)

The Indians laughed, chided one another for being unarmed, and speculated as to where it had gone and what it had said when it saw us. They followed the spoor to the edge of the forest, where it vanished.

I wondered, absurdly, if it might be the same puma whose tracks Jim had seen. At first the animal had seemed a thing incredible, almost a specter. What business had it there? Now it appeared a link with the past.

Benito had wandered farther down the beach, and I saw that he was digging in the sand.

"Airplane," he said. There was a piece of aluminum sticking up a few inches out of the sand, with a rusted red scrap of metal bolted to it. I knelt down and examined it. It was from Nate

A JUNGLE GRAVE

Saint's airplane, a piece that fitted above the door. The ceaseless rise and fall of the river had buried the rest of the plane. Nate had flown each of the other four men in here, one by one, with all of their gear, which included the boards for a tree house. It took highly skilled flying to get down into this canyon of trees and land on a two-hundred-yard sandspit.

Kimu waved toward the trees downriver. "That's where the plane came—bbbbb—right over those trees. Then it went out there" (gesturing in the opposite direction), "bbbb—and flew away to where we couldn't see it, where it looks blue, far away."

When the Aucas killed the five, they stripped the fabric from the plane, "because we thought it might fly home by itself," they explained to me.

I asked Gimari where she had first stepped out of the jungle to greet the foreigners. She pointed across the river.

"Your husband saw us. He came across and led us over here." She laughed.

"And the men, when they came to spear, where did they come from?"

"The same place," she said. "They watched the men in secret for two days. Then they brought women with them. The women wanted to see the foreigners too. They came out first and sat down—here, here on the beach. The men had built a little house here to cook in, so the women fanned the foreigners' fire. The foreigners sat down too, and they all laughed together. They ate some meat and some wasp's nest [this is the Auca word for bread]. Akawu, my mother, fanned the fire—wih, wih, wih, wih, she fanned Then suddenly, Gikita and Minkayi jumped out with spears. Dyuwi and Nimunga and Kimu leaped out—from right over there. They speared all of them."

She was very casual and pleasant about it all.

One of the Indians asked if I wanted to see where the men were buried. Yes, I wanted to see, though I knew there was nothing there. Valerie saw us walking back up the beach and raced over

165

breathlessly. This trip was a lark for her. I had told her of course that we were going to where her friends had killed her father. But since she had no recollection of him this meant little, while any trip by trail or canoe with the Indians meant much. But now she wanted to know when we were going to see her daddy. I explained that we were not going to see him—not, that is, until we saw him in God's house—but we would see the place where other missionaries had buried him.

The Indians led me to the reeds at the edge of the forest and broke through them a few feet to a spot a little higher than the level of the river.

"Here." One of them pointed. I saw a slight depression in the ground, covered by a heavy growth of reeds. Buried here were four men: Roger Youderian from Montana, Pete Fleming from Seattle, Nate Saint from Philadelphia, and Jim, my husband, who was from Portland, Oregon. The body of Ed McCully from Milwaukee had not been found. The Curaray had washed it away before the search party reached the scene.

Wordsworth's simple words about Lucy came to me:

> *But she is in her grave, and oh,*
> *The difference to me!*

My reflections were brief. Kimu picked up a scrap of aluminum nailed to a rotted two-by-four, remains of the tree house the foreigners had built.

"Ah! Here's a fine piece of tin for me to mend my canoe with!" he said. To him, this was worth coming for. The others kicked around in the bush hunting for more. There was nothing, except a very rotten stump nearby which they said was once the tree where the house had been. The jungle had reduced everything to indistinguishability.

We went back into the sunlight of the riverside. The water flowed deeper and more smoothly here than farther up. It was medic a few yards up the trail, and his breath caught in his chest. Even though she knelt in the dirt, her profile was the same. He'd looked at it for months during Seth Black's trial. Rachel. He was the one man assigned to her to keep her alive through her testimony, and then he'd had to…give her away. She turned, and he saw her face, easily identifying her button nose, high cheeks and soft lips. Yet, everything else about her seemed different. The way she carried herself. There was a confidence in her movements that she had not possessed before.

He closed the distance. Another shot rang out, hitting a rock formation close to him. Instinctively, he lunged toward Rachel, knocking her to the side, covering her body with his to shield her against additional gunfire.

What he hadn't expected was her coworker considering his actions nefarious instead of protective, and the stout man shoved him off Rachel as easily as if he were flicking an insect off his skin.

Kyle reached for his badge and flashed it in the big guy's direction. "US Marshal Kyle Reid. Back off and get your head down."

At his statement, he heard Rachel inhale

sharply. She turned back to look at him, her light blue eyes wide.

Rachel scurried back to the supine woman. "Moose, I need you."

Kyle drew his weapon and tried to determine the direction the shots came from. He could hear sirens in the distance—local law enforcement coming in answer to likely dozens of 911 calls. He saw a metallic flash in the sun and aimed toward it, but he couldn't in good conscience shoot with so many tourists in the area. He shielded himself behind the nearest tree, which was like hiding behind a toothpick.

"Rachel, we need to get you out of here," Kyle said. He glanced back toward the victim. Rachel held a needle in her hand and was aiming it at the crook of the woman's elbow. The big guy, the one she'd called Moose, applied an oxygen mask to the woman's face and then dived back into their trauma pack. He pulled out a package of gauze and began piling the squares up against the wound, slapping tape down around the edges. The blood dripping to the ground mixed with the fine dirt, creating a crimson paste. There was a hint of iron in the air. One thing Kyle didn't like was blood, but Rachel's actions mesmerized him. She exuded tenacity. Something he'd not witnessed from her before. No longer the mouse of a woman who could do little more than cower in the courtroom.

"Just tape it on three sides," Rachel said to Moose as he placed the dressing.

She inserted the IV and connected the bag of fluids. She looked back at Kyle. "Hold this."

Kyle glanced her way, eyebrows raised. "I'm the only one protecting you," he said, keeping the gun aimed at the tree line. "We need to move the three of you to a more protective place."

Rachel scanned the terrain, then looked at him, her eyebrows bunched. Her perplexed countenance was warranted. There was nothing around but high rock walls, small boulders that wouldn't hide even her slight frame, scrub brush and thin trees.

More gunshots. Moose grabbed his right shoulder, coming off his haunches onto his butt. Rachel placed her body over the injured woman while still holding the IV fluids up to keep them dripping in.

"Moose," she called out. "Are you still with me?"

He'd lain down more to keep a low profile

than because of the injury. "Just winged me. Gonna take a lot more than a bullet to take me down."

Kyle laid a few rounds of suppressing fire up into the tree line, high enough not to injure anyone but hopefully low enough to get whoever was firing at them to seek cover. After he emptied his magazine, he wiped the sand and sweat from his brow and ducked down, pulling his spare from his holster and reloading. Once these bullets were gone, their best shot at a defense would be throwing sand. Kyle shielded his eyes, scanning the trees, his chest tightening at the predicament. Then he found some hope—an indentation in the rock wall that would take them out of the direct line of sight.

"Let's pull her back into that cove."

Rachel glanced to see which direction he pointed. Moose gave a thumbs-up and crawled to the woman lying unconscious.

"On three, I'll shoot in their direction as you guys move her."

Moose nodded his understanding and tucked the small green oxygen bottle under his arm and grabbed one of the trauma packs. Rachel, looking far less certain about the plan, slung the other pack over her arm and put the IV bag between her teeth. Each grabbed an arm and readied themselves. Kyle inhaled deeply. He had twelve bullets left to keep them from getting hit. If they could get themselves tucked into an improved defensive position, hopefully additional officers would soon swarm up the trail and they'd be in a safer situation to evacuate the woman. Kyle lifted one finger, then two, then three.

"Move!"

Kyle stood, gun high, shoulders taut, scanning the ridgeline, sidestepping slowly toward the cove as he discharged his weapon. A flash in the distance. He fired two bullets in that direction.

He heard Moose huffing. Moving the victim off the sandy trailed proved harder than Kyle anticipated.

"We're going to have to lift her," Rachel said.

Kyle glanced sideways. They were trying to hoist her between them without losing any of their gear. He wanted to instruct them to leave it, but he also knew if the woman was as critically wounded as she appeared, they'd need it to keep her alive until the situation resolved.

Off trail, it was bumpier and more difficult for Rachel and Moose to find footing. Moose tripped, dropping to one knee, his hands raised above him to keep the woman steady.

Kyle fired another two rounds toward the tree line to keep Moose protected as he righted himself.

"Inspector Reid! Glad we found you."

The taunting voice came from the tree line. The shooter. Kyle's arms prickled. He continued to shuffle sideways to keep from falling. "Who am I speaking to?" Kyle yelled back. There was a mantra—if they were talking, they weren't firing. Male voice. Young. Twenty to thirty, he guessed. From his peripheral vision, he saw Rachel and Moose were close to the cove—not perfect cover, but in a better position.

"One down, one to go" was the only answer.

Kyle continued moving, listening. Silence was the answer. Had the shooter made his point and decided the battle was over for the day? Kyle made it to the crevice and folded himself against the rock. Even though the temperatures hadn't climbed to their highest point of the day, it felt twenty degrees cooler in the shade.

Moose and Rachel had the woman lain snug against the rock. Rachel was taking her blood pressure as Moose held up the IV bag.

Rachel lifted the stethoscope from her ears. To Moose, she said, "Blood pressure is on the low side of normal. The fluids will buy us some time, but we need to get her to St. George."

Kyle looked at the woman's face, and his blood chilled. The dark hair, now with tendrils of gray, and aquamarine eyes were a dead giveaway. There had been two star witnesses in the trial of Seth Black, infamously known as the Black Death.

Rachel Black, now Rachel Bright, and Heather Flores. One alive and uninjured, caring for one flirting with death.

The marshals had scurried both into Witness Protection after the trial.

Now each had been discovered. How had that happened?

TWO

Rachel stood outside the trauma room at the local community ER where the medical team was working to stabilize Heather. Sweat trickled down the back of her neck despite the air-conditioning. Her fingers ached to rush in and help. It had been her job once, working as an emergency physician at a level-one trauma center, but after her ex-husband and his crimes were exposed, she'd left that life behind for safety. Her skills were probably rusty after three years, but doctors in these parts rarely dealt with gunshot wounds. In her old life, she'd dealt with them every shift.

Through the parted curtains into the room, she could see Heather's monitor. The bullet had collapsed her left lung, and the air and blood that filled the space were shifting her heart dangerously to the other side of her chest, making it difficult for the organ to beat properly. They'd successfully placed a chest tube, which was helping, but they were struggling to put a breathing tube in to help her oxygen levels climb. A medical team was flying from Salt Lake City to take her from St. George Regional Hospital via helicopter, but time was running out. Doctors called it the golden hour for a reason. Response time from Salt Lake was over two hours, and that was after they were airborne. All the closer air medical teams were busy. Rachel leaned against the wall and closed her eyes.

Lord, Heather has been through so many things. Surviving my ex-husband should have been the only trauma she'd have to deal with. Please help her overcome these injuries. Help the medical team make the best decisions and give them the skills and attention to detail to keep her from dying.

Though her eyes were closed, she felt a presence sidle up next to her. First, there was a sensation of heat caressing her skin. Some things about Kyle Reid had changed, but the one constant was his cologne, a mildly musky, woodsy concoction that tingled her nose. His presence in her city without a beckoning phone call from her end meant her worst fears had been realized.

Rachel opened her eyes and looked at him, reexamining the features she'd become so familiar with during the trial. Her hand ached slightly to reach up and touch his face. The sensation surprised her. Maybe it was needing to reconnect with something stable, something dependable from her past when everything seemed so uncertain again.

"Why are you here?" she asked.

Kyle offered her a cup of coffee. She took it from him and gripped it between her hands. His gray-blue eyes always looked troubled. Maybe it was the prominent brow line overshadowing them that increased the look of worry. Maybe it was the things he'd seen protecting the hunted that caused the look as well. His jaw was angular, with a hint of five o'clock shadow. Dark blond hair trimmed relatively short. Had she ever seen a smile cross his face? Had she ever seen a look of peace?

Not that she could remember.

A chill tickled her spine. Was it the words he was going to say or something else?

He leaned toward her. His voice was low. "How is Heather doing?"

Rachel sipped the coffee. Nutty and heavy with caramel flavoring. A hint of char. What else could you expect from a hospital coffee machine?

"We'll be fortunate if she makes it. They're awaiting helicopter transport to get her to the University of Utah Hospital. It's the closest level-one trauma center that had an available flight team, but between now and definitive care is a lot of minutes to survive."

Kyle nodded. "She'll make it. She survived Seth and all he put her through."

Rachel turned toward him, leaning her shoulder against the wall. "Bullets take down even the strong. Want to answer my question now?"

"Not really." Kyle took a sip of his drink.

"You've always answered my questions before."

"That's because I was getting you through the trial and ultimately moving you to a safer place. I'm not sure that I can say that now."

A nervous ache spread through Rachel's chest. The bitterness the coffee left on her tongue was inching through her psyche. There was no leaving her past behind, no matter how hard she tried.

Kyle cleared his throat. "They've released Seth from prison. He's a free man—for now."

Though Rachel was trained to take in

shocking news and keep her emotions under wraps, this news tasked that skill. A man she'd divorced nearly five years ago upon finding out about his criminal behavior was now free to hunt her openly.

"How?" Her voice squeaked through her vocal cords.

"Juror misconduct. A woman with an extensive history of being a domestic violence survivor didn't disclose it on her jury questionnaire. Investigation has shown that she lied in other areas, too, during jury selection. Of course, they're going to try him again, but it's going to take time."

"He and the Black Crew are trying to eliminate any potential witnesses that could offer evidence against him."

Kyle puffed a breath out through parted lips. "There's enough circumstantial evidence to put him back behind bars, but eyewitness testimony persuades juries more. You were a very persuasive witness."

"Heather was more than me. Now she may not be able to testify again. It's going to be hard for her to survive this gunshot wound."

"How did Heather know where to find you? She's a long way away from Chula Vista, California."

It was a question Rachel was loath to answer because she had violated the stringent rules Kyle had lectured her on prior to entering WITSEC. Contact with anyone was highly discouraged, and he meant *anyone*, from her previous life. It was a quiet death. Something lived but not memorialized.

Her silence led him to his next conclusion. "The two of you were keeping in touch?"

Rachel felt like a child with her hand in the cookie jar. "We're the only two women that I know of who survived Seth Black. No one else can understand what we went through. I didn't think going to counseling and talking through all my issues with a stranger would be a good idea, either."

"We could have set you up with someone trustworthy," Kyle said.

"Heather was better. She's what I needed. How do I know the Black Crew didn't follow you here?" She pointed a finger at him. "They called *your* name from the tree line. You know they keep tabs on everyone. They've probably been tailing you since the trial. Time has no meaning for them. They're all playing the long game. And you came here, directly to me."

"If I hadn't, do you think you and Heather

would have made it off that trail alive?" he countered.

Rachel bit her lip. He had a point. They could both be reasonably held at fault. Perhaps her first instinct had been the correct one—that the shooter had followed Heather here and naturally thought, *what else would she be doing here other than trying to find Rachel?* Particularly when news of Seth's release hit.

"When did this happen?" Rachel asked.

"They released Seth last night. Heather was informed. Did you change your phone and email again without telling me?"

"I had your number."

"If I had gotten hold of you last night, none of this would have happened today."

"So I'm responsible?"

He placed an assuring hand on her shoulder. "No, only the people choosing to commit crimes are responsible, but you can't stay here. We need to go back to your house and get some essentials, and we're hitting the road."

Would she even live that long?

Kyle followed Rachel's older-model red Toyota Camry to her home in Rockville, Utah, which was approximately six miles from Springdale. The Camry, covered with a fine layer of reddish-brown dust, was a far cry from the posh black Mercedes-Benz she'd driven before. Part of the suspicion surrounding Rachel was that she and her now ex-husband had kept many of their finances separate. This led people to believe Rachel had done so to protect her assets should Seth's crimes be discovered. Nowadays, that choice didn't seem highly unusual to Kyle, but the thought niggled in his mind, wondering if Rachel had truly had no inkling of her ex's other life.

One thing Kyle knew about witnesses—each carried a secret. Some harmless.

Some that proved deadly.

It was a hard position to be in. Many WITSEC inspectors couldn't see how Rachel could not be involved in or, at the very least, knowledgeable about Seth's endeavors. Many witnesses were duplicitous in crime. Long ago, Kyle decided it wasn't his place to judge their actions—only to protect them. It kept his mind homed in on the task at hand. For him, having that core conviction helped him believe that even bad people could be redeemable. His faith was a cornerstone to keeping that thought at the center of his actions.

All people were redeemable through hope and mercy.

That didn't mean his mind was always in agreement.

He exited his black SUV and followed her into the house. A completely nondescript one-story beige and brown home. It was shrouded in the shade of several cottonwood trees interspersed with a few ponderosa pines. He could understand why she'd picked it—the property would be hard to surveil from the street. Another departure from the home she'd had before, which had been a stunning three-thousand-square-foot Boston brownstone, which had sold for nearly $4 million. The only benefit to this property he could see was the stunning view of the surrounding bluffs.

Rachel unlocked the door, and he followed her inside. She locked the door behind him.

Stepping around him, she motioned him to follow and brought him to the kitchen. He sat at her two-chair farm table, which looked as if it had been rehabbed from a curb somewhere, and she grabbed two glasses, filling them with ice and lemonade. She brought one to him and took the open seat. He couldn't get over the change in her appearance, in the way she carried herself now. Before, her hair had been short, cut just below her ears. A double chin. Matronly dresses. She still wore her EMS garb, but he saw fitness gear strewn over the couch near a treadmill. Her hair was long, dyed blond. Only her blue eyes seemed to hold a vestige of her past self. She took her jacket off and draped it over the back of the chair, revealing a short-sleeve T-shirt and well-muscled arms.

"Am I ever coming back here?" she asked.

Kyle took a sip of the drink, letting the sour yet sugary liquid linger on his tongue. It was exactly what he needed to chase away the grit that lingered in his mouth.

"Would you want to? It's not exactly the living conditions you had before. You certainly could have afforded something nicer."

Rachel leaned back. "That would make me more noticeable, though, wouldn't it?"

Kyle chuckled. "You have a point. So, you followed one of my rules, at least." He twirled the glass between his hands, rubbing the condensation between his fingers before he captured her eyes with his. "You're so different."

She shrugged. "Many of the changes came out of necessity, to be honest. The first time I had to huff it up a trail to get to a patient, I knew I had to do something. It would have crushed me if someone had died because I didn't have the physical stamina to make it to them. I hid here for months and didn't venture out. I completely lacked cooking skills, so I learned to survive on protein bars and yogurt." She fingered her blond locks, twisting them around her index finger. "The hair was the most intentional change. Once the weight came off, I decided I really didn't want to look anything like my old self." She dropped her hand back to the table and grabbed her tumbler. "The physical change I went through is probably what saved Heather's life today."

He couldn't disagree with her. His legs still ached from the quick sprint up the sandy path.

"One suitcase for now," Kyle said. "We'll worry about the rest later."

She nodded and stood, resigned to her fate. He followed her, eager to keep her within view. They had to travel through the living room to get to the bedroom on the other side of the home, and the walls that he hadn't been able to see from the kitchen revealed something unfathomable.

Lining two walls were what Kyle would term murder boards. There were photos of many of Seth's victims, along with pictures of women he didn't recognize as known victims of the Black Death. He felt nauseated. His feet cemented to the ground.

"Rachel, what is this?"

She stopped and turned. "It's some of Seth's known victims. And some other women I think he might be responsible for killing."

"I *see* that." The images of Seth's victims were hard to erase from Kyle's mind. "But why are they all over your wall?"

Like trophies.

"I owe them," Rachel said simply.

"Owe them what?" Kyle asked.

"Everything."

Kyle placed his hands on his hips. Seeing this didn't support Rachel's assertion that she was unaware of her husband's misdeeds. It would lend credence to all the surrounding suspicions.

"These aren't good," Kyle said. "If people find out about this, they'll think you were involved in what Seth did. It looks like you have an unhealthy fascination with his crimes. I could regard these as trophies."

"If I study the victims we know about, I'll be able to find the ones they have not prosecuted him for. I owe them justice for not being aware of what Seth was doing for all those years. It's how I'm...paying penance, I guess. I want the families of these missing women to have closure. Everyone is worthy of a grave. Something that marks the time they were on this earth. Families deserve a place they can connect with their loved ones when they're gone."

Kyle scratched his head. His hearted pounded, barely caged by his ribs. He couldn't wrap his head around her actions. Then he saw the scrapbooks on the table. He crossed the room and opened them up. Pages and pages of news stories about Seth's criminal run. Never had he seen a spouse memorialize the deviousness of an ex-partner in this way.

Unless they'd been involved.

He looked up. She was watching him. He swallowed past the tightness in his throat. The acidic lemonade added to his stomach roiling.

"Rachel, I've never asked you this. I always believed your prior statements, but I can't protect you unless I know the whole truth. *Did* you know about Seth's predilections before finding Heather Flores in that cabin?"

THREE

"I was never a part of Seth's crimes."

Rachel brushed past him, and he followed. She went into her garage and picked up a shovel. Going to the other side of the living room, she slid open the glass doors to her backyard and walked to the spot, a suitable distance from her home, where she had buried extra cash and new identity documents. If Kyle felt she was hiding something, this would not help. She found the tree, put her back up against it, took three steps—heel, toe, heel—and sank the metal blade of the shovel into the dirt.

Kyle had followed her out and was standing a short distance away with his arms crossed over his chest. "What are you doing?"

She threw soil off to the side until metal clanged against metal. She bent down and smoothed the earth away from the edges of the coffee can and wrestled it free from its grave. "Getting provisions."

Kyle closed the distance and took the rusted coffee can from her hands, flipping off the dirt-encrusted plastic cover. He reached in, pulling out several bound wads of $100 bills.

"You didn't need to do these things, Rachel." He put the bills back in the can and snapped the lid into place. "You had...*have* me. I know when I put you into WITSEC, I told you you'd be living a solitary life, but I thought I impressed upon you that I would always be here for you. Especially if someone was coming after you."

Rachel turned away from him and settled the shovel against the tree. He was right. Though she had planned and developed several exit strategies predicting that Seth and/or his followers would come after her someday, the day it happened, Kyle had shown up as he had promised her he would.

Suddenly, there was a loud crash inside her house, like wood splitting from wood. Kyle dropped the canister to the ground and unholstered his weapon, motioning her to step behind him.

She paced quickly to him, and they sidled

toward the house, stopping near the sliding glass doors.

Before Kyle could peek, a voice bellowed from inside, "Springdale Police! Show yourself with your hands up!"

Kyle secured his weapon and eased the sliding glass door open a smidge. He then raised his hands and slid it open the rest of the way with his foot.

"I'm US Marshal Kyle Reid," he said as he edged into the home.

Rachel followed with her hands raised similarly. There was one local law enforcement officer with a weapon drawn. Once he saw Kyle with his arms raised and Rachel following, doing the same, he lowered his weapon.

It didn't take long for the officer to notice Rachel's murder boards.

"Do you have a warrant?" Kyle asked him. When the officer shook his head, Kyle proceeded. "What cause do you have to come into this woman's home without a warrant?"

The officer turned slowly away from the photos and faced Rachel. "One, we need a statement from you regarding the shooting this morning. Two, we got a call from the hospital that the lady who was transported pleaded that we come protect you because your life was in danger. That people were coming to murder you."

"Fine," Kyle said. "You had exigent circumstances."

The officer was from the Springdale Police Department. Rachel didn't recognize him, even though it was a small department. She did, however, recognize the woman who emerged from her bedroom. Amanda Williams, a park ranger whom Rachel had worked with on multiple occasions. Since the shooting had happened in a national park, the Park Service would lead the investigation with conjunctive help from the Springdale Police Department. Amanda's hair was black, tucked into a tight bun. Her green eyes piercing.

"Rachel, why do you have these?" Amanda asked as she eyed the photos on the walls.

Kyle looked back at Rachel. She guessed this was the question that every law enforcement officer would naturally ask. Most presumed guilt before innocence these days.

"It's a project I'm working on," Rachel said.

Amanda came closer to her. "I can see you now where I was blind before." She reached up and fingered Rachel's hair. The park ranger's demeanor changed—no longer the friendly camaraderie they once had. Just another thing Seth ruined in an instant. Amanda's eyes narrowed. Her breath was hot against Rachel's cheek as she spoke. "All those women—and it looks to me like you knew about it. What are these? Your trophies?"

Kyle stepped between her and the park ranger and faced the Springdale officer. "There's a lot you don't understand here."

"Regardless, we need to sort this out," the officer said. "It will be best to take your statement down at the station."

"She'll ride with me, and I'll follow you in," Kyle insisted.

The officer seemed perturbed but didn't verbalize his disagreement.

Amanda pushed Kyle aside. It surprised Rachel he'd allow her to do that. She was armed and clearly upset, the paint of anger red on her cheeks.

"I thought we were friends." Her voice broke.

An achy hollow opened in Rachel's chest. "We are."

"We *were*. How could you have kept something so important about your life from me? We've known each other for three years. I shared everything with you, and you kept this big secret from me."

Not anger. Betrayal. Rachel understood the disconnect in her friend's thoughts. Amanda had fled from a violently abusive man. Rachel had suffered far worse in her eyes. It was something they could have helped each other through.

Which was why she'd kept in contact with Heather.

"It's not her fault—" Kyle attempted.

Rachel cut him off. "I don't need you to fight my battles for me." She turned to Amanda. "I know it makes little sense to you what you're seeing here, but I'm trying to find justice for these women. There are certain rules I had to follow in WITSEC. I can't share why I'm a protected witness, even with those who are close friends of mine."

"Seems like someone let your secret out," Amanda said. "Otherwise, why would they be shooting at you?"

They sat in Kyle's SUV in the parking lot of the Springdale police station. Rachel's hands were clutched tightly in her lap, white from the force, and she stared out the passenger window. She had said little during the drive, sitting upright and pensive, and it was one of many times he wished he had a mind-reading device to get straight to the truth.

"Are you okay?" he asked.

She inhaled deeply and settled her back against the seat. "I'm worried…about Heather. About whether she'll make it."

Kyle wondered the same thing. He hadn't received any updates from Heather's WIT-SEC inspector, who was guarding her at the hospital, since Heather had gone into surgery.

"I need you to let me handle this police issue," Kyle said. "It will not be surprising if the Black Crew has been searching for ways to get you into trouble and get you confined to a jail cell. You're a simple hit if that happens. No doubt they know you're here by now. The media photos of you with Heather… You look different, but on close inspection—"

"I'm the same."

"No, you definitely don't look the same, but it's your eyes. There's only so much you can change about those—about the memories behind them. Let's get this done. Stay put a sec and let me make sure no one is waiting in the parking lot to surprise us."

Kyle exited the SUV. The sun was high in the sky, and temperatures were escalating. Reaching underneath his suit jacket, he placed his hand on his service weapon, scanning the parking lot as he rounded the front of the vehicle and opened the door for Rachel. Amanda and the Springdale officer seemed petulant, waiting for them at the doors. Rachel climbed out, and he placed his hand on the small of her back as they walked into the building.

"This way." The officer motioned and took them into a small interview room. Once inside, Kyle pulled a chair out for Rachel and then took the seat next to her.

"I think it might be best if I talk to the chief of police," Kyle said to the officer. "The longer Rachel and I stay here, the more dangerous it is for your community."

The officer huffed and exited. They knew who Rachel was and her importance in a national case. Kyle had taken away a big interview from a small-town officer, and feathers ruffled easily when that happened.

He'd retrieved his suit jacket from the trail and tried to brush off the debris, but it had little effect. There was fine dirt driven between the fibers of his suit that only a good dry cleaning could fix. It wasn't the image he wanted to portray—that of a tired, disheveled agent. He didn't want to give the impression that he wasn't good at this job.

Kyle thrummed his fingers against the tabletop and Rachel settled her hand over his to stop the movements. The warmth from her touch spread up his arm, hitting his heart like a jolt of adrenaline. He couldn't remember the last time a woman had caused this type of physical response. As soon as his fingers stilled, she settled her hands back in her lap.

The chief of police entered the interview room and held out his hand to Kyle, who stood and shook it. The more respect and humility he showed, perhaps the sooner he and Rachel could get out of town.

"I'm Chief Bailey," the man said, sitting. He stood about the same height as Kyle, putting him at about six feet. He was gangly—all bone and sinew with little muscle covering. His bushy, untrimmed mustache a compensation for his bald head. "You put a dangerous witness in my town, and you don't notify anyone about it?" he asked, his dark brown eyes boring into Kyle.

"Sir, it's not required that WITSEC notify local law enforcement of a protected witness in their jurisdiction. Doing so would defeat the purpose of our organization, which is to keep their new identities known to only a few trusted people. The more people that know, the more incidents like today are apt to happen. Rachel has lived and worked productively in your community for three years. Her talents as an EMS provider have undoubtedly saved countless lives. It's been a net positive for your city to have her."

From Kyle's peripheral vision, he saw Rachel's head turn, a look of surprise on her face. Perhaps she wasn't used to people paying her compliments—or maybe just men. Among Seth's many crimes was how emotionally abusive he'd been to Rachel. He reportedly never laid a hand on her, but his words of condemnation had been as damaging to her psyche as a punch was to the body.

"There's nothing you can share, officer to officer?" The man winked at Kyle, as if Rachel wasn't present. "Criminal background? Was she forced into hiding? Who is trying to kill her? We're in the middle of an attempted murder investigation. You've got to give me something."

Kyle pressed his lips together before speaking. "If you had spent even a few minutes on the Internet before coming into this room, it would answer the majority of your questions."

"Problem is, we've been getting reports that Rachel lured the victim here so she could be…executed."

"This information came from where?" Kyle asked.

"From an anonymous source."

Kyle smoothed his hand over the surface of the table. "Do you have any other evidence that would implicate Rachel?"

The chief tapped his knuckles. "Just her utter fascination with her husband's crimes, as reported to me by my officer."

"That's not proof of anything. I'm sure you could find hundreds of people across the US who are keeping tabs on Seth Black's case."

"None that were married to the perpetrator," the chief countered.

"Look," Kyle said, "unless you're making an arrest, we'll be leaving. Rachel won't agree to any questioning without a lawyer present. We came here as a courtesy, out of respect for your organization. Rachel will leave you a written statement of her account of the shooting, but after that, we'll be vacating the area."

The chief stood. "And dare I say, good riddance. We don't need her kind around here."

FOUR

Kyle took Rachel back to her home. The finality of packing and leaving her jewel in the desert was hitting Rachel harder than she'd expected. In this house—some would say a definite step down, more like a hovel compared to her previous lifestyle—she had found her true center. Discovered who she was without Seth Black's shadow stunting her growth. In the sand and sun of Utah, in the crevices of Zion carved out by centuries of clear, cool water running through it, she had been cleaved into something new.

Something strong enough to withstand the onslaught Seth was sending her way.

Kyle stood near her closet as she sat on the bed. A paralysis swept over her. Just like when evacuation orders were issued ahead of an impending natural disaster, they were under a time crunch. Kyle hadn't said definitively how much time he would give her, but she could tell from his mannerisms that the clock was ticking faster than the time she needed to catalogue her memories of this place. To sort through those things she needed to take and items she could emotionally leave behind.

He bent into her closet and tossed out several suitcases. "Rachel, which one?" It would be almost comical if the situation wasn't so serious. Like the comedies from early television, shown in black and white, the husband trying to get the wife to move, exasperation dripping from his face like the sweat streaming down Kyle's forehead.

"If you took your jacket off, you wouldn't be so hot," Rachel said.

"Why did you pick a house with no air-conditioning?"

"You said nondescript."

"Does ordinary have to be paired with misery? I didn't mean you had to be suffering. Witness protection isn't designed to be a prison for you."

"Isn't it, though?"

Kyle dropped the items he held in his hands and sat next to her on the bed. "It's not, but I get the sense it was for you. It's meant to be a new lease on life, but disconnecting from everything you knew and everyone you loved is hard."

"It's worse than Seth got. He still has easy access to his family, no matter how delusional they are in thinking he's innocent. He can call his mother directly. I have to use WITSEC as an intermediary. He has his horde of followers bowing to his every whim, even when it entices them to commit crimes. When people find out who I am, like Amanda today, they disown me and wish me convicted immediately despite my innocence. They're not interested in learning my story. I've been alone here, and even though I wasn't confined..."

"You feel Seth is living a better life than you, with more freedom of association, even though he's behind bars."

"Not anymore. He's free and I'm running again when I did nothing wrong."

She flopped backward onto the bed. For so long, she'd put aside these feelings. It surprised her that she'd opened up so much to Kyle. Perhaps it was because he was the one adult she was supposed to trust, and with him she could be angry, be disappointed and let her true feelings show. She didn't have to guard her tirade for fear that saying the wrong thing would cause a backlash of poisonous words.

Maybe she had more freedom than she thought—with Kyle, at least.

Kyle stayed seated but took her hand in his. Rachel's heart fluttered. During Seth's trial, he'd been nothing but a tight, buttoned-up specialist. Not one hundred percent emotionally unavailable, but he exuded an air of professional distance. Any touch before had been only for protection.

This was not one of those situations.

Kyle had been true north for her during those dark days. She could trust his interpretation of the events that were taking place. He was loyal to her. Always timely. And though he never said a word to the media about her, the hundreds of times he pushed overzealous reporters and their recording equipment out of her way to and from the courthouse said more than anything he could say in words for print.

As much as she'd changed, there was a shift in Kyle as well. Little things she'd noticed from the moment he came back into her life. Bringing her coffee at the hospital. His curious introspection regarding her hobby of trying to solve crimes she knew Seth was responsible for. The first thing she expected him to do was order her to burn them—he hadn't.

More important was the way he defended her to the local chief of police. The kind words he'd said about her being a net positive for the community. She'd served years as an emergency physician and had never received such an accolade—let alone from Seth.

Something had happened to Kyle over the last three years.

He squeezed her hand. "I'm open to suggestions on where you want to go. Preferably someplace we can stay for several months until the prosecution is ready to retry Seth."

Her heart gently leaped. *We?* Did he intend to stay with her until the trial started? And through it again? Didn't he have a place already planned? Or was this just an effort to help her feel more in control of the situation?

"I have a place about four hours from here in South Jordan, Utah. A house that was willed to me after my grandmother died. I've gone there a few times to check on it and make sure it's ready, just in case I needed to leave quickly."

"Does Seth have any knowledge of the property?"

"He doesn't. I inherited it before I met him. It was something I didn't disclose. I'm not sure why I didn't. I was always very close to my grandmother, and I guess it was something I wanted to keep between the two of us—the memories that are there."

"Maybe something in you knew Seth was never worthy or didn't have it in him to hold precious those things that you did."

His comment echoed a pervasive thought in her mind. Had her subconscious known what Seth was all along and her conscious mind had stomped out the warning? Early in their relationship, everything had been fairy tale–like. The handsome young man from a wealthy family. They'd met in medical school. She'd gone through college on full-ride scholarships. Her parents, hard workers, were unable to assist with college expenses. She'd known all along that would be the case. When she and Seth were dating, Rachel had been enamored by the exquisite dinners, the fancy cars and the Boston town house he owned, where they would lounge and drink bottles of wine from foreign countries. Those accoutrements blinded her to some of the early warning signs. His anger toward her when she'd score higher than he did on exams. When he'd wanted her to pick a more lucrative specialty, like his neurosurgery.

"Ready to pack?" Kyle asked.

"No, but I will."

"One suitcase."

"I know. You already said that."

He released her hand and stood up, going back to the closet, and picked up the two suitcases he'd previously held. "Which one?"

"Kyle, I'm taking them with me."

"Who?"

"The women. The boards. They're coming, too."

Kyle had insisted they leave Springdale under the cover of night. They'd be harder to track and hopefully the Black Crew would take the night off. The four-hour drive to South Jordan had so far been uneventful.

"White Ford F-150 trailing. Looks to be a female driver," Rachel said, scrutinizing the car behind them in the passenger side-view mirror.

"Even in the dark you could make that out? I'm impressed, and I agree. I taught you well about peripheral awareness, and you've honed your skills. Is that person a threat, do you think?"

"Unknown. All depends on what she's carrying on the inside. She could overtake us, powerwise, but I think we're in the more agile vehicle, so we might be able to outmaneuver her."

That was always the issue. Those things that couldn't be seen. What was Rachel hiding?

Eventually, Rachel fell asleep. He understood why. Long days with scattered bursts of adrenaline always levied a heavy tax on energy levels. He was used to going without sleep during times like this. WITSEC did not afford to a normal lifestyle, and he'd never wanted to subject a wife and kids to the uncertainty of his work. Not only the time away, but the level of danger.

In moments like this, his mind would drift and he'd think about what most people considered a normal lifestyle. Weekends and holidays off. Dinner at home. Getting to keep track of an entire series on television. Seeing a movie in the theater. He'd had a lot of wild adventures. He didn't crave the adrenaline surge as he once had.

All that had changed a year ago, when a protected witness, a woman not unlike Rachel, had died in his arms.

Shaking off the troubling memory, Kyle double-checked the address Rachel had given him and pulled up in front of the cottage. The sun had risen, and he got a good look at the property.

It was an upgrade from Rachel's desert abode. What would be the correct term for a high-end cottage? It wasn't a mansion, but more than the fifteen hundred square feet Rachel had lived in in Springdale. Two stories. A double staircase that wrapped skyward to a deck on the second level. Brick exterior on the first floor. Gray siding on the second level. Three dormer windows peeked from the top that likely had an amazing view of the Wasatch Mountains.

He looked at Rachel. She was slumped against the window. He nudged her shoulder, hating to interrupt the peaceful look on her face. She opened her eyes and stretched, accidentally hitting him in the face.

"Sorry," she said.

"I've suffered worse." Kyle laughed. The lightness in his spirit felt good. He felt a sense of peace around Rachel. He didn't have to pretend to be stronger than he was—not anymore.

He opened the car door and stretched.

When he went to the back door to grab the poster boards, Rachel grabbed the other end at the same moment, and removing them became a tug-of-war between the two.

"Please," she said. "I'll worry about these."

He let the boards slip from his hands. It bothered him, her obsessiveness with these women, and he hadn't quite put a finger on if her interest was one hundred percent innocent.

He pulled their suitcases from the back of the SUV and followed her. She unlocked the front door and led them into the living room. It was kept up. Fashionably decorated in a French country style. Muted pastels. A lot of cozy furniture. A stone fireplace with an ornately carved mantel. Kyle set their suitcases down and walked farther in. The fireplace had bookcases on each side, which held photos. Kyle perused them, watching Rachel grow older in each successive frame. From the lanky kid to the heavyset, awkward middle school years that she'd grown out of during high school. Kyle's stomach turned at the photo of her med school graduation, with Seth sidled up next to her. From that moment on, her physical appearance deteriorated, the weight of Seth's abuse clear in the fact that she'd lost the ability to care for her own needs. Her energy had been focused solely to the care of her patients and surviving an abusive marriage. He lifted his fingers from the mantel. It wasn't dusty. Someone was getting paid to keep this place neat and orderly.

"Do you trust the person keeping tabs on this place?"

"She's been with me since even before I knew Seth. She's like a mother to me."

A person who was likely a poor substitute for the mother she'd been instructed not to keep in contact with anymore, for both of their safety.

Rachel stepped into the kitchen. "The only thing we'll need to do is get groceries. Nothing but cold water in the refrigerator."

Kyle followed her. There was a center island painted a light denim blue. The cabinets were whitewashed. Two modest chandeliers hung over the island, and chairs surrounded it. There was likely a formal dining room elsewhere. Kyle's phone pinged. He picked it up and read the message.

"Is there a television around here? Something that will get national news?"

Rachel motioned him back into the living

area. There was an armoire off to the side. She opened the doors and pulled out the television. Turning it on, she then handed the remote to Kyle. He panned through several news stations before he found what he was looking for.

A familiar scene for him—an upscale Boston property with the periphery cordoned off with crime scene tape. He took the television off mute.

"Dr. Lewis was a fellow neurosurgeon in practice with the formerly convicted serial killer Seth Black. Today, questions surround his whereabouts, and anyone with information concerning his disappearance is asked to contact the Boston Police Department at once. It is feared that Dr. Lewis's life is in immediate danger—if, in fact, he's still alive. As has been reported, Dr. Lewis's wife came home to find a ransacked property, blood marring the walls and doors, and her husband missing. Since Seth Black's release from jail, several witnesses who testified at his trial have come under attack. One unidentified female is currently clinging to life at an undisclosed medical facility after an assassination attempt. Now this previous trial witness has disappeared under mysterious circumstances.

Police say foul play is suspected. As of now, we don't know the safety of Seth's ex-wife, Rachel Black, or where she might be."

Rachel took the remote from his hand and turned the television off. "I'll be surprised if he's still alive. He was too easy for the Black Crew to find." She turned to him. "None of this will come back to Seth. You get that, right? He'll find a way to escape this just like he did the first time. Just like he did prison. And the only thing that will happen is more innocent people will die."

Kyle hoped she was wrong, but he feared the worst.

FIVE

Rachel gripped the handle of the shopping cart in the parking lot. They'd gone to a grocery store located two hours away from the cottage, hoping to prevent the Black Crew from nailing down their location. The news of Dr. Lewis troubled her more than she wanted Kyle to know. She wanted to present a tough exterior, but no one had firsthand experience of how brutal Seth Black could be—other than the women who had been close to him or nearly died at his hands. She carried those who fell victim in her heart always. Wanted to see justice done on their behalf. Now, none of that seemed possible. How long would she have to fight this menace? Would she ever feel wholly free of Seth—both mentally and psychologically?

What could Kyle do at this point? They could keep moving from location to location, but the Black Crew's fingers were like metastatic cancer. The unknown of when that one cell would populate another area and cause unchecked disease to grow was an unnerving, never-ending mind game.

Kyle walked a few steps in front of her, his head swiveling from side to side, looking for any threat. It was in that same moment that a man rushed her, grabbed her from the side and pulled her tight against his body, the sharp edge of a knife pressed against the fabric of her collar. A slip upward of half an inch and her carotid artery could easily be severed. Rachel kicked the cart forward, reached up and grabbed his forearm, tucking her chin into the crevice of his elbow to protect her ability to breathe and shield easy access to her throat. The sound of the quickened pace of the cart's wheels over the pavement caused Kyle to turn around. Sensing danger, he already had his gun drawn.

Just as Kyle turned toward her, another man tackled him from behind, knocking Kyle's head into the trunk of a nearby car. Stunned, he slumped to his knees, holding the side of his head, blood dripping between his fingers.

Rachel, her heart in her throat, bent at her

hips, pivoting her body behind her attacker. Once he was slightly off-kilter, she brought both of her hands behind his arms and shoved her head backward through his grip. As her head slipped through, he turned back on her. The knife flicked out with a glint of a silver flash against the sun, slicing down her arm, splitting open her flesh. Ignoring the pain, Rachel moved toward the cart and quickly grabbed a bag of groceries and swung it with all her strength into the side of his head.

Unfortunately, the bag of lettuce and fruit did little to stun him, and he smiled mischievously in her direction. Rachel reached behind her and grabbed two more bags. She threw the lighter one at his face to distract him and then clocked the side of his head with the second. The man staggered and fell to his knees, his back toward Rachel. She ran with all her might straight at him, lowering her body mass to slam into his backside, forcing his face into the pavement, and then wrenched his knife-wielding arm behind his back. He dropped it, and Rachel kicked it off to the side.

She looked back at Kyle. He sat on his haunches, his gun aimed at the other man.

"Can you hold him, Rachel?"

"I've got him."

Kyle pushed himself up against the car, leaning against it heavily, keeping his weapon fixed on the other man. "Put your hands up, turn around and get down on your knees."

The man ignored Kyle's request. Kyle pointed the weapon skyward and fired a warning round, pointing the gun back toward his assailant.

"I don't ask twice."

The man reluctantly acquiesced. Once down on his knees with his hands clasped behind his back, Kyle approached and cuffed the man's wrists with zip ties and then patted him down for weapons. He then got to his feet, holstered his weapon and walked to Rachel, swaying slightly as he got down to his knees and put the other man in zip ties.

After that, Rachel looked up. A few passersby had cell phones up, recording the whole incident. Kyle worked to get on his feet and approached them, gathering the handful of men and women like a father would wayward children, asking them with all the deference he could muster to secure the footage. Hopefully, appealing to their inner humanity would convince them not to put the video up on social media and put Rachel's life at further risk. Now Rachel wished they had gone to a store in the next state, closer to a metropolitan center, to throw the Black Crew off. They'd barely settled at their new location. Would they have to move again?

The yelp of police sirens drew her gaze to the road. Two police cars swerved into the lot. Kyle walked toward the car, where the first officer stepped out, his hands raised, and began a conversation.

The man lying prone on the ground rolled onto his side and looked up at her. "You think you're smarter than he is, but he'll get you. There's no way he's going back to jail."

Rachel looked down. The first thing she noticed was her blood dripping onto the pavement from the laceration on her arm, and she placed her other hand over it to control the bleeding.

"How did you find us?" Rachel asked.

"Like I told you. Just a matter of time before you have to face your fate. Flushed you out of your hidey-hole like the insect you are. Now all we have to do is stomp your life out of existence."

The words were not as eloquent as the man likely wanted them to be. Seth was highly intellectual and could persuade his followers with flowery words and speech. This thug's emulation of that had fallen flat.

"I've survived worse than you. I survived Seth once. I'm better now than I was then. And the only insect in this scenario is you—feeding on the death and destruction that Seth leaves behind."

Rachel zipped up her jacket and put her hoodie up.

Kyle shielded his eyes from the sun. Never had he been photosensitive. Now, even with a pair of sunglasses on, the light was too much. He was nauseated and weak. If Rachel hadn't been able to defend herself, the worst-case scenario would have happened to him…again.

"For the safety of my witness, I need to get her out of here and back to a secure location," he said to the officer. "We can submit written statements regarding the incident, but I think reviewing the security footage and…" Kyle reached into his pocket, gathering the contact info of the few who had taped the incident "…if you reach out to these fine people, they've agreed to share what they have as well."

"You're not worried about them leaking it to the press?" the officer asked.

"I may have said something about payment down the road if they kept it quiet. Not as much as they'd get from the press. Explaining it could put Rachel's life in danger seemed to seal the deal, if my ability to read people is still intact."

"That's quite a cut on your head. Sure you don't want me to call a rescue unit for you?"

Kyle looked Rachel's direction. "I've got easy access to a highly qualified doctor. I think I'll be okay in her hands."

The officer flipped open a notebook. "Why don't you give me your address and I'll send someone out for those statements?"

Kyle shook his head. "I'm sure that under the circumstances, you can understand why I can't tell you our location. There are just too many unknowns right now. I don't know who I can trust. Even if they wear a badge."

The officer withdrew a business card from his wallet and handed it over. "I get it. Must be a lonely place to live in."

Kyle took it and offered him a weary smile. "We'll be heading out."

Kyle waved for Rachel to come his way. He went to the car and sat in the passenger's seat, surrendering his keys. He didn't feel well, and there was no hiding it from her. His head was killing him. The nausea a close second in what would cause his demise.

Rachel secured her seat belt. He could see her sweat jacket was wet with blood, yet her first instincts were for him. "How are you feeling? You don't look well."

"Headache. Nausea."

"What's your full name?"

"Kyle Reid. I'm in some unknown city in Utah getting groceries. It's July."

"Can you tolerate a two-hour car ride? I've got meds back at the house that will help you feel better and supplies to stitch your cut up."

"I'll make it. Let's get going."

He glanced behind him and noticed the torn grocery bags piled in the back seat. The thin white plastic was splattered with blood. When Rachel was back on the highway, he watched their wake for anyone following.

"I've got you, Kyle. You taught me well. Please, just rest. I know to check to see if someone is following."

"I know you do. You already proved it to me."

He resituated himself and closed his eyes, gritting his teeth against the nausea. He'd never been in a vulnerable position like this before with a witness. Right now, he couldn't defend Rachel against a tick. Every time the car swayed, he wanted to vomit. He gripped the grab handle, trying to hold himself steady, and reviewed the incident in his mind. Mostly to keep his thoughts off how bad he felt.

Rachel was not the woman she was before. That much was clear. It was more than the physical changes and the few self-defense skills she'd picked up. She didn't need him. Maybe that was too strong a statement. She hadn't looked to him first, called out his name, when the man came at her. She'd just taken action. Had defended herself and subdued her foe without his help, even after being injured.

She was not a victim anymore. She was a survivor.

He reached out and touched her shoulder lightly. "Are you okay? Your arm?"

"I'm fine. Just rest."

His hand slumped off her body, and he pressed his face into the cool glass of the window. It helped a smidge. He'd never been attracted to a witness before. Always had held the professional line between his job and the client.

Now, that line was blurring. Her presence, her touch, caused a physical reaction within him.

Unaware of how much time had passed,

he felt Rachel grip his thigh and jumped at her touch.

"Sorry," she said. "We're back."

He'd slept the whole length of the drive. As soon as he opened his eyes, a wave of pain and nausea washed over him.

"Can you walk?" Rachel asked.

He nodded and followed her inside. She directed him to the couch, but he stood in one place. He reached out to her, taking the zipper of her hoodie in his fingers, and slid it down. Her eyes met his, and she didn't resist his touch. It was almost as if she was as desperate for a connection as he was. He slid her jacket off her shoulder and looked at the laceration on her arm. It was open. Deep. Would definitely need stitches.

His mind traveled back a year to the woman he'd held, a witness he was supposed to defend, shot in the chest, who had taken her last breath in his arms. The witness had disclosed their location to her criminal boyfriend, who'd been stalking her. She'd been testifying to his laundering money for a drug cartel. She'd mistakenly thought he'd changed his ways and wanted to see him one more time. His goal in seeing her was to silence her testimony.

He'd been successful.

"I can do stitches if you tell me what to do," Kyle said.

She shook her head. "You're not feeling well enough to do that. Besides, we're taking care of you first. In a few hours, we'll see how you feel. We've got twelve hours to address my arm." Rachel reached for his hand and guided him to the couch. "You're going to let me take care of you by doing everything I tell you to do. I'm pulling rank as your doctor, so you must do what I ask." She put him through a brief neuro exam.

"Am I going to die?" he said, attempting levity.

"Hopefully not today. No focal signs of weakness, so I don't think you're bleeding in your brain." She pressed her hands against his chest and eased him back onto the couch. "Be right back."

He heard her go outside and start the car. She was hiding it. An extra effort to keep their location hidden. Maybe the garage was used more for storage than for a vehicle. When she returned, she searched the house and made all the same maneuvers he would. Checking that doors were locked. Windows shut and secured. She pulled the curtains closed.

Returning to his side, she had her medical kit. She unbuttoned his cuff and rolled up his sleeve. "I'm going to start an IV and give you some medications to help you feel better." The poke was nothing as brutal as he'd had in the past. Most doctors weren't good at bedside skills, as they rarely performed such tasks, but Rachel had been getting a lot of practice in the field over the last several years. She brought a standing lamp over and hung a bag of IV fluids on it. She took two medication vials and showed them to him.

"One for the nausea and one for the pain."

He'd never been so thankful for modern medicine. He could feel the medicine swirl up his vein.

"I'm going to stitch the cut on your head. This is just lidocaine—might sting a little. When was your last tetanus shot?"

His eyes closed, and her words became a sweet sound at the end of a distant tunnel.

SIX

Rachel stood at the window and opened a section of the vertical blinds. She'd paced the interior perimeter of the cottage, looking through each window more times than she could count, in the last few hours. For the moment, they seemed to have slipped through the grip of the Black Crew. Unfortunately, with so much heightened interest in Seth's case, she didn't know how long that would last.

Kyle stirred on the couch, and she felt it best to return his weapon to the table where she'd first picked it up. There were other guns in the house, but she hadn't wanted to stray far from his side while he was sleeping. A change in his breathing pattern could indicate swelling in the brain, but his respiratory rate had been easy and regular. Her farthest venture had been to the kitchen to get some dinner started. Hopefully, he'd feel better enough to eat.

He opened his light denim-blue eyes. They were clearer than before he fell asleep. She sat on the coffee table next to the couch. "How are you feeling?"

Inhaling, his eyes widened in surprise. "What is that amazing smell?"

"Spaghetti sauce. A secret family recipe."

"The Prego we got from the market, I take it. I'm surprised you didn't crack the jar when you slugged the man's head with it."

"It served more than one purpose. They likely won't use it as a marketing venture, though." Rachel chuckled and leaned forward, pressing the skin around his cut. "You seem better. A patient near death can't crack jokes."

He stretched. "Definitely better. The headache and nausea are gone." He lifted his hand in her direction, indicating his IV. "I think we can take this out, and it's time to take care of you."

"All right. But you need to tell me if you start feeling worse again."

"I will. I promise."

She took the catheter out of his arm, held pressure at the site with a cotton ball for a few minutes and put a Band-Aid over top. Kyle sat up.

"Probably best to do my stitches in the kitchen. There's better light in there, and I sterilized the instruments," Rachel said, picking up the trash and trekking that way. She stopped at the sink and pulled out the supplies. "I've already washed the cut out." First, she handed him a syringe. "This is lidocaine. Go into the wound and inject several areas, infiltrating the tissue with the medicine."

"Got to wash my hands first, right?"

Kyle turned his back and scrubbed his hands at the sink. It might be common sense, but he scrubbed his hands like a surgeon before going into the OR. "And these?" He picked up a pair of gloves.

"It's okay. Don't worry about the gloves. It's already going to be hard enough if you're not used to handling these items to get the stitches in place." Rachel rested her arm on the table. The cut ran from just below her deltoid muscle to the crook of her arm and was several inches.

After he injected the lidocaine, Kyle inspected the suturing material and then looked at the wound. "Have any dissolvable sutures?

You probably need some on the inside to pull this thing together."

Though surprised, she simply handed him the requested item.

He opened the package and clamped the needle in the hemostat. With the blunt curve, he tapped her skin. "Can you feel that?"

She shook her head, and he pushed the needle internally through both sides of the laceration and approximated the wound's edges. A perfect horizontal mattress closure. Kyle had skills he hadn't been forthright in disclosing.

"You said you could do this if I walked you through it. Clearly, you don't need any instruction."

"As soon as I became a WITSEC inspector, my mother taught me a few things about sewing. She's an avid quilter."

"Why did she find it important to do that?" Rachel asked.

"Because she said no woman would ever want to be with me because I'd never be home, so I'd better learn some basic lifestyle skills to keep myself alive. I guess she considered sewing buttons and repairing torn clothing essential to life."

"I mean, if that button is the only thing holding your pants up...she could be right.

Can't run from nefarious people with your trousers falling to your knees. You know more than that, though. You know the right suture material to use."

"Online videos are very instructional in a pinch."

Meaning he'd had to do this with another witness at some point, likely when they were on the run.

He clipped the loose string and then picked up the other suture material. "She gave me a motto that you're probably not going to like, though. She'd always say, 'It just has to be functional, not pretty.' I can't guarantee the cosmetic closure that you would likely do."

Rachel watched him work, numb to the sharpness of the needle. "Was she right?"

"About the motto? I guess you'll have to tell me after my job here is done."

"No, I meant her comment about women."

Kyle tied off and clipped a stitch. "It might be mutual, I guess."

"How?"

"Early in my career, I tried to hold down a few relationships. The unpredictable schedule didn't foster growth. Guarding other women became a point of jealousy for some of my partners."

"What about your dedication to your work? I have a feeling that didn't help, either. It's good for me, but…"

"No, you're right. After a few failed, short-lived relationships, I thought it best to just stop trying. Seemed pointless."

"You're not lonely?"

"Are you?" he asked, holding her eyes, and the question sank into her soul.

"Yes." Her reply was a whisper.

"Then why should my experience be any different from what I ask a witness to go through? At least I can still fully enjoy my family relationships. I can see my nieces and nephews at Christmas. I'm not entirely cut off. Having a shared experience, in some part, with what I ask my witnesses to do keeps me humble and puts me in their mind-set."

"So you can sympathize."

"Maybe *empathize* would be a better word," Kyle said. "I feel like the word *sympathy* means that I feel bad for you in your circumstances and maybe say some kind words about it, but I'm not going to do anything to help you. It's like watching the news and seeing a crime. *Empathy* to me denotes action.

I'm in the dark hole with you, and I'm going to help you get out."

Rachel swallowed hard. She felt tears well up and turned her face away from Kyle. Maybe he knew she was crying and wanted to give her the space that he could while he did his work, which he was far more gifted at than he'd given himself credit for.

Her view of men had become skewed from being involved with Seth Black—living in his world had imprisoned her mind to believe that all men were the same when, clearly, they could be different.

In some ways, Rachel didn't feel she deserved another relationship. One, could she have a healthy one after the years with Seth? Two, didn't men always have an ulterior motive? With Seth, living a married life with a woman had provided cover. Surely a man with a wife and a stable, profitable career serving the community could not also be a serial killer. Looking back through her years with Seth, she had bought into this deception herself. Red flags she should have recognized she'd put aside for those very reasons.

But was Kyle different?

His touch was tender without being greedy. He wasn't expecting anything from her. He didn't dismiss her needs as trivial. Even allowing her to cry without telling her she was weak and needy was something she had not experienced with a man before. In medical school, she'd felt like she had to work twice as hard as her male counterparts for the same respect—particularly in her chosen field of emergency medicine, which was dominated by men. With her free hand, she wiped the tears from her cheeks. She looked back at him and offered a weary smile.

He gathered up the instruments. "I think I'm done unless you want me to redo part of it."

Rachel glanced down at the laceration. He'd closed it nicely, though not expertly. He'd done a far better job than she'd expected. "It's fine. Thank you," she said.

"Of course." He gathered up the pair of scissors and needle holder and placed them back in the pot of boiling water Rachel had used prior. "What type of dressing do you want?"

Rachel pointed to her medical kit. "The antibiotic ointment. There are a few nonstick pads you can place over the top of the cut and then wrap my arm with Kerlix."

Kyle followed her instructions, his movements sure and steady. He was more practiced in providing first aid than he'd let on.

"Did you try to date at all while you were in Springdale?" he asked as he dressed the wound.

"Is this a background question or personal interest?" Rachel asked. Another one of her bad habits—assuming nefarious intent behind any question that a man asked. Seth's interactions with her had often been piercing questions about her day and her whereabouts. She'd taken them at first to be a genuine interest in her well-being. Proof of his love and how committed he was. After a few years, her opinion changed. He'd asked the questions because he didn't trust her. Was obsessing over her movements. Stalking her. In reality, he was trying to determine if she'd discovered who he really was.

"Sorry," she said. "With Seth, there was no innocent question."

Kyle wrapped her arm snugly in the gauze and then looped the material to tie it in a knot. "Rachel, I understand why you don't trust men or wouldn't want to have a relationship. Why it would be easier to just stay single. Maybe we made the same choice for different reasons."

She pulled her arm away and settled it in her lap. "I never tried to be with anyone. It wasn't something I felt I could handle, or that I deserved."

"Do you still feel that way? After three years? That you don't deserve to be loved by someone?"

She couldn't lie to him and because she couldn't be deceptive, she couldn't answer. Her silence was an answer in and of itself.

Kyle closed the lid to her first aid kit and snapped the locks. "What you've told yourself is not true, Rachel. You deserve to have a man love you properly. As an equal. As a partner. A man who wants nothing from you other than just to be with you. You've probably earned it more after what you've been through."

Her lips trembled, and she bit the inside of her cheek to keep from crying harder.

"It's been a long few days. Go take a hot bath or something. I'll have dinner ready to eat in an hour." He reached for her hands, and when she stood, he pulled her into a gentle hug. The stubble from his chin tickled the side of her cheek. His breath was warm in her ear as he whispered, "I've got you."

Kyle gathered up supplies to finish the spaghetti and rifled through the kitchen for a cutting board and knife.

He'd crossed a line with Rachel, and he knew it. Providing a comforting hug to a witness at a time of stress was one thing, but that wasn't the reason he'd embraced Rachel. He'd wanted to be physically close to her. To know what it felt like to hold her in his arms. It was everything he'd expected it to be. What he should do was enforce proper boundaries with her. For her safety. For his. Getting overly emotional with her would blind his thinking. It would put them both more at risk.

Above anything else, he didn't want to feel the pain of another lost witness. Maintaining a professional distance was the best way to ensure that didn't happen. No matter how difficult that might be.

As he chopped vegetables for a salad, he'd received a few texts giving him updates pertaining to the case. Heather was in critical but stable condition. He'd always found that phrase somewhat of an oxymoron but had learned that it meant the patient was still flirting with death, but their vital signs were stable for the moment. No news on the missing doctor. It looked like a kidnapping. No valuables had been taken, and his wallet, car keys and vehicle were still at the residence.

There'd been no ransom note.

Kyle didn't know what to make of it. Seth and his followers didn't seem shy about killing people in broad daylight. Why not just kill the doctor if they didn't want him to testify again? Was there really a reason to hide their motives at this point?

He set the table and checked his watch. He was about to holler out for Rachel when she came down the stairs, dressed in jeans and an airy light pink cashmere sweater, along with a silver necklace with teardrop earrings. Her long blond hair was down and blown dry in gentle waves. The citrus scent of body wash filtered through the room.

She wasn't making it easy to maintain any sort of distance.

"Feel better?" he asked, rubbing the back of his neck to dissipate the trickles of nervous sweat.

"Much. I didn't even get my dressing wet." She took a seat at the table. "You didn't have to go to all this trouble." She fingered the place setting and cloth napkins—the embroidery likely done by a distant relative. "But it's nice. I haven't had anything besides yogurt and protein bars in ages."

"Let me fix you a plate," Kyle said, accidentally dropping the tongs on the table. He grabbed them quickly and drove them into the mound of noodles, hoping the action would hide his shaky hands. Her physical presence was doing a number on him, and his rational mind was dissolving in her presence.

She could do this perfectly well on her own, but it was one way he could spoil her. Another action that blurred the distance he'd said he wanted to maintain. After piling spaghetti on her plate, he loaded it with meat sauce and sprinkled freshly grated Parmesan cheese over top. He filled a bowl with salad and put the dressing next to her. He'd found a bottle of white wine and chilled it quickly in the freezer. Now he poured her a small glass and then took the seat across from her.

The tension eased from her shoulders. A soft smile appeared on her lips. "You missed your calling as a server."

"In my household, whoever cooked dinner didn't have to do dishes."

"Aw, I see the fine print now. Well, I don't mind doing dishes." She took a bite of spaghetti, and a noodle landed against her chin, leaving a slice of red sauce, which she slurped into her mouth. She took the cloth napkin and wiped her chin. "I'm violating one of my mother's golden rules for first dates…or just eating with a man in general."

Kyle caught the redirection. It felt like a first date in every sense of the word. "What was that?"

"To never eat spaghetti for this very reason. Getting the sauce everywhere. It's not very dainty."

"No need to pretend to be someone else around me, Rachel. You may look…delicate, but I know you're made of tough stuff."

"My mother was all about pretense. Not that doing your hair and makeup is an illusion, but almost putting yourself aside for the pleasure of someone else. I never felt like I knew to the core who my mother was. Only who she was in relation to my father."

Kyle sipped water in lieu of wine, though he wished he could have a taste of the sweet essence liven up his tongue. The last thing he needed was a bit of alcohol to lure him into doing something ill-advised. More than what he'd already done. "I've never asked you this before, but what was it like with Seth, in the early years?"

"If you had asked the woman who'd married him at the time, she would say it was a dream come true. If you ask me now, with twenty-

twenty hindsight, I would say I was in a nightmare that I didn't wake up from until it was too late. What I took for love was a jealous obsession—and not over my being beautiful, but as a cover for his crimes. I was the facade he put forward so that he could commit his devious acts. It's strange. Even though I'm glad we're divorced, it still hurts at times, as if he died. Not the death of the man he was, but of who I imagined him...who I wanted him to be."

"I don't think that's atypical. Grief can be a normal expression of emotion when something we believe in wholeheartedly turns out to be not what we expected."

Rachel took a few bites of her dinner. "Some people would call me crazy over feeling emotional after divorcing a serial killer."

"You lost the man you thought he was. The life you were building together. We all make mistakes. Some people just aren't honest about them."

She set her fork down and sipped her wine. "Have you?"

Heat spread through Kyle's chest. "Made a mistake?"

Nodding, Rachel leaned forward. "I mean a dreadful one. Something that you have difficulty living down."

"I lost a witness once." The words were out before his mind edited them. Clearly, revealing this secret could cause Rachel to doubt his ability to protect her. Maybe that was his goal. She'd proven she could be a partner. That she could defend herself. They would need one another to survive this. He hadn't ever been in a position before where so many unknown people were hunting his witness. In all his previous cases, the threats were known. He knew who to look out for. But the Black Crew was a completely unique element.

"What happened?" Rachel asked.

Kyle set his fork down and wiped his lips, taking a sip of water before he started.

"She was due to give testimony about a boyfriend who was laundering money for one of the Mexican drug cartels. Unfortunately, he also had a penchant for stalking, and it caught her up in that entire cycle of domestic violence. She loved him and had a hard time separating herself from him. Like you alluded to, sometimes people find it hard to tell the difference between obsessive traits and a healthy, mature relationship."

"I guess exhibit number one is sitting right here."

Kyle smoothed his palms over his thighs, trying to dry the sweat. His heart pounded behind his ribs. He hated thinking about that day. Why was he sharing this with Rachel? He'd never shared more than the bare details of what happened with his colleagues. Only what was necessary for the report and investigation into his actions. Reliving the day would open a well of emotion he didn't know if he could lock back down.

"What I didn't know was that she had disclosed her location to him. She wanted to meet with him one more time. Ultimately, I think she wanted to be back with him again and, though consciously she would say she was done with him, her subconscious needs overruled."

"I can't blame her. Some people can't stand the thought of being alone."

"When we left the hotel we were staying at to go to court, he ambushed us. He shot her in the chest. The bullet passed through her and nicked my left side." He pulled his shirt up and showed Rachel the scar. "The force of the bullet threw her into me. I caught her and laid her down. Fellow officers returned fire, and the threat was extinguished."

He exhaled slowly, picking up his unused

knife, and tapped it mindlessly against the table. "When I looked at her eyes after that, I could see the look of betrayal she felt. Her lips, blue from lack of oxygen. I…tried…to save her. To do CPR. Nothing helped. They pronounced her dead at the scene."

The ache from his throat as he shared this tale spread through his body. He couldn't bring himself to look at Rachel. He heard a slight rustling as she stood from the table. He pushed his chair back, intending to stand up, too, but Rachel settled into his lap. Kyle embraced her. She placed her hands on his cheeks, easing her thumb over his lips. The other hand caressed the back of his head, sending electric tingles down his back.

"Rachel…"

She briefly pressed her index finger against his lips to quiet his protest and then lightly brushed her lips against his before pressing in. The wine he'd hoped to sip before now tasted sweet against his mouth. He pulled her tight into an embrace, his lips melding with hers.

She eased back, a soft sigh on her exhalation. "I just wanted to know what it felt like. To kiss someone who never intends to hurt me."

Kyle wanted those words to be true. Forcing a professional distance was going to do the very thing he dreaded. How could he keep her safe when his emotions were all tangled up with his physical attraction to her? He was flirting with dangerous territory.

He eyed Rachel intently, holding her gaze, caressing her arms gently and avoiding her injured side. "Rachel, there's always something a witness will hide from me. Always. I've never found an exception."

"I'm not hiding anything."

He wondered how long it would be before those words would prove untrue.

SEVEN

Rachel hadn't slept well. For most of the night she'd lain in bed staring into the darkness, questioning what she had done. Why had she kissed Kyle? She knew why—to prove to herself that men could be different. That a man could be attracted to her for who she was and not just what she could offer. That experiment had pulled hard at her heart. At the realization of how closed off she'd been to pursuing a close relationship with anyone.

It also proved to her it wasn't just a lab-based analysis. Something she could view from the outside and make an objective assessment of the study's goals. Clearly, she was attracted to Kyle. His kindness was tear provoking because of its uniqueness in her life. Because of that, the feelings she'd stifled over the last three years—of wanting to share her life with someone—were growing fresh shoots.

Throughout the night, she'd listened for him. He was sleeping on the couch on the first floor, putting himself as the only line of defense. After she'd kissed him, they'd finished dinner. He'd insisted on doing the dishes despite his previous statement. An attempt to stay busy, no doubt. After putting everything away, he'd asked her to show him the other weapons in the home and picked a small handgun for her to have in her bedroom. He'd checked the weapon to make sure it was in good working order—surprised when he learned that, every other month, she would visit this property and do maintenance. Making sure the guns were oiled and cleaned, so if she needed to fire one, they'd be ready. At varying times each hour, she'd hear him rise and walk through the house. He'd come upstairs and open her door, go to the window to be sure it was locked, and leave as quietly as he'd entered. Most often, she'd been awake, feigning sleep when he'd come through.

From downstairs she heard the doorbell ring. Rachel's heart skipped a beat. She heard footsteps cross the hardwood floor and then the sound of two male voices. She rose from the bed and put on her jeans and an olive green tank top. Even though this home had air-conditioning, it was still in the middle of the desertlike environment.

When she approached, Kyle and another man were in the kitchen, sitting at the table. The other man, dressed in a suit, was familiar to Kyle. Likely a superior in the way Kyle showed deference to him in his mannerisms. Kyle was scrolling through photos on an iPad.

"Rachel, this is Javier Armijo."

The man turned to her. He stood a few inches taller than Kyle. Olive skin. Jet-black hair. Nearly as dark, chocolate-brown eyes. His goatee was well trimmed. A pair of blue-tinged prescription shades complemented his black pinstripe suit. There was something about him that pulled at Rachel's memory. She'd met him before but couldn't put a finger on where.

Kyle's words brought her back to the present. "He's my WITSEC supervisor. There's been a development in your case that we need to talk about."

"You mean Seth's case," Rachel said.

He was short and to the point. "No. I mean a case that Seth's prosecutor, Elijah Nguyen, is developing against you…for murder."

Rachel's limbs felt heavy as she took a seat at the table. What she had hoped would never happen was now a probability. Seth had always told her he'd never let her be free. It seemed he was cashing in on his promise.

Everything about Kyle's demeanor had changed. It was almost as if they were meeting for the first time.

He positioned a photo on the tablet and showed it to her. "This is—"

"Penelope Schmidt."

"You know her?" Armijo asked.

"Not personally, but I've been looking into her being one of Seth's victims."

Armijo continued. "Twenty-eight-year-old female. She was a nurse at the hospital where both of you worked. Disappeared just prior to Seth's trial."

"Right," Rachel confirmed.

"Why did you think she was one of Seth's victims?" Kyle asked.

Why did you? Past tense. Meaning they had found her, and not alive?

"Seth had a type. Brown haired. Relatively fit. Pretty. He also had a radius—they found only one of his victims outside it. One hundred and twenty miles. Two hours' drive. The hospital dead center. It was enough time to be gone to hide a body, but not too long to draw anyone's suspicions."

"The cabin was that distance," Armijo said. "Exactly."

Kyle rubbed his hands over his face. "They found Penelope's body three nights ago in the woods around the old cabin."

Rachel swallowed hard. She waited for the punch line.

"They estimate she's been dead a week."

She could see the multitude of calculations Kyle was making. That Seth was still in jail at that time, and she was free. She and Kyle weren't together then. He couldn't vouch for her innocence. A week ago, she'd taken a few days off and although she had traveled nowhere, there wasn't anyone who could confirm her whereabouts, either. A clear downside of choosing to live an isolated lifestyle. Was there someone who knew her work schedule and could have given that information to the Black Crew—in order to more perfectly frame her for the murder?

Risky moves like this weren't unknown to Seth. If she'd been working, it would have been an easy alibi. Regardless of what television purported, it could be difficult to nail down the actual time of death, considering the factors that played into the decomposition of a body. Time. Temperature. Animals and insects.

What had been done to the victim prior to death.

Kyle cleared his throat. "They found your DNA on the victim's body."

"What?"

"A hair sample. DNA matches your profile," Armijo added.

"Why would you test my DNA against it?"

"There was a tip that you were involved in the murder," Kyle said.

"Let me guess—an anonymous source."

To prove her innocence before, Rachel had allowed the police to collect her DNA. Fortunately, because of Seth's obsessive habits in erasing evidence from his crime scenes, there had been no trace of her at the cabin.

Seth and Rachel had married young. Each close to twenty-one at the time. Rachel had filed for divorce the day Heather had been found—almost ten years after their nuptials. She hadn't been to the cabin for more than five years prior to the separation once Seth stopped taking her there. It was a property that his parents had given to them as a wedding gift. At the beginning of their relationship, they had visited it frequently. Later, he'd gone alone, choosing it as a cover. Honestly, his solo trips had been a relief for Rachel. A break from his emotional abuse.

Kyle held her gaze. "Can you explain it?"

There was an edge of betrayal to his words. Seth had made it a pattern to always accuse her of things she was innocent of, acting like the hurt partner.

"No. I had nothing to do with her murder."

"Then how do you explain your DNA on her body?" Kyle pressed.

"I can't."

"So someone is framing you for her murder," Armijo said, a snide statement. He didn't believe in her innocence. Many didn't.

Kyle once had.

Now, the look in Kyle's eyes held an edge of uncertainty, and she could feel a canyon open between them. He was questioning himself. Her prior statements cast doubt in his mind, based on the way he averted his gaze. Likely he was revisiting how he felt about everything.

Including her.

"Yes, someone is framing me." Rachel searched Kyle's face. He wouldn't make eye contact with her. She reached for his hand, and he pulled it away. "Kyle, I didn't do this."

"Then how do you explain it if you've

never left Springdale—your DNA being there? Your hair on the body?"

"I don't know..."

Truly, she didn't know, but she'd have to tell Kyle the truth.

Then who could guess how he would really feel?

Kyle's heart raced. His headache was back. Inwardly, he chastised himself. His instincts were correct. Clearly, she hadn't been one hundred percent honest. Many said the most accurate predictor of future actions was past behavior, and he'd let slide that Rachel had thumbed her nose at the rules and maintained contact with Heather.

In his disregard of the significance of that action, he'd let his guard down. Now he looked foolish. This coming as a surprise from a superior made it look like he didn't have a handle on his witness.

He stood from the table. His eyes bored into her. "You know how this might have happened and you need to tell me now." There were likely legal implications of forcing her to tell him. She could plead the Fifth. Ask for a lawyer. It intrigued him to know what she'd choose.

"I visited my sister in Boston," she confessed.

"When?" Kyle asked.

"Two Christmases ago. She'd had a baby. I couldn't take the thought of never seeing her."

"Any other adventures? Did you have contact with anyone else other than your sister and Heather?"

"No. That's it."

"Did anything unusual happen on your trip to Boston?" Kyle asked. Inspector Armijo seemed to melt into the background.

Rachel's hand went to her throat—her breath quickened. Panic? Difficulty breathing? Both? She pressed her mouth into her upper arm and turned away from him for a moment. Composing her thoughts? Or creating a believable lie.

She faced him. "Someone broke into her apartment when we went out driving to look at Christmas lights."

"What was taken?" Kyle asked.

Rachel blew her hair from her eyes. "Only items from my bedroom."

"Like?"

"My hairbrush. Toothbrush. The water glass that had been on the bedside table."

Now she understood the significance of

those items. They all contained her DNA. How could she have been so blind? What she and her sister took as a teenage prank, a defense mechanism they'd both employed to shield themselves from feeling watched and hunted by the Black Crew, hadn't been just that. The Black Crew was collecting items that could be used as evidence against her.

"Did you report this to the police?"

"Of course not. First, it didn't seem that serious. We didn't want to draw attention to the fact that I was there."

Kyle pressed his fingers into the table. "You hid it from *me*."

"As if you would have given me permission to go."

"You're right. I would have talked you out of it for this very reason. Do you now realize how serious Seth and his crew are? They've likely been watching every member of your family since I placed you into WITSEC hoping for this very opportunity."

"I'm sorry," Rachel whispered.

"We have to consider other possibilities," Armijo said.

Kyle slumped back down into his seat. "I know."

"Like what?" Rachel asked.

"As big as Seth's network is, it would be difficult to monitor each of your family members for this length of time. The other option is they're getting inside information from someone in WITSEC," Kyle said.

"Like who?" Rachel asked.

"That's the million-dollar question," Armijo answered.

Kyle stood from the table and walked into the living room. He needed a break from her. He wanted to trust her, but doubt poisoned his ultimate belief in her innocence. The law and justice part of his psyche pushed him to consider that she was guilty.

His prevailing thought pushed those ruminations away. Not that a doctor couldn't be a murderous leech. A woman, though? Using such violent means? That was unusual…rare.

If Rachel was innocent, then who in WITSEC would have as much intimate knowledge as he had? Someone who could predict that Rachel would break protocol?

The first name that popped into his mind was Dr. Nora Allen.

Unbeknownst to the public was the battery of hoops that witnesses had to jump through prior to being put into the program. It wasn't as if WITSEC just scooped them up and put them in new towns, washing their hands of those people and their lives. All went through a risk assessment with a Bureau of Prisons psychologist. The purpose was to help predict how the witness would do in the program. What would be their barriers to holding the line? The psychologist reached out to them every three to four months. Any information from the family to a witness or vice versa was supposed to come through WITSEC.

"How did you find out about your sister's pregnancy?"

"Dr. Allen called me. Gave me her due date. Said if I wanted to send any cards or gifts, she could help coordinate delivery."

"Did you do that?"

"No, once I knew the delivery date, I just made the plans to go back to Boston. I figured the fewer people who knew about it, the better. I could slide in and out—"

"Undetected," Kyle finished.

Armijo pulled Kyle off to the side. "You really want to go down that road and investigate a member of our own team?" he whispered harshly when they were out of Rachel's earshot. "You believe in her innocence that much?"

"I don't know what to believe, and it's not just about believing in Rachel's innocence—"

"Because you're probably the only one."

Kyle pressed his lips together. Hearing his superior's statement clarified Kyle's thoughts. Armijo didn't think he was being objective. That was a problem. WITSEC inspectors handled criminal types all the time. Justice wasn't always well balanced. Sometimes, it was about getting the guiltiest behind bars. Other people who deserved justice certainly went free.

"We're used to handling shady people," Kyle said. "It's the nature of our job. Whether or not Rachel is truly innocent doesn't change our objective here. Keep in mind, Heather's movements also seem known. It's not just one witness who has been exposed. Due to that, I think it would be in our best interest to do some internal investigation, because it would be nothing less than a firestorm if it came out before we investigated it ourselves that someone inside WITSEC was putting protected witnesses in harm's way."

Armijo considered Kyle's statement. "Dr. Allen also did Heather Flores's risk assessment. She was her contact as well."

In that moment, Kyle saw the red laser light land on Armijo's right shoulder, then heard a tinkling of glass, saw a spray of blood, and his superior dropped in front of him.

EIGHT

"Rachel, get down!"

Kyle barely had time to hit the floor before the spray of bullets punctured through the walls. From the direction of the projectiles, it seemed two shooters had descended upon the cottage. How could they have found them so quickly? One night and they'd already been discovered.

In his peripheral vision, he saw Rachel scurry up the stairs. At the first break in the gunfire, he grabbed Javier by the shoulders and pulled him into the kitchen. There was a large pantry there where he could secure him until they handled the situation. He opened the door and pulled him inside. He was alive, his breaths quick, a slight tinge of blue to his lips. Kyle pulled opened several drawers and found a stack of towels. He opened his superior's shirt and pressed the towel against his wound. Javier cried out in pain.

Kyle found his phone, but when he pulled it out, he noticed it had been shattered by a bullet. How close had he come to death?

In the rush of adrenaline, he hadn't even felt it.

He found Javier's phone and scanned the wounded man's face to unlock the phone, but he didn't find a good signal. No bars, but he still tried to call 911. The call didn't go through. He sent a text message to their headquarters and prayed it would find home. Though headquarters was miles away in another state, hopefully they could notify local law enforcement and a rescue unit.

"Javier, you need to hold pressure to the wound. I've got to get out of here to help Rachel before they pin me down." He pulled Armijo's weapon from his holster and put it on his belly. "If you hear someone coming, shoot unless they announce themselves." Javier nodded, his face glistening with sweat, reflective of both pain and fear. Though they handled dangerous witnesses often, it wasn't every day they took oncoming fire.

Kyle exited the pantry and looked at the floor. There was a definitive blood trail that led from where Javier had fallen to his current position in the pantry like grisly breadcrumbs. Nothing Kyle could do about it now. Since the first barrage of gunfire, Kyle hadn't heard anything, and all the doors remained closed.

With his weapon at his side, he paced back to the living room and peeked out the window. He didn't see anyone. Where had they gone? What was their plan? To kill Rachel or take her with them? He was hurrying toward the back of the house, toward the screened-in porch, when he heard the explosion toward the front of the house.

He had to give them credit for the awe factor. They weren't attempting to be stealthy in any measure.

Kyle exited the screened-in porch to the backyard and made his way to the front of the house. He moved quickly, knowing that as soon as the gunmen found the red trail leading them straight to Javier's position, Armijo would have little time or strength to defend himself. When he rounded to the front of the house, he saw smoke clawing its way toward the peaceful blue sky. A small, likely improvised, explosive device had obliterated the entryway. He stepped through the hole, acrid smoke filling his nostrils. Part of the wood frame was on fire. If that wasn't controlled, it could take the whole house, but his priorities were making sure Javier and Rachel got out alive.

Making his way through the rubble, his gun held out ahead of him, his eyes roving to keep any potential targets in his sight, he found the first gunman heading into the kitchen carrying a weapon that was more powerful than needed for the intended job. As the man reared the weapon up to shoot through the closed pantry door, Kyle laid a round into his back, and the man dropped. Kyle approached him quickly, taking the automatic assault rifle from his hands and holstering his own weapon. Likely, his partner was using the same armament.

Kyle bent down to one knee. The man's face was toward him, his eyes open, but it was clear he could not move his arms or legs. He was breathing, but his shoulders heaved with each attempt. The shot had landed in the man's back, exactly midline. If he had to make his own medical diagnosis, the shot had pierced his spinal cord. He was no longer a threat, and the difficulty breathing would make it impossible for him to yell out and warn his partner.

Now to find Rachel.

Rachel bounded up the steps and went into the main bedroom. In there, she had several weapons hidden for an occasion such as this. From her nightstand, she pulled out her handgun. From the same drawer, she pulled out a sheath that held a large knife. Quickly, she lifted her pant leg and secured the knife. If things got close, that knife would be her last line of defense.

In less than three days, she'd been hunted three times. Instead of making her wearier, it made her angry. *Why do I have to spend my life running when I didn't do anything wrong? Getting mixed up with the wrong man shouldn't be a life sentence.*

A resolve set within her. She'd been hiding for three years like she was the guilty one, holding a defensive position and praying that this day would never happen. It wasn't that she'd become the next ninja warrior, but she had taken it upon herself to learn a few things for just this scenario.

Because if she knew anything about Seth,

she knew he'd never give up on trying to kill her unless he was dead himself.

Well, I'm not running anymore.

Rachel stepped out of the bedroom. She had a plan. She didn't know if it was a wise one, but if it worked, she could dispense with the situation quickly.

She'd seen Inspector Armijo go down and hadn't waited to see any additional fallout. Kyle was armed and better trained. Hopefully, he was still engaged in the situation, because there seemed to be more than one person trying to eliminate them.

She peeked out into the hallway. The only sound was that of a door closing on the first floor. Someone was moving around below. Hopefully Kyle. She patted her back pocket and then remembered her phone sat on the kitchen table downstairs. No calling for help in the short term.

If Kyle was down or otherwise detained, she was on her own. Just like she had been for years.

The sound of the explosion pushed her back into the bedroom. The smell of smoke wafted up to the second floor. She had to give Seth credit. Why had he changed his MO so much? These attacks had been in daylight. Full-frontal assault. It would be easy to identify the assailants.

Which meant they hadn't figured they would leave anyone alive to make an ID.

Rachel pressed her back against the wall next to the open door. Just because she was going on the offensive didn't mean her body didn't feel every ounce of her fear. Her fingertips tingled. She forced herself to take slower, deeper breaths. If she continued to hyperventilate, her hands would cramp and she'd be unable to hold a weapon.

Stepping out onto the landing, she looked down the stairs and made eye contact with a black-clad assailant with a ski mask over his face. He reared his weapon toward her and fired off a multitude of successive shots.

Rachel scurried back into the bedroom. The doors to the closet at the end of the hallway shattered. Broken remnants of splintered wood and drywall showered her face.

Part one of her plan was complete. The assailant knew where she was and would come after her.

She skirted to the other side of the bedroom and went into the bathroom, closing the door and locking it, and then paced through it to the bedroom on the other side.

Veiled from her attacker, she hid behind the door and waited for the black blur to run past the doorway. After he did, Rachel darted into the hall, tracing his steps, and found him at the bathroom door, poising the weapon to fire at the lock.

"Drop your weapon or I'll shoot you," she stated to the figure from the doorway. His shoulders eased down as he contemplated his next move.

The masked assailant dropped his left shoulder, not in a motion to surrender, but in a move to flip his direction and fire at her. Rachel released a round before he could fully turn, hitting his body on the left lower side. He tumbled to the floor, clutching his back.

That's when she felt someone rush up behind her. She almost turned and fired when Kyle wrapped his arms around her waist, bringing his hand up to her arm and drawing down her weapon.

"Great job, Rachel. I've got this guy. Armijo is in the pantry. He needs your help."

Rachel pocketed her gun and headed down the stairs. The front entryway was fully engulfed in flames. She stifled a cough as she rounded into the kitchen.

First, Rachel came upon the body of the

first assailant. A gunshot wound to the back. Kyle had restrained his hands. The ski mask was askew, and Rachel took it off his head. The man's eyes were closed. He was still breathing, but too slowly. Rachel figured he wasn't long for this world.

Grabbing the man by the legs, she pulled him back and opened the pantry door...and came face-to-face with Javier Armijo raising a weapon with shaky hands, his finger settling on the trigger.

She instinctively lifted her hands in surrender. "It's Rachel!"

Armijo dropped the weapon to the side, and Rachel stepped in and knelt down next to him.

"Can I see?" she asked, taking one of his trembling hands in hers.

He nodded assent. She pulled open his shirt, exposing the wound to his upper right shoulder. Considering his difficulty breathing, he'd likely collapsed his lung. She backed out of the space and headed into the kitchen to get her medical kit. Stepping next to the sink, she grabbed a pitcher and set it in the sink to fill it with water. From the trash, she gathered the IV tubing she'd used on Kyle.

Not sanitary, but she had little choice in the moment.

Honestly, she didn't know if the maneuver was going to work. But she had no alternative. They were miles away from the nearest trauma center, and local EMS were likely first responders and probably didn't carry any advanced medical equipment.

Kyle came up behind her. "We need to move Javier onto the dining room table," Rachel said.

As she turned, a beam from over the front doorway fell to the floor, burning embers cascading down like fireworks. The beloved cottage, the last remnant of her life that she could fully claim as her own, was falling around her. All that her grandmother had left for her, torched by Seth's darkness. Losing this piece of serenity was making Rachel feel unhinged. Even if she beat Seth in this current chess match, there was nothing left for her to go back to. She shut the thoughts down and forced herself to focus on her patient. They entered the pantry, and Rachel pulled Javier by the ankles as Kyle leaned over and scooped him up by the shoulders.

They wrestled him onto the table. Rachel pulled all the chairs from one side away so she'd have easy access to perform the procedure. Kyle raced back to the pantry to gather additional supplies, and Rachel grabbed a few needed items from the kitchen.

Standing next to Javier, as his color paled and his skin dotted with droplets of sweat, she opened a clean kitchen towel and placed the instruments she'd use on top. This didn't match the sterile procedure in the hospital, but habit forced her to at least try to do all she could for her patient under these circumstances. Secondary infection could be just as brutal a killer as the primary injury.

"Help me get his jacket and shirt off," Rachel ordered. Each took a shoulder and lifted, wrestling him out of his clothes. Rachel cupped his head as they laid him back down on the table. Javier was not responsive other than a few moans as they moved him.

Rachel yanked several disinfectant hand wipes from a canister. Iodine was the preferred antiseptic, but this would have to do. She scrubbed his side and then picked up a scalpel, palpating down his rib cage to the spot between the ribs she'd need to cut into. "This is going to hurt." She sliced through his skin. Javier reared up slightly and protested. Not a strong yell, which would have been reassuring, but a huffed-out mew because of his body's lack of oxygen and his inability to take a deep breath. Her patient continued to try to sit up. Swatted at her hands to drive them away.

Kyle gripped his shoulders and forced him back down to the table. "It's okay. She's helping you."

Armijo blinked rapidly. "You...sure?"

Rachel knew Javier didn't believe in her innocence, and she also knew he'd likely chastised Kyle for giving any credence to her assertion that she had nothing to do with Penelope Schmidt's murder.

Sweat poured from Armijo's face. Kyle grabbed an extra towel from the pile and wiped it clear. "I'm sure," he said, attempting to reassure his coworker.

"Sorry, a little more pain." She pushed her index finger between the ribs, the IV tubing nestled next to it, through the incision, and left the tubing behind. Taking the pitcher of water, she pulled a chair back next to her and settled the end in the water. A poor man's chest tube with tubing that had too small a lumen, but despite the hindrances, air and blood bubbled through the water. Not as fast of a pace as she hoped, but the measure should buy him some time.

Rachel returned her attention to her patient and stitched tight the skin around the IV tubing. From her kit, she grabbed some gauze and smothered it with antibiotic ointment, placing it around the site and securing it in place with foam tape.

"Can you go find him a blanket?" Rachel asked Kyle.

"Of course."

Kyle skirted off. Rachel laid a reassuring hand on her patient. No matter his attitude or opinion about her, she was a physician at heart and had a duty to treat. Could she blame him for his feelings? He wasn't in the minority.

"Thank…you," he said. "My…breathing… little easier." She patted his hand, but he gripped hers in response. When patients felt near to death, they always reached out. At that moment, thoughts, feelings, barriers didn't matter. Just a human touch. Not wanting to be alone.

And yet that's the sentence she'd been living out. Being alone. Forced to, in some senses. Voluntarily in others.

"I've bought you some time, but we need

to get you to a hospital quickly," she reassured him.

Finally, the welcoming sound of sirens came from the distance. At the right time. The smoke from the front entryway was starting to billow more into the house.

"I may have been...wrong about...you."

Rachel was relieved both by his words and his ability to string more words together, even though his speech was still choppy. It meant the tube was helping with his breathing.

Kyle returned and laid the blanket on Javier. "You look better. A bit of color."

"How's the man upstairs?" Rachel asked.

"He'll live. He's breathing fine. I shredded a few bed linens to put a dressing in place to control the bleeding. More than he deserves. How about the other guy down here?"

"Depends on the capability of the responding EMS. He needs help breathing and oxygen pretty quickly if he's going to survive."

The acrid smoke caused Kyle to cough. "We need to start moving people out of here. It won't take long for that entry fire to take hold."

In that moment, there were men at the back door, in EMS uniforms, carrying a backboard. They could use that to get Javier to safety. He'd be her choice to evacuate first.

It tore Rachel's soul seeing the gunman lying there in distress. Emergency medicine was all about triage. It wasn't a fair system but a necessary one. Using the available resources to help those that could be saved. The bullet wound to the back. The lack of movement to the extremities. How the man's shoulders heaved to take each breath showed a high spinal cord injury. She could have used her knowledge and slim medical supplies to save him, but she'd chosen Javier instead.

Kyle waved the EMTs over. At the same moment, water spray spewed into the home. A team of firefighters was working to knock down the flames at the front door.

Rachel held a hand up. "Turn him toward me and put the board underneath." They did as she instructed and moved him onto the hard blue plastic. Rachel grabbed the pitcher of water. "You need to keep this next to him or lower to help get the air out of his chest."

"We got it. We'll get him to the rig and start a line and oxygen."

When this story came to light, they would judge Rachel for picking Inspector Armijo over the more injured assailant, and few would be interested in her explanation of the principles of triage. They would claim revenge, not understanding that she couldn't save both men.

If the men's injuries had been reversed, would she still have chosen Javier?

Probably, because her heart was tired of evil triumphing over good. She was desperate to put a win in the column for her team. Justice had been served to the one man who had tried to kill them, even though she wasn't supposed to be the one who determined who lived or died. Now she felt guilty about feeling all those things.

Which was why she could never be a murderer. Why she had turned Seth in to the police.

The guilt of not doing something against evil would have killed her first.

That's the one thing she wished everyone knew.

NINE

Kyle paced the hall. There was too much waiting in hospitals. They were back at St. George Regional. WITSEC thought it best to keep their resources concentrated in one place. Rachel was across the room in a chair sipping watered-down cafeteria lemonade. Javier had been evaluated in the ER. Rachel getting praised for saving his life. She did still hold her medical license from Boston, which probably protected her from liability. Though, from a past case he'd been involved in that dealt with medical malpractice, he knew you had to prove both negligence and harm to get a payout. A medical provider could be negligent, but if they did no harm to the patient, there was no case. And vice versa. There could be harm in a patient outcome, but if the provider hadn't been negligent, it was the same outcome.

Could he say the same thing about himself

right now? He was being negligent in his duties as a WITSEC inspector. There was no doubt about that. He was emotionally involved with a witness, and it was clouding his judgment. If he stepped back and analyzed the case from the point of emotional detachment, there were several things that a curious inspector would have seen as red flags concerning Rachel.

One was her overall insistence that she had known nothing about Seth's crimes. Of course, anyone could look back with twenty-twenty lenses and analyze things now that should have been apparent then. Most spouses whose significant others were of the deviant type went through that process. However, the number of bodies that Seth had piled up rivaled the most prolific serial killers. Could she have been so enamored by his lifestyle and wealth that she'd ignored those red flags? Of course, it was plausible. That was human nature.

Denial was the specialty of humanity. Particularly when getting something that someone felt was missing from their prior life. It was hard to give up wealth after experiencing its advantages.

Second, there were the murder boards. That had left him unsettled since the first moment he'd laid eyes on them. A reasonable explanation was that she felt guilty and had wanted to make amends for not acting sooner on the things that she should have. But if he were honest with himself, it felt more than seeking justice. It felt like an obsession.

Third, her DNA at a crime scene when Seth was imprisoned. Had Penelope Schmidt been kept alive since the time she'd gone missing? Or had her body been stored in such a way to prevent decomposition? The medical examiner hadn't ruled either way at this point. Was Rachel the true criminal?

Though rare, there had been female serial killers. The brutality of the crimes lent to a male persuasion. Women tended to be cleaner when they were involved. Even if they used a weapon like a gun or knife, torture was rarely involved, as it had been in Seth's crimes. Women didn't hold victims for days unless there was perhaps a monetary payout. Something like caring for an elderly person while establishing a way to cash in on retirement money and then doing them in. Most likely, if Rachel was involved, she and Seth had worked in partnership. That was more common in the literature. If that was the case, was she still fully under his spell and had he been directing her from prison?

He neared a window, pulled out his phone and dialed Gage Carter. "Hey, it's Kyle."

"How's Javier doing?" Gage asked.

"Should make it," Kyle said.

"I guess he's fortunate, considering who treated him in the field." Another reminder that most in WITSEC didn't consider Rachel's hands clean.

"When's the last time we inspected Seth's communications?" Kyle asked.

"Considering the developments in the case, we're poring through them as we speak."

"Anything unusual pop up?"

There was a shuffling of papers on the other end of the line. "About one year ago, it seems Seth was using a code."

"A code?"

"The letters are written in normal fashion, but at the top and highlighted in different colors for each correspondent is a code made up of numbers of letters. There are three different codes. Likely, the notes have something embedded into them, and the top code is either instructions on how to decipher it or it directs who it should go to," Gage said.

"Has anyone broken it yet?"

"Too soon. We're trying to gather more samples."

"What about his phone calls?" Kyle asked.

"Seth is a more prolific letter writer. He only calls one person, and that's Mommy dearest—who, of course, still believes in her son's innocence."

"Mothers usually do."

"What's your plan?" Gage asked.

"I'm trying to track down Dr. Nora Allen. Evidently, she hasn't been seen in a few days."

"Correct. Missed a few days of scheduled interviews. We sent some agents over to her place, but nothing seemed amiss. No signs of foul play. She took what a woman would normally take for a trip. Packed a bag. Purse, car keys and vehicle were gone. She's made regular charges to her account, so someone is using her credit card. Without other evidence of foul play, we're not going further with an investigation. Many people are upset that you would even consider that she's involved in criminal activity. She's a lot more liked around here than you are. She's not beholden to us to tell us every move she makes."

That stung, but it was the truth. Kyle's defense of Rachel had put him in the clear minority.

"You can't afford it, Kyle. The witness you lost—even though she broke WITSEC rules—is a mark against you. You should have been monitoring Rachel more."

"They may have their own life to some degree," Kyle argued. "They're not criminals."

"At least not criminals that have to go to jail. Come on, Kyle, you know quite a few people who we've had in WITSEC have not been the most trustworthy individuals. We've had felony murderers."

"And if so were ordered by the court and served jail time."

"Yeah, in our posh private facility to keep them out of gen pop, or even a private cell with a guard who might want to pervert his own justice. Listen, Kyle, I like you, but I see how your mind is getting fuzzy, and I'm trying to help you, as a friend. Rachel was in communication with Heather Flores. She had contact with her sister. Whether this break-in during her stay with her sister accounts for her DNA being present on the latest victim is yet to be seen, but you've lost your objectivity. You need to, one hundred percent, maintain professional distance. You cannot get wrapped up with this woman. If you do, it wouldn't surprise me if you became a victim yourself."

"Point taken."

"You're a good man, Kyle. You *cannot* trust

her. You need to keep your head on a swivel, as they say. Watch your back."

As he looked at Rachel across the room, he didn't know if his heart could abide by what his mind and professional ethics dictated must be done.

Rachel could see Kyle's distress oozing from every pore. He paced and frowned. Whomever he was talking to intensified his mood for the worse. She was losing him. Not in the relational sense. One kiss didn't signify a liaison, no matter how much she wanted to explore it. She was losing his trust. If a physical thing could represent an emotional change, then he was slowly building a brick wall between them. A strong one that she didn't know if she could break through. Even Rachel could see how guilty she looked, despite what she knew in her heart.

He disconnected the phone and paced toward her but stood a good three steps away. Too far away to have any intimate conversation. She stood, reached her hand out and placed it on his chest. "I'm sorry about your friend."

He grabbed her wrist and removed her hand from his body. "He wasn't my friend, but I appreciate the sentiment." He raked his fingers through his hair. "Rachel, I owe you an apology. I never should have allowed physical contact between the two of us. Nothing outside what is necessary for protection. It was irresponsible of me." He inhaled deeply and let the air slowly escape from his lips. "I must maintain my professional perspective. You can see how not operating that way puts all of us at risk."

Rachel's heart caved. She briefly glanced down to her chest to see if an open wound existed. The pain was so real. She was alone again. The trust she'd put in Kyle felt tainted. Perhaps men didn't change.

Rachel folded her arms over chest. "I understand."

"Do you?"

She bit the inside of her cheek, hoping the pain would dissuade the tears from falling. It didn't work. Rachel swiped at the tears and came up with a different reason for her emotional distress. Anything to keep from admitting the truth—that his words had wounded her, and she didn't know how many more inflictions she could take. Death by a thousand cuts. An emotional demise could still lead to a physical one.

"I'd like to see Heather before we go."

Kyle looked at his feet, shuffled them from side to side. "Why?"

"To check on her. She is a friend—my only friend."

Kyle's eyes widened at her statement. Briefly his lips parted, but a refutation of her statement was not forthcoming. He relented rather than argue with her. "For only a few minutes."

They walked to Heather's room. Kyle ushered her in but stayed outside to talk with the police officer who was standing guard near her room. It would be hard for WITSEC inspectors to cover a witness 24-7, and their resources were likely stretched thin with the Black Crew being so active.

When she first entered the room, Heather was sleeping. Rachel pulled up a chair and sat down, first noting the IV fluids that hung, how much oxygen she was on and how much blood still drained from her chest tube. These would likely be the same things Inspector Armijo would have after his surgery.

Rachel laid her hand over hers, comforted by the warmth—not feverish, which was a good sign.

Lord, we're alone, Heather and I. There's no one we can trust except for one another.

Even those fighting to protect me don't believe in my innocence. Please, bring Heather back to full health. She has already endured so much pain and trauma. Don't let this event sideline the progress she has already made. She loves You. Please make it clear to her You love her just as much...

She'd whispered the words in her mind, but at the end, Heather turned her hand and gripped Rachel's. "Why are you here? You know it's not safe."

Rachel smiled and gripped her hand back. "There was an incident at my grandmother's cottage. I probably can't ever go back there. The Black Crew shot an inspector. They transferred him here."

"Will he make it?"

"I think so...hope so. How are you feeling?"

Heather struggled to sit up. Rachel stood and used the bed controls to get her into a more upright position. Heather leaned forward, and Rachel instinctively adjusted her pillows behind her. Heather sank into the fluffiness.

"You should have been a nurse," she said, motioning for her water cup.

Rachel grabbed it and helped guide the straw into her mouth. "No. I don't have the patience that nurses do. I'm fine with a shorter interaction and having them do all the heavy lifting."

A knock came at the door, and a nurse walked in.

"Your ears must be burning," Heather said.

"Really?" the nurse replied.

Rachel checked the clock. It was two in the afternoon. Ward nurses usually made rounds at eight, noon, and four o'clock.

"Where's the nurse I had this morning?" Heather asked.

"Late lunch break. I'm bringing you your medication."

Rachel's heart settled a bit until Heather spoke.

"I didn't think I had anything scheduled until this evening." Heather sat up more and straightened her sheets, bringing out her hand that contained the IV port.

"What medication?" Rachel asked.

"Um…an antibiotic. A new one."

Strange. Most antibiotics were hung as a piggyback, in a small bag, to an existing IV solution.

"What's the name of the medicine?" Rachel pressed.

The nurse eyed the syringe, and Rachel

did so with equal scrutiny. It didn't bear a patient label. She took in the nurse's attire. The whole outfit came across as trying too hard. New scrubs. Starched to perfection. These days, nurses typically had a more laid-back vibe. It was almost as if someone was trying to exude what they thought the perfect professional nurse would look like in order not to draw suspicion.

His badge was turned around, so she couldn't read the name. "Can I see your badge?" Rachel asked him.

Heather reached out and took Rachel's hand, squeezing it tightly as a warning. Heather always was kind and loath to be embarrassed. "Rachel, I'm sure it's fine. There aren't boogeymen around every corner. We're in a safe place. There's an officer right outside my door."

The nurse turned it over and showed it to her. The photo was covered by a sticker of Kermit the Frog. More appropriate for pediatrics than an adult unit. Some nurses did this when they didn't like their photo or wanted to protect their information, but the badge looked worn, and the sticker was new.

"Heather, what was your nurse's name this morning?"

"Tyler."

It was the name on the badge.

"Male or female?"

"Female."

The interloper abruptly took Heather's hand and connected the syringe without cleaning it with an alcohol wipe. An infection-control no-no.

This wasn't a nurse providing care for her patient. It was attempted murder.

"Kyle!" Rachel yelled, and in the same second she slammed one foot on the pedal to unlock the bed while her other plunged into the side of the bed, sending it into the perpetrator's midsection and knees and knocking him down. The man righted easily and stomped back to the bed and grabbed for the syringe. In one motion Rachel reached over and ripped the IV out of Heather's hand.

Kyle broke through the door without hesitation and drove the man into the ground. "What's going on?"

"The syringe. You need to test it immediately. He tried to poison her."

Suddenly, the man laughed. A maniacal, mind-altering heckle. "None of you are safe. We're going to keep coming and coming and coming."

TEN

There was a full-force war in Kyle's body between his heart and his mind. He knew what everyone else believed about Rachel, but she'd also saved the last two victims—even himself and his more minor injuries—that had nearly been killed by the Black Crew. How could this amount to her working on Seth's behalf?

The intruder in Heather's room had been detained by the local police. They found Heather's nurse—whose badge the perpetrator had stolen on the outskirts of the hospital grounds—alive but severely beaten. Most often, smokers couldn't be close to the hospital these days, particularly staff, and it had been an easy opportunity for the man to knock the nurse unconscious and steal her badge to give him access to Heather's room and prevent questioning from the trained officer who sat outside the door.

The syringe had contained a combination of a paralyzing agent and Valium. At least in that way, the assassin had tried to be kind. Heather would have slept through suffocating to death. It still surprised Kyle that he'd taken the chance with Rachel in the room. Maybe he'd also had plans for Rachel that hadn't come to fruition. A happenstance he would have acted upon.

Or the Black Crew was continuing to frame her. If Heather had died in Rachel's presence, it would have added to the belief that she was Seth's accomplice and not simply his unknowing ex-wife.

Both stood outside the interrogation room, on one side of the two-way glass, where the nurse impostor sat, waiting to be questioned. None of the Black Crew members that they captured had been willing to talk. It would not stop Kyle from trying.

He faced Rachel. "Are you okay? You've said little since we left the hospital."

"Is there anything to say?"

They were alone. The other officers were doing business elsewhere.

He knew what she meant without expanding

on her words. Maybe there was nothing else to say to her right now. His words had been clear. She understood them and was shielding her emotions in the same way he had.

Which meant there had been emotions to guard on both sides.

"I'm going to go back to the hospital," Rachel declared.

"For what reason?"

"I want to spend more time with Heather... while it's legal."

"You'll need to be escorted," Kyle said. He turned to the officer standing nearby. "Would you mind taking Ms. Bright back to the hospital and staying with her? I'll come relieve you after I talk to this character."

The officer agreed. Kyle tried to meet Rachel's eyes, but she turned to leave. An ache settled in his gut. The sensation troubled him. He was clearly falling for her. Thoughts of what life could be like with her had crossed his mind more times than he could count. Was there a way for them to be together? Could they come through something like this and be able to fully express what they both were feeling? Kyle closed his eyes. He did believe in prayer, though he didn't utilize it as much as he should.

God, this feels like an impossible situation. Bring Rachel and those she loves safely through this situation. I'm so afraid of losing her. If there's a way for us to be together, help us find it.

Kyle opened his eyes, turned the knob and entered the interrogation room.

This was what he could do right now to try and help Rachel. The other things were out of his control. He had to trust God was watching over those details.

Watching over Rachel when he couldn't be with her.

The assailant was tall, muscled, his body used to spending time in the gym. Shock of red hair. A smattering of freckles across his face. Fair skinned. Dark brown eyes. Not someone who blended into a crowd easily. Kyle dragged the metal chair out from the table. The shrieking sound as it scraped against the floor unsettled his nerves. It was the first time Kyle had felt the paranoia that his witnesses dealt with every day. When you didn't know who to trust and there were villains around every corner.

The man was a no-name to law enforcement. Cody McHale. No priors. Had never been arrested or charged with so much as a speeding ticket. His primary residence was in Boston, and he worked in pharmaceutical sales, which could explain how he became, presumably, closely connected with Seth—and likely explained his access to the medications he had brought with him to the hospital.

"I'm US marshal Kyle Reid."

"Marshal." The man returned Kyle's statement with an awkward, mocking salute. Attempting to raise one arm while simultaneously forgetting his wrists were handcuffed together. Trying for bravado. Coming across as a clown.

Kyle showed his badge. "I work in witness protection, and you're coming after my wards. I don't like it."

The man brought his well-defined arms to his eyes and mocked rubbing them—like a mime mimicking crying. "So, so sad." He slapped his hands onto the table. It took everything within Kyle not to jerk back. "Too bad I didn't get her. But as Seth says—we'll die trying."

Kyle crossed his arms and eased back into his chair. "Why do you follow him?"

"Why not? We're setting him free. An innocent man has been wrongly charged. It's about time he gets justice."

"Why would you want a serial killer out of prison?"

"So he can do as he wants."

"You're fine with him killing innocent women?"

"Someone has to thin the herd."

Kyle groaned inwardly. "You see the dichotomy here, don't you? You've just said you want to release an innocent man, but you know he's guilty of his crimes."

"All depends on how you define murder."

It didn't happen often, but there were truly evil people who wanted to see mayhem happen. It seemed Cody was one of them. It was the thing that fueled Kyle's belief in God— the balance between good and evil. The world was full of opposites, and one could not exist without the other.

"You would ruin your life for this ideal? You'll be brought up on attempted murder charges. Plus the assault on the nurse whose badge you stole. There were witnesses to your crime."

"If Rachel's believable, that is."

"What's that supposed to mean?" Heat flared in Kyle's chest. His hands fisted in his lap. Some days it took every rational cell not to physically strike out.

Cody smiled coldly. "I think the tide is turning against your most favored one. You seem to be only one of a few who believe in Rachel's innocence." He slid the handcuffs over the table. Kyle's skin prickled. "Some say she's a wolf in sheep's clothing and you're too blind to see it. You might want to beware. She ultimately could be setting a trap for you."

Kyle swallowed hard. It unnerved him, to be honest. Evil could more easily identify evil. It was a kinship. A look in the eye recognizable when you contained the same characteristics. Good people could more easily be fooled—because of their nature, they sometimes didn't buy into the twisted essence that could be the human heart. Was Kyle being foolish to continue to believe in the possibility of Rachel's innocence? Was he the only one who could see her goodness?

"You'll be going to jail for a long time. I'm wondering if you checked the state statutes," Kyle said.

"Meaning?"

"Massachusetts doesn't have the death penalty, but that's not true for Utah. The view on criminality here is a little different from out East."

"You're saying I could get the death penalty," Cody tried to verify.

Likely not, but that wasn't something that Kyle was obligated to share with McHale. Law enforcement could lie to a witness. He'd been read his rights and declined an attorney. For now, Kyle was well within the scope of the law to try to scare him a little into confession.

"You said it, not me."

The man inhaled sharply, contemplating his choices. Kyle used silence to let him sit and ruminate through them. One weakness of people was that they talked too much. Silence could be just as easy a generator of truth as pounding a suspect with a tirade of questions. People didn't like silence and would intentionally or otherwise fill the gap. Sometimes the information was useful—other times not.

"What if I helped you?" Cody asked.

Kyle leaned forward. "Depends on what kind of help you're offering. It would have to be a big help to take something like the death penalty off the table."

"What if I gave you inside information?"

"Depends on how significant it is."

"I don't mean inside information regarding what you call the Black Crew. Selling them out would easily mean my death—even in prison. I meant inside information about your highly esteemed organization."

Kyle leaned in. "That would be significant. If you expose a mole inside WITSEC, I can promise you it would be beneficial to any judgment handed down against you."

"I thought so. Wouldn't look good if someone on the inside was developing hit lists for those you're duty bound to protect. Right?"

"If proven true, of course," Kyle countered.

"Have you ever wondered how your two past locations have been disclosed? I mean, a grocery store in the middle of nowhere and a house Rachel was gifted that she thought was under the radar."

"Of course. But I didn't even know those locations myself. Nor did anyone inside WITSEC."

"That is, until you arrived there. Correct?"

Kyle stood and paced the room. Cody's deceptive language was a ploy, but hidden in the puzzle he was trying to weave was the clue Kyle needed to latch on to. Then it dawned on him. He exited the room and made his way to the parking lot, breaking into a run until he came to his car. Winded from the sprint, he got down on all fours and looked under his vehicle.

It didn't take him long to see what he feared was present.

A tracker on his vehicle. Likely placed by someone back at WITSEC before he had left to meet Rachel in Springdale.

There was one man Kyle could think of who would do that. Kyle grabbed the tracker and stomped it until it fractured, got into his car and hightailed it back to the hospital.

What was it they said? It was easy to continue to break a moral boundary once someone had surpassed it the first time. If so, Rachel was living up to the saying. She stood at the nurses' station in the ICU. It had been her intent to come back and visit someone, and she would stop by and see Heather again. It might be the last opportunity she'd have. But that wasn't her primary intention.

Her real reason was to visit Inspector Armijo. Something about him—his persona, his mannerisms, his looks—had bothered her ever since he'd set foot in her grandmother's cottage. Now it was time to see if her suspicions were warranted.

Peering through the glass window of Javier's room, she didn't see any medical personnel in attendance. The officer seemed fine taking a seat in the hallway for her to go in and have a private conversation. Without knocking, she breached the door and quietly closed it behind her. His eyes were closed—likely facilitated by a painkiller. Rachel stepped to his bedside and checked the medical equipment, just as she had in Heather's room. Basic IV fluids, a morphine drip and oxygen delivered through nasal prongs. His vital signs marched by on his patient monitor. Heart rate slightly elevated. Oxygen level normal, though on the low end. Perhaps the perpetrator's bullets had done more damage than she had initially thought. It was definitely plausible.

Rachel smoothed her hand over his until he opened his eyes. He startled and jerked his hand away. She pulled up the wooden chair and sat down next to him.

"How are you feeling?" Rachel asked.

"Better. Obviously thanks to you," he said, gathering the bed linens closer to his chest. "Can't say having this tube in my side is any fun—" He coughed, covering his mouth with his hand. Coughing was the result of the chest tube irritating the lung lining. It echoed Rachel's feelings "Happy to be alive, considering how far away the hospital was."

"When did Seth first come to you with his proposition?" Rachel asked.

"I have no idea what you're talking about," Armijo replied.

Rachel nodded. "About seven years ago, your daughter was severely injured in a car accident. She would have died without Seth's help, isn't that correct?"

The man remained silent, but Rachel could see he swallowed heavily multiple times in a row. A sheen of sweat broke out on his hairline. She was close to the truth, and she would pull it out of him. An ER physician was just as good as any law enforcement officer at getting the truth from a person wanting to keep it hidden.

"I almost didn't recognize you," Rachel said. "People look so different in a hospital setting—particularly when a loved one is close to death. It was both your wife and daughter, right? I'm sure, in your memory, I'm just one of the many medical personnel you crossed paths with. We all blended together. People rarely remember the first person in the hospital who comes to assist them. Usually they remember the one credited with saving the life, even though all the people along that path had a hand in it. But I digress."

Javier reached for his nurse call button, and Rachel tugged the cord to pull it out of reach. She would not allow him to signal for help to get out of this conversation. He then pulled the oxygen from his nose, and Rachel watched his numbers tick down. The ploy was a good one. A monitor alarming would bring help, probably more quickly than a nurse call button. Rachel grabbed the tubing. He brought his hands up and tried to force her away.

"Put this back in your nose and let us have a reasonable conversation about your misdeeds. If you don't, I'll reach out to Seth myself and tell him you disclosed his location."

"That would be a lie."

"You think Seth cares about differentiating the truth from a lie? He only cares about killing. Just knowing you had a conversation with me will be enough to get you marked for death. If you cooperate with me, your reputation, the love you have for your wife and daughter—you might be able to save all of that, because once Kyle knows about this he's going to become unhinged. If you choose to testify against Seth, you'll be fortunate if they put you into the very program you've tainted."

Javier put the nasal prongs back in his nose and inhaled deeply, bringing his oxygen numbers back up.

"The suit and tie threw me off. When I first saw you, you were dressed in jeans and an old college sweatshirt with bloodstains. Flecks of blood in your hair. You'd beaten your family to the ER. They were being helicoptered in."

Armijo lay there frozen, unable to move past the truth spilling from her. No doubt his mind was petrified by the thought of the prison sentence awaiting him.

"Seth recognized your daughter's devastating brain injury and hastened her to the OR… We could barely lay hands on her. It's probably why you think I wouldn't remember you, but I remember your distress. That's not something any physician casts easily from their mind. The darkness that can swallow a whole being when the fear of death of a loved one grips them."

"If you think there's some grand confession coming from me, you're more delusional than I thought you were."

Rachel stood and walked to the window. "I've always found it interesting that the things we despise in ourselves are almost always the things we're guilty of. When I was overweight, I was always much more judgmental about those who suffered weight issues. Here I was, a physician, and I couldn't follow my own advice. I think it was the anger at myself that perpetuated the judgment. Hating the weakness in others I couldn't self-resolve."

"Cry me a river."

Rachel turned back to the bed. "But that's exactly what you did. You accused me of the very thing you were guilty of. You betrayed everything you stood for. Did it surprise you when the Black Crew shot you so indiscriminately?"

Armijo's eyes widened, as if he hadn't considered the possibility.

"The last thing I saw before I ran up the stairs was the red laser on your chest...not on Kyle's. On yours. Once you've fulfilled Seth's wishes, he disposes of you. Once you make a deal with the devil, he'll kill you in the end. Whatever promise of safety and security he gave you was all a lie. And it won't end. He'll keep coming and coming...and not just for you, but for your family. For the wife and daughter you think you're protecting by

giving Seth what he wants. It wouldn't surprise me if they've already gone missing."

Armijo's heart rate ramped up, the beep
on his monitor driving faster. "It's not true."

"What? That Seth would hold to his word?
His work as a doctor was a cover. He didn't
hold to those ideals. The Hippocratic oath
was a joke to him. You merely need to look
at what he's most proud of."

Tears streaked down his face, the realization of Rachel's words bringing forth the
emotion he'd likely bottled up as a defense
mechanism.

"I was broke when we were in that car accident. I'd gotten into some trouble. A few poor
investments. My daughter was hospitalized
for several months. Over that time, you get to
know your doctors pretty well. Seth is very
easy to talk to. I shared about our financial
struggles. Concerns about paying her medical bills on a government salary. I disclosed I
worked with WITSEC. Seth, seemingly out of
kindness, finagled it so that most of our medical fees would be waived. If I promised him I
would repay him at some point. Of course, I
didn't know what he was. I thought he would
ask me to raise money for a good cause, not
betray everything I stood for."

"You didn't study Seth well enough. He's all about undoing people. What deal did you make?"

"He kept tabs on my career. I thought transferring out to the west coast would put distance between us but it played into Seth's hands."

"Did you recommend Utah as my placement?"

"It was a group decision."

"Did you force it so I'd be close enough to keep tabs on? Did you recommend Kyle's transfer out to the west coast as well so you could keep a close eye on him?"

"Kyle volunteered for that himself, though it did help that I became his supervisor."

Kyle ruptured through the doors. "Rachel, are you okay?"

She nodded, and Kyle turned his attention to Javier. "Want to explain to me how a geotracker made its way onto my vehicle?"

Armijo sighed. "Can we first check on my family and make sure they're okay?"

An announcement came overhead. "Code silver. Code silver."

Rachel bolted for the door.

ELEVEN

"We need to go," Rachel said.

"What does the code mean?"

"Someone is brandishing a deadly weapon."

Kyle motioned her away from the door and tugged down the blinds. He reached for his phone and reported to 911. Once he disconnected, he neared Armijo. "Did you do this? Did you give the Black Crew Rachel's whereabouts?"

His mute response seemed an answer in itself.

"You're working with Seth Black, aren't you?"

"I'm not answering any questions without a lawyer present."

"Whatever happens, you'll be on your own."

"Kyle, we can't stay here in this room like sitting ducks," Rachel told him. "We need to leave now."

He positioned himself in front of her, opened the door a crack and then pulled Rachel through the opening. "Where can we go with a locked door?"

"Patient doors can't be locked. Med rooms will be badge access only. Most supply areas will have a door with a punch code. That only leaves restrooms."

"No, they're too small of a space. Easy for someone to shoot through the door and hit one of us."

The halls were eerily quiet. Rachel could hear doors closing and then slams against the wood. Staff barricading themselves into patient rooms, trying to protect what charges they could. Kyle pressed against the wall and motioned her to do the same. Rachel pointed to the ceiling, where the red Exit sign was.

"Then our only option is out of the building," Rachel said.

"Not ideal. I don't want to get trapped in a stairwell, but it may be our best option at this point."

Kyle peered down the hall, his heart hammering in his chest. The ICU was on the third floor, so they had two floors to go down. There was a distant scream, then the sound of two gunshots.

Whoever it was, the gunman was on their floor. Kyle reached behind him for Rachel's hand and pulled her to the stairwell door. Stopping before it, he paused. Rachel braced herself. As silently as he could, he opened it. That's when the piercing beep flooded the floor.

As Rachel feared, the door was set to alarm if badge access wasn't used. It was a security measure to keep patients from fleeing without being detected. In this instance, it was a beacon to their location.

Kyle pushed her to the front, and she scurried down the cement stairs. They were down one floor when the alarm signaled again, followed by a few bullets pinging against the walls.

"Keep moving. Faster," Kyle urged. He stopped to pivot, firing a few shots upward into the stairwell.

Rachel cleared another floor, Kyle coming up fast behind her. The next door let them out of the hospital. They ran through. Kyle motioned her to hide behind a nearby tree as he waited for the gunman to exit.

When the door opened, Kyle had his weapon in position, ready to shoot. "Drop your weapon."

The gunman looked toward the sky, exasperated, but did as Kyle instructed. That's when Rachel felt a presence behind her, bringing his arm around her waist. Before he could get her body pinned, she dropped down and elbowed her assailant in the groin. The pain plummeted the man to his knees. Rachel scurried to pin him to the ground, her weight over his back, and saw that his exposed hands didn't hold any weapons.

Kyle pulled out a zip tie from his pocket and secured the gunman that had exited from the stairwell. Then did the same to Rachel's attacker, who curled into the fetal position as soon as Kyle had secured his wrists.

"Nice move," Kyle told her, resisting the urge to pull her into a hug.

"What do we do now?" Rachel asked.

"Stay away from anyone in WITSEC. Until I know how deep Seth's claws are into that organization, we can't trust anyone there. If Seth was able to turn a well-respected supervisor against us, who knows who else might have gone astray."

The flight from St. George, Utah, to Boston, Massachusetts, had been a quiet one so far. Kyle had disconnected himself from anything WITSEC could use to find him. He'd purchased burner phones for himself and Rachel. He was wholly alone, trying to keep someone alive with just his own skill set, and he didn't know if it would be enough. As he sat beside her on the plane, he prayed.

Lord, I need You to work through me. Give me the power, the insight, the knowledge to keep Rachel safe. Help me find who is at the center of deceit within WITSEC so it can be a trusted organization again. Bring Seth Black and anyone who has helped him to trial. I know we don't always see justice prevail here in our time, but for the sake of humanity, help me end the reign of this madman.

Before he left St. George, he'd secured enough cash to operate off the grid. There were one or two agents he did completely trust—inspectors he knew had turned down a bribe in the past—but he would not reach out for help until he absolutely needed to.

"I know you blame Javier for what happened. For the tracker on your car. For the assault on the hospital," Rachel said, breaking into his thoughts. "But people will do extreme things to protect their loved ones. If Seth hadn't saved his daughter after that accident and made Armijo feel like he owed him something on a personal level when he never did, this wouldn't have happened. It's

Seth's manipulation that twisted him. Sometimes I feel like we shouldn't be so hard on people when they've been emotionally manipulated to such a degree that they don't even see themselves anymore."

He turned to look at her, assessing her. "Was that you? And how you feel about how others judge you?"

Rachel wiped the condensation from the plastic cup she held. "Even very intelligent people can be gullible. Self-deception is the strongest of all defense mechanisms. I'm not saying Javier shouldn't be held responsible for the things he did in abandoning from the ideal of his job to do the bidding of a mass murderer. But clearly there were mitigating circumstances."

Kyle stared at her in disbelief—that she could offer such grace to a person who had set her up to be killed. Upon their first meeting in Springdale, she'd been all about exacting justice. Now she seemed to want to deliver more grace than had been afforded to her. He thought through other witnesses he had worked with, and never had he protected one who had such a sense of forgiveness.

"I am amazed by you," Kyle said, the words slipping out before he could pull them back.

Rachel smiled, shyness causing her to drop her eyes from his. "I don't know why. You see things like this every day working in the justice system. People making choices they shouldn't be driven to by extenuating circumstances. People will do lots of wrong things to get control back over their lives."

"I'm amazed by your forgiveness. True forgiveness is rare. I think victims and their families say it a lot because it's the *right* thing to say. And they want to seem above it. But you can tell they don't mean it in their hearts. That if the one who perpetrated the crime against them left the courthouse at that very moment, they would be the first to attack them and seek their own vengeance. How do you explain it?"

"I was talking to Javier before you arrived about how I sensed he was involved in exposing our location. I said to him that the very thing we accuse others of we are often doing ourselves. Perhaps the opposite is true as well—the thing we also need the most is the thing we're most willing to offer someone else."

"What you want most desperately is for people to forgive you?"

She nodded, fighting back tears.

It made Kyle wonder—what did she need forgiveness for?

TWELVE

It was dark. Kyle had convinced Boston PD to help him enter Dr. Allen's house. They were at the front door to her posh brick home that sat on the outer edge of the city near the water. The smells of salt and fish were heavy in the air, thick. A hint of electricity charged the atmosphere. A storm was brewing off the coast, about to make its way inland.

Nora Allen still hadn't been seen, and Kyle's badge had done enough for the local cops to believe his story that she could be missing or otherwise suffering under some mysterious consequences. Her ex-husband, Theo Allen, had a key and insisted on accompanying them inside. Kyle allowed it if the man promised to not intrude on their search of the doctor's things. Theo okayed it if they were respectful and didn't trash the place.

Despite Javier's actions, Kyle knew his next

steps would not be looked upon favorably by WITSEC.

It would be helpful to have the ex-husband there. Hopefully, he could help them gain access to some areas of Dr. Allen's life that she wanted to keep hidden.

Once inside, with a few lights turned on, they got a good take on the posh interior. The home was valued at close to $10 million. Seemingly, the good doctor was earning a lot more than just her income from the Bureau of Prisons. Government employment didn't pay this well. From what Kyle understood of her divorce, she was paying her ex alimony and not the other way around.

Kyle walked slowly through the rooms, looking for anything that might be amiss. He'd seen no signs of forced entry as Theo had punched in the code to disarm the security system at the front door. Neither were there signs of a struggle inside. The home seemed to be in its neat and proper sentinel state. Nothing knocked over or out of place. Some houseplants were starting to wilt, indicating Nora had perhaps been delayed longer than expected—or might have been detained against her will.

It was risky involving the ex-husband, and Kyle couldn't disregard his training. Theo could be responsible for her disappearance. Statistics bore that possibility out.

Theo went up to the nearest shelf that housed several plants. "She'd never allow this to happen. These plants are more important to her than people. If she had planned to be gone for an extended period, she would have hired someone to come and take care of these."

"Can you check with any service she might have used?" Kyle asked. "See if she made arrangements? Even excellent companies have people who flake out from time to time."

"Won't be able to do that until morning. I can send a few emails, but I doubt they'd be checked until normal business hours."

Kyle watched Rachel walk through the space. It was important to have her perspective as well. Women picked up on different clues than men did. Also, if Seth was involved, she knew his habits. His modus operandi. She could be better than a seasoned investigator in that sense.

"Does Nora have a home office?" Kyle asked.

"This way."

They followed Theo up one level. Off the bedroom was a good-size room, perhaps an old, swank master closet that had been converted into a home office. Rachel lingered in the bedroom while Kyle sat down at the computer and powered up the screen. "Know her password?"

Theo nudged him off to the side and made several attempts, without success. Kyle tried passwords that were associated with previous Black Crew members. What opened the computer was Seth's birthday.

Not a good sign that Nora Allen's hands were clean.

He began a search of her files. Checked her sent emails. Nothing too incriminating there.

"You know, she has a safe. Want me to open it?" Theo asked.

Kyle didn't believe in good fortune. But then again, few partners had friendly relationships with their exes. Perhaps this was Theo's way of getting back at her.

"I'm surprised she trusted you with that information and that you still have a house key," Kyle said.

The man shrugged. "I gave her all the house keys she thought I was in possession of. Doesn't mean I didn't make a copy."

For what purpose?

"Were you keeping tabs on her?" Kyle asked.

"I was worried about her. About some of her actions. Her suing for divorce…well, it came out of nowhere."

"When did that happen?"

"She filed shortly after Seth Black's trial."

"Do you think she was involved with him?"

"I don't know if I would say him specifically. But she had an unhealthy fascination with the case…and maybe with him. It was hard for me to tell the difference."

What was it about evil men that entrapped others so easily? Kyle could testify that there was a hypnotic quality to them. He could feel himself persuaded by their arguments until his law enforcement background kicked in and snapped at his ear to pull him back to reality.

Behind him, the man lowered a lever that opened a compartment on the bookshelf. It never surprised Kyle the lengths rich people went to hide their money.

"Does anyone else in your family have this birthday? February 28?" Kyle asked, trying to verify a non-nefarious reason that Dr. Allen might have used that for her password.

"Not that I'm aware of. We don't have any children. Her parents' birthdays were in the fall. She's an only child."

Curiouser and curiouser.

"There's a stack of letters here. From the prison," Theo said, pulling them out from the safe.

Kyle took the stack from his hands. They were from Seth. This didn't bode well for Nora Allen keeping her professional distance from someone who could influence her to do harm to the witnesses.

Maybe she and Seth were two peas in a pod.

Kyle pulled out the most recent note. He found the code at the top. The letter was unusually bland. What he'd had to eat. What books he was reading. Certainly nothing incriminating. There had to be something here. Why would Nora keep these notes unless they meant something to her?

Rachel came into the office and laid several beauty products on the desk. "These are all Seth's favorites."

Kyle raised an eyebrow. "Meaning?"

"Seth was very particular about my perfume and the shades of makeup I wore." Rachel motioned to the pile. "Versace Bright Crystal was a must. In my line of work, I couldn't wear it. Aromatic scents can be offputting to patients and…well, you only need to make someone's nausea worse once before you learn that lesson. He would insist on this scent whenever we would go out... and I hated it."

It didn't surprise Kyle. Criminal types wanted to control everything in their sphere of influence. Dictating what a partner wore, their hairstyle, their makeup, was an additional way of exerting control. Almost building a prison without bars.

Theo picked through the items. "These are not what she used to wear. It makes sense to me what Rachel is saying. Around the time of our divorce, there was a drastic change in her appearance. Here, let me show you."

Theo pulled up several photos on his cell. "This is about a year before the trial. She's blonde. Her hair and makeup are very..."

"Natural-looking," Rachel offered.

"Exactly. Almost what people consider California chic. Airy. She wore more flowy clothing. Jeans. Casual slacks. With long, drapey tops. A relaxed vibe."

He scrolled through a few more pictures. "I took these a few weeks after our divorce papers were signed. We ran into each other by happenstance at a local coffee shop. Her ending our marriage was a surprise to me. I loved her...still do. Nora never fully explained to me what changed. Just kept parroting the words *irreconcilable differences*. Maybe there were slight changes before that."

"Like what?" Kyle asked.

"Almost as if she was trying to cast off the life we had lived to try on something that didn't fit her. When she first started working for WITSEC, it was all about helping the victims. She was burned out in private practice. Not that those people didn't deserve therapy—she just couldn't relate to the high-society nature of their problems, I guess. She was raised in a lower-middle-class community. She worked odd jobs to get through college. Her parents gifted nothing to her when they died."

"And then?" Rachel prompted.

Theo cleared his throat. "Nora wanted to take part in the very lifestyle she said she detested. Started seeking out invitations to high-society parties. Sought court with the Boston elites. Supported candidates that were oddly more lax on crime."

Kyle inhaled deeply. It didn't take someone with a law enforcement background to see what had happened. Somehow, along the way, Seth had sunk his hooks into Dr. Nora

Allen. And WITSEC hadn't ferreted it out, and now they were going to pay dearly for it.

"And then this." Theo held his phone out at arm's length, and Kyle saw the photo of Nora after the divorce. The difference was striking, and it brought a heaviness to Kyle's chest as he put it into context. He couldn't help but realize it was as if Rachel and Nora had switched places in their physicality. Nora had dyed her naturally blond locks to a deep brunette with bold red highlights. Her makeup was gothic. Heavy eyeliner. Dark eye shadow. Bold red lipstick.

It was a mirror to the past and how Rachel had dressed at the trial. Once Rachel had been free from Seth, she'd almost assumed what Nora Allen had once looked like.

"Can't you see it?" Rachel asked.

"That she's become Seth's preferred type? Yes, I see it. Mind if I take these?" Kyle asked Theo as he gathered up the pile of letters, not really intending to leave them behind regardless of the answer.

"Of course. I still care for Nora. Do you think something bad has happened to her?"

"I think she's gotten tangled up with Seth Black," Kyle answered. "I know when women do that, it's not usually a good outcome. We need to figure out what this code at the top of the letters means. I think once we have that, it will give us insight into where Nora might be."

The evidence linking Dr. Allen to Seth shouldn't have been that much of a surprise to Rachel, but if she were honest, it was like tremors to her foundation. Was there no safe place? No entity she could trust? Was Seth's reach that far and wide that she'd be his prisoner forever even though she wasn't locked up?

She pushed her way out of the house to sit on the stoop. She needed to breathe, but the stifling air from the incoming storm wasn't helping her to calm down. Where could she live to get away? Antarctica? At least the air there would be crisp and cool.

Kyle and Theo parted ways after Kyle gave him some reassuring words about keeping in touch and giving him updates if they discovered anything on Nora's whereabouts. Kyle had almost seemed grateful for Theo's deceit. That he'd had a key Dr. Allen didn't know about. Some of her most secret information was still in his possession. He could go into her home any time he wanted, and she didn't know it.

Were men all that different? Or did each of them manipulate, just on a scale? Zero being the lies of omission. Many didn't even consider that lying—just intentionally withholding the truth to spare someone needless worry. The noble lie. Was there any such thing? Didn't a lie always harm someone, whether it was withheld or twisted out of some sense of altruism? Was a ten on that scale taking another's life? Obviously, most men didn't reach the level of her ex-husband, but did they still have the manipulative component to their genetic makeup?

Kyle sat next to her. "What's on your mind?"

"Probably things you don't want me to share."

"I want you to tell me even those things. Even if you think it will hurt my feelings. We can't move forward unless you're able to do that."

"You mean move forward as far as my case? Or as far as you and me?"

"Is there a difference?" he asked.

Evidently not to him, but there was a difference to her. Maybe it currently explained the chasm between them. Kyle was fully back in professional mode. Those things that they had shared—clearly, he felt they were a slipup on his part. She wanted to break down the barrier between them but also didn't know if she had the strength, considering all the other things she was currently fighting. Like trying to prove herself innocent of murder.

The trait of an ER physician took the better of her. Forcing the truth out of reluctant people. Or maybe drawing out greater insight.

"Doesn't it bother you?" Rachel asked.

"What?"

"That Theo continues to manipulate Dr. Allen?"

"How is he manipulating her?" Kyle asked, drawing an evidence bag out of his briefcase and tucking Seth's letters inside.

"By hiding from her the key he has to her house."

"What if he did it because he cared about her and what was happening? Maybe it's his love for her that's the explanation behind his action. He noticed a change in her behavior and was keeping closer tabs on her. Isn't that something you might encourage a family member to do if they were concerned? We both know not every mental health issue warrants an emergency evaluation and inpatient treatment. What is the plan that you institute if they sent someone home who might have been having thoughts of wanting to hurt themselves or others?"

"A safety plan."

"And could an ex-spouse be part of that plan?"

"Depends on what their relationship was like. Does that patient trust them?"

"So, not so far afield, wouldn't you say?"

"Theo could sneak in any time he wanted to."

"But there's not any evidence that he did that." Kyle cleared his throat. "Rachel, each of us has our biases. A scope that is colored by our choices. By our life experiences. You come from the perspective that someone that you loved deeply was working every second to deceive you, and I think that makes it hard for you to consider that Theo might have good intentions for keeping that key. He still loves her and wants to look out for her, to keep her safe. He's willing to do that even though she broke up their home and marriage."

Was this so different from God? How many times had she read biblical accounts of entire populations of people turning their backs on God, and yet time and time again, He tried to get them to see that by allowing Him into their lives, they would be so much better off?

Rachel set her elbows on her knees and pressed her palms into her forehead, trying to stave off a headache. Her arm itched from the healing laceration. She could normally quiet these sensations while her body was busy, but now that her mind was engaged in heavy thoughts, it seemed as if all these nuances were flagging her psyche for attention.

Kyle was right, in one sense. Being an ER physician brought that to light. It always amazed her how a clinic-based doctor and she could have wildly different assessments of patients who were referred into the ER. It took a few years in medicine before she'd sorted it out. The clinic doctors operated from a well bias. They assumed that most patients weren't that sick and would do fine without a lot of intervention. She operated in the opposite—all patients were knocking on death's door until proven otherwise.

What Kyle suggested was that Seth had forever tainted her view of men and their motives. That was probably true, but had Kyle shown her any difference at this point?

Kyle placed his arm around her shoulders—seemingly to interrupt the quiet space, to focus her attention back to what he was going to say. "I think Theo's intentions are true. He's still in love with her and anxious about what's happened. The divorce came as a surprise. From my perspective, sure, it wasn't great of him to hold on to her key without her knowledge, but if it saves her in the end from being murdered, then his actions proved beneficial. They're altruistic. He's not using his access to harm her...only to help."

Was he? Or were his actions just a means to an end? Rachel swallowed hard. Was her mind so bent that she could not see the good in anyone? Particularly men?

"What's our next move?" Rachel asked.

Kyle tapped his briefcase where he'd put the evidence bag with the prison letters. "We need to figure out this code. I think once we break that, we'll be able to get insight into where Dr. Allen might be and what Seth has planned."

They both stood and walked down the steps.

A white van accelerated to the front of the property. The door opened, and two men brandishing assault rifles pointed them directly at Kyle and Rachel.

"Ms. Black. Would you come with us, please?"

THIRTEEN

Kyle dropped his briefcase and went for his sidearm. The warning shot the assailants fired into the air halted his progress.

"Ms. Black. If you'll step inside." One of the men bowed to her and motioned with his arm to the inside of the van.

"She's not going anywhere with you," Kyle said. "You'll have to go through me first." He moved to position Rachel behind him, and they fired a round at his feet, chunks of sidewalk spraying his suit trousers.

"We don't mind doing that." The man snickered. "But Rachel could save your life if she merely came with us."

The men wore black ski masks. This seemingly had become the dress code for the Black Crew. This team was comprised of two men and the driver, who had waited patiently for this kidnapping to come to fruition. The exact moment when Kyle and Rachel would be alone. Kyle glanced sideways, trying to take in Rachel's demeanor. What he saw bolstered his spirt. Absent were trembling hands and tight shoulders. Instead, her jaw was set tight, and her nostrils flared.

Her body was priming for a fight.

"Ms. Black, we've asked you nicely two times now. Get into the van."

"I don't think your request meets the definition of *nicely* if you're holding a gun on us. You have fully removed the sense of choice," Kyle said.

"I'll give you three seconds," the man responded.

"These are the tactics you're going to use? How an adult would reason with a toddler?" Kyle responded.

"Fine. We'll pick a more adult choice. Rachel, if you don't get into the van right now, Mr. Reid, your proverbial knight in shining armor, gets a bullet. This time, not to the ground he walks on."

Kyle went for his gun but couldn't pull it in time. At first, he didn't hear the gunshot, but he felt the hot projectile slice through his flesh. The power knocked him backward into the brick steps. Blood seeped down his side, and he pressed his hand to the wound to stop the flow. The bullet had hit him on the lower left side of his abdomen.

When he had a moment to gain focus back on the street, he saw Rachel stepping inside the van.

"Rachel, no!"

He pulled his gun from his holster, pushing himself to a standing position and taking several wobbly steps into the center of the street as the van pulled away. No license plate. He aimed at the rear tires—and was rewarded when one of his bullets hit its target as the vehicle escaped into the night.

The punctured tire would stop them eventually, but Kyle knew a lot could happen to Rachel in those moments. She could lose her life.

He holstered his weapon and got into his rental car, leaving a bloody handprint on the side. He pulled out his burner phone and called 911.

"This is WITSEC inspector Kyle Reid. I'm in pursuit of a white van that has kidnapped a woman by the name Rachel Bright, aka Rachel Black. I'm heading down Washington Boulevard—taking a right at Harrison. I'm in pursuit but am injured. Took a bullet to the gut."

Kyle sped up as soon as they were on a

straight thoroughfare. The van took a hard left, and as Kyle whipped the car to turn the same direction, the seat belt dug into his wound and he cried out in pain. Perhaps it was more than just a flesh wound he was dealing with. Gunshot wounds to the belly were one of those things that rarely killed immediately but could take their toll over time.

His body shook and his mouth grew drier by the second. Shock setting in. Wet, bloodied hands made it hard to grip the steering wheel. The coppery smell of blood combined with the salty, humid air, nauseating him.

A nightmare was repeating itself. Another witness at risk of losing her life. It was more than his professional reputation at stake if Rachel died. His heart was at risk. Each moment he spent with her made it hard for him to imagine a life without her. He couldn't lose Rachel...not this way. Not on his watch.

She'd chosen to give up her safety for him. It had seemed reckless in the moment, her decision to step foot into that van. But if she hadn't, the gunmen would have had no compunction about sending more bullets his way to get her to comply. She'd had a decision to make, and she'd opted to save his life.

Who else did that remind him of?

* * *

Once inside the van, which reeked of marijuana smoke, Rachel was forced to sit in the back seat. The three men executed several celebratory, juvenile high fives, nonplussed that they'd just shot a federal agent. Kidnapped a woman.

Seeing Kyle down on the sidewalk, bleeding, yet still trying with all his effort to stop the assailants from taking her, tugged at her heartstrings. The look of terror in his eyes she'd seen more than a few times in her career.

That facial expression came when someone thought they were going to lose their loved one permanently. The depth of anguish was so pervasive it felt as if thorns of agony were being pushed deep in her soul. Rachel carried several of those barbs with her, and it was easy to recall the story behind each one.

Despite Kyle's words, Rachel could see she meant more to him than he alluded to. More than he was willing to expose at this moment in time. Would he ever risk it?

She turned away from her kidnappers and looked out the window. That was when she noticed there was something wrong with the vehicle. It tilted to one side and took a lot of handling from the driver to keep it between the faded street lines. Rachel glanced behind her and saw a set of headlights looming fast.

She prayed it was Kyle.

If Kyle was giving chase, his wound was likely survivable, though people could do amazing things with a cardiovascular system pumped full of adrenaline. Plenty of research supported that.

She needed time to figure out a plan.

Rachel flexed her fingers and cracked her knuckles.

The kidnappers' use of her married name was like a gnat buzzing in her ear. No matter how much she swatted at it, it just came back with its annoying high-pitched sound, aggravating her nerves to hysteria.

Just like Seth. He was unshakable and had likely insisted the kidnappers use Rachel *Black* for that very reason. He knew it would plunge a dagger into her heart. Signify, somehow, that he still had ownership over her. Show that he could exert control over her no matter where she was or who she was with.

Even if it was armed protection.

"What's the reward? What price is he willing to pay you to take me?" Rachel asked the kidnappers. She assumed the least threatening posture as possible. Legs crossed. Hands folded into her lap, though her fingers squeezed so hard together it was painful. It kept her from striking out when the moment wasn't opportune.

Certainly, Seth's family funds were helping their efforts.

There was a drag on the vehicle. The young men were eyeing one another, the driver revving the engine to get it to go faster. She could hear a car honking behind them. She turned and saw Kyle's face through the windshield. But he was not the one making the noise. It was the car behind him that was laying on the horn to get everyone to move faster.

"What's the reward?" one of the kidnappers yelled. "Infamy!" He pumped his fist into the air.

Unfortunately, Rachel knew that could be payment enough for some people. Just the minute possibility of having fifteen minutes of fame was enticing. Especially to this crowd.

"Where are you taking me?" Rachel asked.

"To see Seth."

Rachel's blood ran cold. No, this had to be avoided at all costs. Who knew what he would do with her.

"Might as well tell her, since she won't live that long, anyway," the driver said to the others, glancing at her in the rearview mirror.

His eyes had lost all semblance of humanity. Though pearlescent green, there was a dark shadow that overcast their luster. Something so heinous that it caused Rachel to tremble. It was easy to see evil in someone's eyes, and this man held copious amounts.

The one sitting next to her smiled knowingly. "It's all in Seth's letters."

"He's been writing to you?"

"Yes…for years. I mean, when you've got a life sentence, there's not a lot to do to pass your time. Have you seen the man lately? He's definitely using his one hour of exercise time and those prison steroids."

Rachel could hardly breathe. They hadn't answered her question, but it was clear Seth had been making plans and wasn't done with her yet. Not in any measure.

"That still doesn't explain how you knew where to find me."

"There's a code in his notes," the captor in the front passenger seat said.

"I know. I've seen it."

"You're a doctor, right?" the driver asked.

"Yes."

"Then you should know what it means. Seth always said it was a famous medical phrase. Something doctors say to patients every day in every hospital around the world."

Rachel searched her thoughts. The saying had to ubiquitous—even common to lay-people for these miscreants to know it. The young men were looking at her, motioning with their hands as if the movement would coax the saying from her mind.

She looked at the driver in the rearview mirror. Though he tried to hide it, he was struggling to maintain control of the lum-bering van.

"You realize this car is dead in the water," Rachel said.

"It's okay," he said. "We only need to make it one more block for reinforcements."

Rachel's heart rose into her throat. She felt dizzy. She wasn't prepared to confront Seth. She'd gotten it into her mind that she'd never have to see him again, and she became mad-der at herself for buying into such delusional thinking.

"You better think twice about that," Ra-chel said. "You know there's a WITSEC agent who was targeted after he fulfilled his pur-pose for Seth, and then they went after his family. Everyone is still alive but suffering the consequences. Once you enter Seth's web, there's no leaving it."

"He'd never do that to us," the thug beside her said, laughing. Her skin prickled at the lack of understanding that the spider was bearing down on them as they struggled helplessly against the sticky, silky fibers.

Except they didn't even know they were entangled.

That was the most dangerous place to be. Just like with illness—some diseases were so silent that the patient could be weeks from death before they even felt ill. And then, if they were fortunate, it became a matter of—

"Two steps forward, one step back." Seth's favorite phrase came to her in a flash. That had to be the code on his letters.

"She got it!" The men set off more rounds of congratulatory pats on the back.

Rachel saw the flash of red on the traffic light ahead. Unfortunately, she also saw the driver's eyes were not on the road. A horn blared behind them, different from the earlier beep. This time it was incessant. She had no time to discern its meaning before the impact.

Glass shards sprayed onto Rachel's face. The back passenger door punched in as the van was T-boned at the intersection. The thug sitting next to Rachel, since he'd been unsecured, flew across her and was ejected from the vehicle through her window. He was tossed several hundred yards down the roadway, screaming wildly when he stopped. It was a reassuring sound, because he could at least take enough of a deep breath to wail. The van was forced diagonally across the intersection and slammed into a light post. The top of it came crashing down, indenting the roof of the vehicle. Rachel ducked, her breath quick in her chest. The assailant in the front passenger seat scrambled out as soon as the van came to a stop. Rachel unclipped her seat belt and lunged forward, wrapping one arm around the driver's neck and yanking him into the headrest to pin him.

"Don't even think about struggling," she whispered harshly in his ear. "You're going to thank me one day for saving your life, even if you think I'm trying to kill you."

FOURTEEN

After seeing the truck T-bone the van at the intersection, Kyle pulled his car to the side of the road. When he bolted from his vehicle, he stopped after a few steps to catch his bearings through the dizziness. He looked down at his drenched shirt. The blood loss was more impressive than he thought.

He staggered to the van. Rachel was still inside and had the driver in a chokehold to detain him. There was a young man screaming in the middle of the road, clearly suffering from two broken legs and who knew what else.

His priority was Rachel and making sure she was okay.

The window on her side was punched out. She and the driver were struggling, even though Rachel had the upper hand. The man attempted to bite her arm, clawing at the exposed flesh, and yet she remained steadfast with her hold. Kyle drew his weapon and pointed it at the driver.

"Put your hands on the steering wheel," Kyle yelled.

The driver did as instructed, and Kyle zip-tied each wrist to the steering wheel to keep the driver contained, and then he fell down onto one knee. The back driver door opened, and Rachel knelt next to him.

Kyle shook his head. They were still in too much danger. The front passenger was on foot. The man could bring more Black Crew members at any time. Kyle worried about the man in the middle of the road even though he couldn't walk. Two hands could still hold a weapon and shoot. He got to his feet and walked toward the man in the street. A quick survey of his wounds lent toward survivability in his non-medical opinion.

"Let me see your hands," Kyle ordered. The man did so, and Kyle restrained them despite the man's moans of pain. After securing his hands, he patted down his body finding only contorted lower limbs.

Now his concern drifted to the one who'd fled the scene.

"Lay down, let me look at the gunshot," Rachel said.

"I can't stop until we find the passenger."

"Kyle, lay down," she ordered, just a hair under a full-on shout.

He acquiesced, and the cooling breeze of the night air kissed his skin as she moved his shirt aside. His thoughts were wandering away. His only focus was on her touch as she gently explored the skin around his wound.

"You've lost a lot of blood. It's probably why you're not feeling all that well."

She brushed the sweat off his forehead. It confused him how he could be drenched when he hadn't run after anyone—simply stopped his car and paced a few steps.

"The bullet might have nicked your spleen. Could explain the degree of blood loss. Probably not too badly, since you're still with me."

With me.

The words were a solace. He could feel something within him slipping. Almost an unhinging of a deep connection he had with terra firma. He felt light and warm. Peaceful and calm. Whatever part of his soul connected to the physical was lifting its anchor.

"Kyle, stay here," she shouted at him.

"We're not done yet. I need you. Hold your hands over the wound."

He popped his eyes open. Forced his vision to focus and find her eyes. His hands sloppily did as she asked. She brushed the fingers of one hand through his hair, then, with the other, reached for her phone to call for reinforcements. Her needing him was the one thing anchoring him back. All he could see was her eyes set against the faint, intermittent lights of the twinkling stars flirting with him from a distance. He turned his head, and she placed her palm on his cheek.

"Stay with me," she pleaded. "We've got a lot to do yet. A killer is—"

But the distant tug became too enticing, and he let himself drift away into blackness.

Rachel sat next to Kyle's bedside, holding the stack of Seth's letters to Dr. Nora Allen in her lap, deciphering them.

Seth's code was simple but devious. *Two steps forward, one step back.* The phrase tried to encourage patients that an upward, unbroken trajectory wasn't always possible with most injury and illness. But now the supportive phrase had been used as the cipher for a killer's devious plans.

Rachel had been right in her diagnosis of Kyle. The bullet had passed through his abdominal cavity but nicked his spleen as it passed, causing him to lose too much blood. At least the doctors didn't think the damage was extensive. They'd given him blood, and the staff would monitor his red blood cell levels overnight to ensure they were stable and likely send him home in the morning. Where they would go was an uncertainty. Kyle needed rest, though he would be loath to do so with Seth loose and a woman's murder unsolved—particularly when Rachel's life was on the line. WITSEC would probably afford him the time, but he wouldn't allow it for himself. Plus, how much did WITSEC know at this point? Kyle had purposely kept them off the grid, but surely this incident had risen to their attention.

Kyle's color was finally pinking up after his third unit of blood. His cheeks held a hint of red, his lips their normal color. His hand was warm when she touched it. The nurse had just disconnected his tubing and was taking her final set of vital signs to monitor for any adverse reactions from the transfusions. He roused as the blood pressure cuff squeezed his arm and saw Rachel sitting next to him.

He pulled the oxygen mask off his face. The nurse didn't make any moves to stop him, as his oxygen levels had been stable over the last several hours and now his blood levels should be near normal. Currently, he had enough red blood cells that he should be able to maintain a normal oxygen level. He rubbed his chapped lips together, and Rachel picked up the cup of water at his bedside.

"Drink?"

He gratefully took a few sips and then eased the cup away. "How are you?"

"I'm just fine other than the expected body aches. I'm not the one who took a bullet."

"It barely grazed me."

Rachel laughed. "I think your spleen disagrees."

When the nurse finished and left, Kyle pulled his covers off to the side, attempting to stand with his overly thin hospital gown barely covering anything. Rachel stood and placed two hands on his shoulders, easing him back down onto the bed.

"Sit down. Doctor's orders."

For once, he didn't argue. "Do we know anything?"

"I'm not sure about the men they apprehended at the scene. They've been detained.

The police knocked on some doors around the neighborhood, but they didn't find Seth. It's not known if he was there or if the men who kidnapped me just thought he would be."

"I get the first crack at him," Kyle said.

"In your condition, there'll be no cracking in the short term. Good news is, we may not need him anymore."

Kyle eased back onto the pillows. "How so?"

"Those men who snagged me didn't think I was ever going to see the light of day again, so they gave me the clue on how to use the code written at the top of the notes to translate what Seth was trying to hide. 'Two steps forward and one step back.' It's a phrase we use in medicine all the time." Rachel held up one note. "See here." She showed Kyle one of the most recent letters Seth had sent to Nora. "I find the first letter as noted—go forward two and then back one and write those letters down."

"What is Seth trying to say?"

"I haven't gotten very far yet. I've only done the oldest and newest letters. Might not seem logical, but I wanted to see the last bit of info he might have been trying to convey to her and the genesis of how everything started."

"How did it start?"

"Nora was a woman looking to live on the wild side. She left a man who clearly loved her. There wasn't any evidence, at least from Theo's telling of their tale, of infidelity or even acrimony on his part. It seems Nora was the one who...felt unsettled. I think Nora reached out to Seth first."

"What?"

"And then joined WITSEC at his behest."

"When did that happen?"

"Keep in mind that Seth's trial didn't begin immediately. He was in jail for a good couple of years as they built the case against him. It was toward the beginning of his jail time. The first letter holds the code. No doubt Seth had used this phrase with her as a clue. It would seem innocuous to anyone who was listening. It's a common enough phrase."

"But how do you know she reached out first?"

"In Seth's first letter to her, he says as much. 'Thank you for contacting me.' Of course, he hides this in code, and it's not as well written as what I just said. It's choppy, but it's clear."

"Does he indicate why she reached out?"

"There are words like *research study*. Serial killers have always been a fascination. It's how the FBI started the Behavioral Sciences Unit. Trying to figure out the crimes from known serial killers to prevent new ones from cropping up."

"You think Nora's interest was benign at first, then?" Kyle asked.

"Unknown. To be honest, Nora was conniving in this way. Maybe a hint that her inner self wasn't as altruistic as she wanted people to believe. If she could be the first to get Seth's story and publish it—that would be more lucrative than even private practice for Bostonian elites."

"Is that conniving or just good business sense?" Kyle countered.

Rachel disregarded the comment. "I'm sure we'll know more as we go through the letters, but Seth's response to her inquiry probably sounded like, 'I'm misunderstood. Let me tell you my story.' Seth's cooperation would be too tempting to ignore, particularly for someone like Nora, who might have been looking to live on the dangerous side. I think her ex alluded to this when we met him. She wanted to be part of the upper echelon. Wasn't happy leading a quiet, homebound lifestyle. It wouldn't surprise me if Seth was reading the Boston papers for clues to his own case when he came across the society pages and saw a recurring theme of her presence. He likely, though maybe not consciously, recognized some of his own qualities."

"What does the last letter say?"

"It gives a meeting time. The letter was sent almost three weeks ago, which is strange, because it means Seth would have had to know that the allegation of jury misconduct was coming. How could he have known that?"

"Good question." Kyle inhaled deeply and rested his head against the pillow. "There was an excellent judge on the case. The jury was sequestered during Seth's trial. In order to know that the jury member didn't disclose that she'd been a victim of violence, it would almost be that each one of them would have to be investigated. The court depends on a certain level of honesty. They don't have the time or resources to investigate whether jurors are being honest on their forms. Someone would have had to discover the fabrication and disclose it to the courts."

"Seth had a lot of time on his hands. A

mind like his will not sit idle—it needs an outlet."

"We need to be at that meeting. It might be our only opportunity to get Seth. If he expects Dr. Allen to be there, we need to be there in her place."

Rachel fanned her face with the letters. "But where is Nora?"

"If she's wanting to live life dangerously, maybe she's the one who is framing you for murder."

"She and Seth could be together now, for all we know," Rachel said.

"They could be, but I'm doubtful. Seth might have her prove herself to know her level of loyalty. He could think she's still part of WITSEC. He'd have to convince her to do something illegal. Something he could hold over her to make sure she's totally under his thumb. If she does certain acts, he'll know for sure she's with him. My guess is when they meet, he'll make it clear that if she ever goes against him, he'll release the evidence he's holding against her and clarify that prison isn't a nice place to be."

"Mutually assured destruction."

Kyle reached his hand out to her, and she

laid her hand in his. "It terrified me to see them take you. Don't do that to me again."

"Why did it terrify you?"

Kyle's eyes widened. She was pushing him to say words he was, perhaps, not ready to say. But she needed to hear them. She had no doubt there were growing emotions between them. She needed to know that what she was feeling was reciprocated.

"I can't lose another witness."

Her heart sank. A professional reason wasn't what she was hoping to hear. But she didn't let her disappointment show. "If I didn't go with them, they were going to kill you."

He gripped her hand, hard, and gave it a tug. Once her eyes met his, she saw the aching there. Something that held her gaze that she hadn't seen before. An inexplicable longing. "Rachel, your job is not to protect me. Your job is to stay alive…even if it means that I die. Promise me you understand this."

She slipped her hand from his. "I can't and I won't. You're asking me to go against every principle that I hold dear. An oath I swore to. Seth might have corrupted every word, but I take it seriously."

"Rachel, please, look at the greater good." Kyle sighed. "We have competing ethics, and I'm going to tell you why mine is more important. It's something law enforcement leverages every day. We let low-level bad individuals go free but get a bigger fish, knowing it might save more people. Trading in a drug dealer for a distributor."

"Kyle—"

"Before you say anything, let me get this out. Your life is more valuable than mine. We need you… *I* need you to stay alive. The world needs Seth to go back to jail. Who knows the influence he would have if he were free, especially now, considering all of his followers? If it comes down to it…you can't let that happen, Rachel. Promise me."

Rachel cleared her throat. "In medicine, each life is held in equal measure. We don't decide like that. The drug dealer suffering from the gunshot wound is treated as decisively as the mother of five suffering from a heart attack."

"You triage based on condition, right? The patient who will die first gets treated first."

"Right."

"Unless it's a mass-casualty incident, and then what happens?"

Rachel settled back in the chair. Kyle was as good as Seth. He was going to use her principles against her, twist them into something so she'd have to obey. This didn't feel good to her. Her heart wanted to acquiesce, but her thoughts were steaming. The same anger she'd felt at Seth when he would do this very thing to her.

"It's flipped. We look at our resources and treat those who are most likely to survive. If you're near death, you'll end up with a black tag on your toe. If there's enough, we might give you a little painkiller."

Kyle braced his side and sat up. "This is a mass-casualty situation for WITSEC. A bomb has gone off in our organization. I don't know how many witnesses are at risk. But what I do know is that if you die, then Seth will become an evil unleashed again—never to be contained. He'll have learned from his mistakes and won't get caught again. My life is worth trading to keep him behind bars. Yours isn't, because you're one of the few who can put him back there."

"Kyle..."

"Rachel, please, promise me."

She stood up and set the stack of letters at the end of his bed. "You're doing what Seth would do to me. You're asking me to trade what I hold dear for something I could never do. If I have any power, I'm going to work to save who I can. This isn't a mass-casualty situation. You're someone that I—"

What word was she holding back? *Admire? Like being with? Love?*

She bit her lip and backed away from him, trying to stave off her tears. He'd made it clear they couldn't be together. Now, he was asking her to let him die to save her own life.

The torment was splitting her in half. She did the only thing she could do. She turned and left the room.

FIFTEEN

Kyle waited outside the interrogation suite for them to bring up the driver of the van who was part of Rachel's kidnapping. How many times had he been in such a position over the last week? Seth's magnetic pull was impressive. To be able to convince a group of people to keep hunting another.

He hadn't seen anything like it in his career.

There were groupies and there were devotees. Groupies followed at a whim. They had adoration but likely wouldn't do anything illegal. A devotee was a different animal. They elevated their admiration to a religious zeal. It became a fever pitch and caused them to do irrational things. Manson had inspired this kind of devotion. Seth Black followed in his footsteps.

It had been two days since Kyle's hospital release. Three days since they'd taken Rachel. His stomach clenched as he relived her kidnapping. At least they hadn't gotten her to the final location. Motor vehicle collisions were never pleasant, but Kyle felt the hand of providence in this instance. If the truck hadn't plowed into the van and the kidnappers had gotten much farther, Kyle wasn't sure he'd have been able to save her.

Seth's underlings seemed to be escalating. So far, they'd been overcome, but Kyle couldn't depend on that to be the case with every contact. Each instance was becoming more deadly. It was probable that Seth had more competent people in his inner circle. It could explain why Dr. Nora Allen was still missing in action.

Kyle rubbed his hand over the stubble on his jaw. Until this crisis was over, there was only so much he could concentrate on and shaving was one thing he'd discarded. His left side ached. There was no denying the pain. It was difficult for him to walk upright. Unfortunately, he couldn't take anything that would cloud his thinking. Before WITSEC released him back into action, he'd had to prove he could physically protect Rachel. Running, climbing, shooting with accuracy. He'd been able to do those things—against doctor's orders. For the physical agility test, he had slipped one of the opiate pain killers the hospital had released him with. Since then, he'd been living on alternating doses of acetaminophen and ibuprofen, which kept the pain to a tolerable level.

Neither his medical team nor the government were happy about it, but when Rachel had insisted he stay on her case, that helped. WITSEC was all too eager to figure out if she was someone they needed to turn over to the law, or if there was a mole framing her that needed to be smoked out of his, or her, hole. Obviously, one over the other was better for their bottom line.

His musings came to a halt when two officers brought up the suspect. To describe their suspect as nondescript was an understatement. There were no unique features about him. He could have been anyone. He didn't look lonely—like someone driven to Seth's group because he had unmet, unidentified, deeply unresolved and thus unconscious issues. Essentially, someone who didn't know themselves and what they stood for. He was a married man with two children. Daughters, even. How could he see himself kidnap another woman and bring her to a certain death? He'd held a job—for several decades. Dedicated to his church—at least in action, though clearly not in spirit. No priors—not even a traffic ticket. What was it about Seth that could get a man like this to abandon everything he believed in?

Rachel was secured elsewhere in the building, being watched over by a member of law enforcement. He just couldn't have this man salivate over her presence while Kyle tried to get him to take part in a plan to trap Seth and end this crisis. Ultimately, proving Rachel's innocence and setting her free.

Once the prisoner was seated and secured, Kyle squared his shoulders and entered the interrogation room. He tried to walk, unsuccessfully, without leaning to his left side. The doctors had admonished him to take it easy. That if he physically exerted himself, the laceration to his spleen could start bleeding again, and if he wasn't close to medical aid, then he was risking his life.

Did it matter? If he didn't keep Rachel safe and prove her innocence, was life without her worth living?

The question paused his thinking. After he lost the prior witness, though it traumatized him, he still had hope and direction.

He hadn't questioned his ability to carry on. Without Rachel, though, the very thing that was keeping him moving forward would be gone, and he couldn't bear to think about life under those circumstances.

Something about Rachel made him doubt his ability to go on alone. They were partners. She had saved his life just as much as he had saved hers. And maybe she was ahead on the keeping-tabs card. She had proven to be a woman that he could see himself abandoning this chaotic life for.

Kyle pulled out a chair and sat down at the table. Mr. Johnson was handcuffed to a chain bolted to the floor. A guard waited in the corridor, constantly peering in. Thus far, though read his rights, Johnson hadn't requested an attorney. Another strange thing about Seth's followers. Was it that they all thought they could beat the system? Few, if any, asked for representation, though the one sitting in the hospital bed with multiple fractures to his legs had done so the first moment he could speak. The other kidnapper who had escaped remained elusive.

"Brad Johnson, I'm Kyle Reid."

"I know you," the man said, his voice deep and full of bravado. "There's not a member

of the Black Crew that doesn't know the infamous WITSEC inspector Kyle Reid. We
study you like we study Rachel—maybe more
so. If we know you and your movements, we
can find her and bring her to justice."

The Black Crew had adopted the same
principles as the Behavioral Sciences Unit.
The thought wasn't comforting.

"Is that what you think you're doing? Helping Seth?" Kyle asked him.

"Of course. The man was wrongly convicted. It's been his wife all along. I hate to
see innocent men go to prison or suffer the
consequences of choosing the wrong women."

That could be what law enforcement missed.
It was normal to run background info—the
obvious things they knew in the short term.
Rap sheet. Criminal history. Times contacted
by the police. But marital history took more
to delve into. Time and resources they didn't
have at their disposal in the moment.

"You're married now. Two teen daughters. Seems like a good match. You've been
together several years. Things not as they
seem?" Kyle asked. Often, when law enforcement interrogated a witness, they feigned
interest in a suspect's personal life to build
rapport, but Kyle was drawn to these aspects

like moth to flame. Brad Johnson's view on how devious women could be could have caused him to sidle up with Seth and make him more able to believe the lies Seth sold.

"Second marriage," Brad said simply.

"And how was the first?"

The man shrugged, trying to appear nonchalant, but his shoulders hinged up a little longer than what the gesture required for Kyle to believe the sentiment.

"Are you paying alimony to your ex?"

The man's hackles raised. Kyle had flipped a trigger. "Do you know what it's like to subsidize a woman who is physically and mentally able to take care of herself? Do you know what that payment takes away from me being able to provide for the family I have now?"

There it was. The tamped-down anger that slowly heated. It was near boiling under the surface. Now Kyle could easily see how Seth had lured him in.

"Did you ever take her back to court to change the arrangement of your alimony payments?" Kyle asked.

"I did…when my girls were young, but I quickly discovered what a scam the whole thing was. The only ones getting paid were the attorneys, and nothing was changing for me. I figured at least the money I didn't spend on attorneys could go to my children. I decided to stop for only that reason."

"Must have been tough to feel that...injustice."

"Have you ever been married?"

Kyle leaned back in his chair. "I haven't."

Johnson backhanded his nose to clear the secretions. His eyes glossed over. Kyle could work with this. "Imagine loving someone with your whole heart. Body. Soul. And then they turn on you in the most fantastically devious ways. The betrayal. The proverbial knife between the shoulder blades. It's as painful emotionally as if it had been done physically."

Strangely poetic for someone in his circumstances. Brad Johnson was an intellect. His language and mannerisms exuded this fact, despite his current financial state. Sometimes, morally minded people couldn't see past their convictions to be able to see when they were crossing a line.

His words were a picture frame for Rachel's life as he'd been led to believe. Only Kyle doubted that Brad's ex-wife had become a serial murderer. "I can't imagine it, but I know someone who has lived that life."

The man laughed abruptly. It was a jarring change of emotion. Kyle jumped slightly. The momentary grin that crossed Brad's face unsettled him. "Don't for one minute try to claim you're thinking of Rachel."

Kyle took his advice. "How did you meet Seth?"

"Online. A support group for divorced husbands."

Kyle doubted that could be possible. They did not give high-risk inmates like Seth Internet access for this very reason. Plots could be made. Not just against others but escape plans to get out of jail.

"You were speaking with him directly?" Kyle attempted to verify.

"Not me, but another gentleman in our group was getting letters. They—"

"Contained a code."

Johnson's eyes widened. "You know about that?"

"There's little we don't know. Seth assumes we're in the dark about a lot of things. Just another thing he's misguided about."

That man inhaled deeply and mirrored Kyle's posture, clearly contemplating whom he wanted to believe in—the convicted psychopath or the member of law enforcement he'd studied for years.

"Why are you helping Seth? Why kidnap Rachel?"

The man fidgeted. Pursed his lips together as if giving himself a physical reminder to keep his mouth shut.

Kyle leaned forward. "This is going to come as a surprise to you, but you bet on the wrong horse. Seth isn't the innocent man he claims to be. Think about what he convinced you to do. He plied you with a story to get you to commit a crime for which you will go to jail. How will you be able to provide for your family then. Did you watch the trial?"

"I did."

"All those witnesses were wrong? You know the famous line—either Seth is guilty, or he is the most unfortunate man that ever lived to have so many people come against him. Coincidences just aren't that common, to tell you the truth."

"What about the most recent victim? Penelope Schmidt?" Brad asked.

"Convenient. Likely a frame job."

"And you don't think the same thing could happen to Dr. Black?"

The deference this man gave Seth churned Kyle's stomach. Seth was the very opposite of a healer. He turned people against themselves and incited them to do things that were detrimental to their lives. It was just another thing that was a thrill for him. People abandoning the truth for a lie. All part of his criminal psyche—to see how his words and actions could cause people to twist in the wind.

"It's easier to frame a person for one crime than it is to frame someone for fifty-plus murders. That's the number of bodies we feel Seth is responsible for, though not all have been found. At the trial, there wasn't any doubt among the jury that Seth was the true killer. No one wavered from calling him guilty on all counts."

"That's the problem. You're holding him responsible for crimes of which you have no evidence."

"The thirty women we found murdered aren't enough for you?"

Johnson looked askance. Kyle was breaking through the facade that the anger toward his ex-wife had made him gullible to. He moved his legs to stand up when he was reminded by the chains bolted him to the floor. If only he realized there was a yoke he carried that he'd placed on himself.

Kyle pressed on. "Why would Seth reach out to a bunch of wounded ex-husbands in a divorce group? He knows all of you have been scarred emotionally and can be plied by his words. Particularly if you are disgruntled with your ex, or the divorce settlement, or are not trusting of women any longer. How much does it take to call a man to action to right a perceived injustice when he's already biased against women?"

Brad dropped his head into his hands to hide his weeping.

"I can protect you from going to jail. I can probably even get these charges against you waived. You can return to your wife and family and go on living as you were before. Put Seth and this whole incident behind you. Few people get that chance. You can get out of this alive with a new lease on life…and maybe a new perspective."

"What do I have to do?"

"Help me set a trap for Seth."

Rachel teared up when Kyle pulled up in front of a nondescript hotel outside Boston. A gift had been given to her. Her sister waited in one of these rooms. Protecting Sofia was part of Kyle's elaborate plan to trap Seth. Rachel's doppelgänger, a WITSEC agent Kyle trusted, was lying in wait at Sofia's house and being very open about her presence with seemingly only one inspector protecting her—dressed as a beat cop. The hope was that Seth would take the bait and they could arrest them there. Rachel knew some of the plan that was designed to flush Seth out and hopefully discover what had happened to Dr. Allen. Kyle didn't discuss his thoughts on whether Dr. Allen was alive or dead.

Something had changed with Kyle. Not that he was any less stressed. In fact, he seemed more so. It was his demeanor toward her. He was soft with his words. Ever since he'd met with Brad Johnson, he'd seemed to want to make amends in whatever way he could, and allowing her to see her sister was part of it.

Sofia opened the door, holding Lyla in her arms. Rachel rushed through and crushed them both in a giant hug. The moment seemed surreal, and she didn't want to let either of them go until Lyla said repeatedly, "Auntie Rachel?"

"I brought you a gift," Sofia said.

"What? Why? Seeing you is the only gift I needed."

Her sister presented her with a small, wrapped package. "It's your birthday in a few short weeks. I didn't want to miss out on the chance when we've missed so many celebrations together." Rachel pulled at the paper, opened the box and saw a pair of peridot earrings. Her birthstone. They dazzled. She was mildly perplexed.

"You don't like them?" Sofia asked.

Rachel, who hadn't worn earrings in years, pressed them through her old holes, feeling a slight pinch as she did so. "They're beautiful. It's just that...you know I swore off jewelry years ago after I got that hoop earring ripped out of my ear by a patient."

"Which is why I chose the studs. You deserve something as beautiful as you are." Her sister fingered her earlobes. "They look great. You're stunning." She edged her back to arm's length. "The desert did amazing things for you."

Rachel gripped her sister's hands. "I brought nothing for you. I'm ashamed of myself."

Her sister locked eyes with her. "You should be." A shadow fell over her countenance. "Remember, things are not always what they seem."

Rachel's heart faltered. What a strange thing to say. Was Sofia trying to pass along some type of message? "Are you okay?"

Sofia took a few steps back, and they held one another with their eyes. Rachel tried to decode the meaning of her words as she waited for her sister to reply. Sofia never did. She merely pulled back Rachel's hair to show off the earrings.

"Doesn't she look amazing?" Sofia's question was directed at Kyle.

A flitter in Rachel's gut signaled alarm. Something was up with Sofia. A forced exuberance when her body language screamed her nerves were on edge. She was trying too hard. There was no ease between them. Even though Rachel hadn't seen her sister in over a year and a half, she could still tell when something was amiss, and her sister might as well have been clanging a cymbal over her head.

Rachel shook the thought from her mind and swept her gaze over her sister's slim figure. "You don't even look like you were pregnant. How did you do it?"

"Slowly," Sofia emphasized. "Lyla is almost two years old. You, on the other hand, have had a complete transformation."

"I had little to do in Springdale other than work and exercise."

"It shows, but it's not just that." Sofia

cupped Rachel's chin. "It's what I see in your eyes. There is a spark of confidence. Of…peace. I haven't seen those two things in years." Her eyes teared up, and she wiped them away. "I only wish Mom and Dad could see you, too."

Kyle stepped closer. "No. You didn't share anything with them, did you?"

Sofia stepped back. "Of course not. I would never…" Her voice trailed off, and she cleared her throat. Something was definitely off with her. Lyla whimpered, picking up on her mother's subtle distress.

Kyle nodded. "That's good," he said, though he didn't seem satisfied with the answer.

"Do you think it will work?" Sofia asked her sister. "This trap you're setting for Seth?"

"I honestly know little about it," Rachel said. Considering Sofia's strange demeanor, Rachel felt it best to feign ignorance.

Kyle tapped at his watch. "Rachel, I told you we wouldn't have much time."

Lyla walked toward Rachel, and Rachel got down on her knees. She reached out and took the youngster's hands. "I'm so glad I got to see you. You've grown so much."

"I'm big girl."

Rachel smiled through her pain. She had missed so much of her niece's life. In that moment, her body felt heavy with despair. "You're right!" She brought the little girl close, inhaling the scent of her strawberry shampoo and trying to forever stamp it into her memory.

Lyla backed up and rubbed her nose against Rachel's.

Rachel nuzzled her back and then hugged her tight. "Eskimo kisses. Thank you, sweet girl."

Kyle reached under her arm to help her stand up. "I'm sorry, but it's time. This was dangerous as it is. There's a WITSEC inspector ready to take Sofia and Lyla to their safe place. They'll stay with them until this is over. I have people watching your parents as well."

Kyle escorted Sofia and her daughter from the hotel room.

As he walked out, her sister waved. "Please, remember what I said."

It was a message she was leaving. Now Rachel had to decipher it like Seth's notes. Only there wasn't a key to go with it.

SIXTEEN

Kyle watched from his post as Rachel and the agent sat in the vehicle hiding in the woods. He was off in the distance, scoping the scene with a pair of binoculars, hoping that what he expected to happen wouldn't take place, but in his heart knowing it would.

He thought back to the meeting he'd arranged between the sisters. The first hint that something was amiss was the earrings that Sofia had given Rachel and the words she'd spoken to her. *Remember, things are not always what they seem.* It had been a clear warning.

Kyle's intentions behind the meeting had been twofold. Truly, he did want to give Rachel the opportunity to see her sister and niece again. But that wasn't the only reason.

Ever since he'd partnered with Rachel again, he'd wondered if Seth had gotten to

Sofia. Kyle had numerous suspicions about the break-in at Sofia's house. The fact that the women had conveniently been gone from the property when the break-in occurred. That the only things taken were Rachel's belongings. His first instinct was that the Black Crew was deep and extensive and was posting 24-7 watch on Rachel's family members. That was certainly possible, but considering the types of people that Seth recruited, was it feasible? Could they keep it up for not just a few days, but weeks to years on end? After the information concerning Dr. Allen came to light, he figured it was more likely that crew members were designated certain duties at certain times.

Kyle knew there was nothing a mother wouldn't do to protect her child. It would be the only way you'd give up your sister—to save your daughter. It wouldn't be done out of spite, but out of necessity.

After their reunion, Kyle reached out to Gage Carter and asked him to look through the plethora of Seth's letters to see if any had been written to Sofia.

A few had been found and decoded. The obtuse language suggested that Seth had his hooks in Rachel's sister.

What Seth's letters suggested in their language to Sofia he hadn't fully disclosed to Rachel, though she was aware that she was in more danger at present than the agent meant to lure Seth from her.

What Kyle did share had broken Rachel's heart.

The earrings Sofia had gifted Rachel had been tracking devices. Both of them. If one got lost, the Black Crew still had the other. The jewelry wasn't a thoughtful birthday gift. They were designed to locate Rachel and bring her to the one person she wanted to see the least.

Seth.

And Kyle was going to let it happen.

The irony of the situation tugged at his heart. Rachel was putting complete trust in him when he wasn't reciprocating. There was an element of need on her part—her ex-husband wanted her dead, and the DA wanted her charged with murder. DA Elijah Nguyen had been making a celebrity of himself with his on-air musings about Rachel's guilt. Kyle suspected he was a member of the Black Crew but hadn't had the time to prove it. Of course, Rachel had other options that Kyle offered her, but she stuck with his plan.

Didn't that speak more to her innocence? That she had nothing to hide? If she had been working with Seth, then it would be exposed in these next moments. That's another reason why he designed the trap as he had.

It was the ultimate cat-and-mouse game, and if he or Rachel failed on any level, both would die and Seth would fade into the wind. Considering Seth's resources and following, law enforcement wouldn't find him before Seth died of old age. Rachel understood the risks and was willing to take them, because she'd never be free until Seth was behind bars. Then again, would she be free even then? Perhaps her freedom could only come after Seth's demise. If they got him back to prison, they'd have to cut him off from all human contact. No more writing letters. The risk was too great. Unfortunately, even Kyle didn't think he could enforce isolation to such a degree.

If Rachel felt that way as well, would she take matters into her own hands? Would she, if she had the chance, kill Seth? Kyle was used to working through the permutations of a situation, but his stomach sank as he considered that possibility. Rachel had done nothing to disprove her belief in the sanctity of life, but he'd also never put her in the same sphere with someone who took so much of it. Some could argue that killing Seth would prevent death—and a lot of it. In fact, he'd essentially made that argument to her in the hospital when he told her her life was more valuable than his because she could put Seth back behind bars.

Sweat beaded his hairline. If Rachel chose something so dire as to kill Seth, it would be the end of him. Not just of his career, but in all he believed about her. His jaw clenched. If he couldn't live with her doing something so against her character, that meant he was emotionally invested in her. In their relationship.

It meant that he loved her.

And he'd put her in a scenario where she'd likely have to confront her biggest fear. And she trusted him to do that.

Did that mean she loved him as well?

His heart skipped a beat as he pondered the question. Then he quickly chastised himself for having such thoughts out here on a mission. The situation could easily turn deadly if he lost focus. Redirecting his attention, he settled prone on the forest floor and looked through the binoculars again. Rachel was sitting in the vehicle with the WITSEC agent, safe. For now.

That was until Seth came for her.

Rachel knew Kyle hadn't disclosed all the reasons behind the plan or why he'd chosen such drastic measures—using her as bait. It went against everything he believed in. The reason she agreed to it? Because she was willing to risk her own life for freedom.

She bitterly fingered the earrings her sister had given her, now knowing the very thing disguised as a gift had been a signal for her ultimate foe.

What had Seth threatened her sister with? It must have been something to do with Lyla. Would Rachel have done anything differently if she had a child? Could she blame Sofia for wanting to protect Lyla at all costs? Was there anyone she would betray her sister for? Rachel couldn't fathom making the choice, and she certainly would lay her life down for her niece—there was just a middleman in the decision.

Rachel had needed to feel close to her sister in their meeting. Instead, it had been like an appointment with a stranger. The words Sofia had spoken to her kept replaying in her mind. Sofia wasn't the free spirit she'd been in the past.

Kyle had used the arrested cult member Brad Johnson to set a trap for Seth. Through channels, WITSEC had sent Seth a message that Rachel wanted to meet with him at Sofia's residence, to discuss a truce, a way to move forward where they could both be free. They were using a doppelgänger for the meeting—or at least for the initial ruse. Rachel had to admit that from a distance, the woman was indistinguishable from Rachel. Up close was a different story.

All the inspector had to do was get close. Once in Seth's presence, she would arrest him with the help of her surveillance team and get him back in jail to be held until they tried him again. Brad Johnson would confess that Seth had paid him to kidnap Rachel and bring her to him. Rachel shuddered involuntarily at the thought.

If part one of the plan failed—Kyle had instituted part two as the backup, using her as bait. This was the plan most likely to lure out Seth since she wore the earrings.

Rachel hadn't met the WITSEC inspector, Daniel Kruger, who was sitting with her in the car. Young man. Early thirties. Brown eyes. Side-swept longish brown-blond hair. He seemed better suited for a movie screen than law enforcement. He was inexperienced. Not that he confessed it to her, but it was clear in each of his movements. His hands either gripped the steering wheel until his knuckles whitened, or his legs fidgeted so much he'd rock the car. At several points, Rachel had to settle a hand on his thigh to stop the movement. Kruger constantly twirled his thumbs or pressed his index finger into his earpiece, listening closely for any incoming message. He reminded Rachel of a new doctor on their first day as an attending.

Rachel could also listen to the team's communications. Currently, there wasn't any cross chatter. They had been instructed to stay silent except for emergency.

Rachel related to what Kruger was experiencing. The weight of the world could be suffocating. Patients held Rachel to account for the training she acquired and expected her to act proficiently in a crisis. The years of school, internship and fellowship were supposed to enable her to succeed under pressure.

Was there a proving ground for WITSEC inspectors? Could going through a simulation many times be the same as confronting a murderous human? Medical simulation attempted to do the same thing. The benefit was being able to make a mistake without costing a life. It was so different with an actual patient, who reached out with frail hands and watery eyes, imploring for just a few more seconds of time on earth.

Another reason Rachel held so tightly to her faith. There had to be more to this life.

Where was Kyle? He'd said he'd keep a close eye, but she couldn't see him, though admittedly she was trying not to look.

Even though the distance between her and Kyle was palpable, she would have preferred to be sitting with him. Was there a way the two of them could ever be together? Or was it a fantasy that Rachel had latched on to that wasn't possible in the real world?

Could she trust the man she was sitting with?

"What time is the meeting with Seth and Sofia supposed to happen?" Rachel asked.

Daniel consulted his watch. His eyebrows narrowed together, the move clearly giving him time to contemplate how much information he should share with Rachel. People young in their profession clung to the rules.

More experienced professionals had ethical boundaries but knew when they could bend the rules—when it was in the interest of the client they were serving.

"I'm sure they have instructed you not to give me a lot of details, but what's it going to hurt if I know the time."

"It's in twenty minutes," Daniel relented with a sigh.

They were in the middle of nowhere. A wooded area shaded by the deciduous trees in full leafy glory. It was a time of year she'd grown to appreciate. How things that once looked dead could bring about new life again. A renewal.

A fresh hope.

The sun was high, though they sat in a shaded area. Rachel powered down her window, inhaling deeply the scent of earth and wildflowers.

That's when she heard the crunching of tree branches.

Reflexively, she unclipped her seat belt, if for no other reason than to exit the car quickly. Seeing the motion, Daniel reached for her hand. "What are you doing?"

Rachel pressed a finger to her lips and slowly depressed the release button on his seat belt as well. She motioned with a finger to the back of the car. They both turned around.

"There's no one there. You're being hypersensitive," Daniel said unconvincingly.

Paranoia was the red flag of a life that had proven monsters lived under the bed. That's when the perceived loss of mind grew into something more life-preserving—hypervigilance—and Rachel's inner alarm system had been fine-tuned to perfection.

Rachel stared into the woods and slowly examined the trunk of every tree. That's when she saw it—the flash of an arm motioning to another individual. How many people were out there? She took the earrings from her lobes and deposited them in the foot well—their purpose fulfilled.

"They're coming." She pointed. "We need to get out of here."

It was never part of the plan for Rachel to surrender herself. The hope was to get Seth in the same geographic area so WITSEC could apprehend him. Plus, there wasn't any way she could allow herself to suffer any such fate. Rachel was going to fight, and it would not be a ruse.

As they both faced forward, Daniel with

his hand on the key to start the engine, two men approached the front of the car. Rachel grabbed Kruger's hand and turned the ignition, reached her leg over his and stomped her foot on the gas. As the car lurched forward, both men jumped out of the way. Daniel took the wheel and steered the car farther down the dirt road.

Gunfire ensued.

It didn't take long before the car couldn't gain traction any longer and lumbered through the dirt and leaves like an elephant stuck in a mud bog. The tires had no doubt been punctured by bullets.

"We've got to bail," Rachel said as she opened her car door, then ran as fast as she could into the woods. She heard Daniel do the same. There was no sense in them trying to stick together. She didn't have any confidence that Kruger could provide protection, and risked it on her own. She slalomed between the trees like a skier fighting for a gold medal on moguls—darting in zigzag patterns between broad trunks to avoid the gunfire. The earth opened underneath her, and she tumbled head over feet into a ditch. After coming to a stop, she scrambled underneath an exposed root ball and stayed still, listening for her pursuers.

They were quiet. She couldn't even hear the faint communication of talking through radios. No voices in her ear of WITSEC agents discussing their plan, which was to fan out through the woods and hunt Seth if the Black Crew showed up. Calling out would disclose her location. How were the Black Crew communicating with one another? Rachel crawled along the length of the ditch. At least she wasn't easily visible from this position. She came to an end and noticed a small river with a few large boulders at its edge. The flow seemed easy enough to traverse, but without knowing the depth, let alone the sound it would make, and the subsequent wet clothes she'd have to deal with, a water escape didn't seem the best idea.

Rachel popped her head up. She could see a man trailing her. She looked upstream and saw a small cottage. It would provide protection but would also be the first place someone would search. It looked well maintained. Would it have a working landline? Cell service in the woods often led people to consider keeping theirs.

Rachel crawled out of the ditch and scrambled to the first boulder by the river. Just as she rounded the back end of it, bullets ricocheted off the top, sending moss-covered rock fragments raining down on her head. She looked at the cottage with renewed interest. Yes, it would be the first place they would look for her, but she could also barricade herself inside, and maybe there'd be a weapon she could use.

Rachel broke into a run and headed for the back side of the cottage. She jiggled the doorknob and found it locked. There was a large window next to the back door. She tested it and found it open. She lifted it and scrambled inside, pulling the window down behind her and latching it. When she turned, she found herself in the kitchen. A phone, harkening back to the '80s, with a long, stretched-out cord, hung on the wall. She yanked off the receiver and listened. No dial tone. She slammed it down. She riffled through the kitchen drawers, looking for something she could defend herself with and strangely found all the deadly knives missing. Nothing better than a butter knife.

That would not help.

Rachel passed through the kitchen door to the front parlor and checked the front latch. It was locked. She tested the windows and quickly pulled the curtains closed. There had to be something here she could use to defend herself.

The fireplace didn't have any utensils beside it. She neared it and was surprised to find the area warm. A few coals glowed red, a faint hiss of steam escaping.

Someone had just been here. Had she just missed someone who could help her? Rachel backtracked toward the kitchen and entered the bedroom. The bed was unmade. She opened the drawer to the bedside table. No gun. She opened the closet doors. No rifles sat inside.

It was almost devoid of anything she could use to defend herself. She looked out the bedroom window and saw a man with a rifle headed her way. She was literally a sitting duck, and the number of men who were trailing her could easily overpower her. She let the curtain fall closed. What could she do? She'd chosen a site that would become her coffin. Seth liked to bury his victims in the woods.

The skin along her spine prickled. The sound of footsteps over creaking, aged floor planks sent electric tingles down her arms and legs, priming her to run, but there wasn't anywhere to go.

Footsteps were an intriguing thing. How

easily someone could differentiate the person behind them. Though it had been years since she'd heard them, they were as easily identifiable to her as seeing someone face-to-face.

Because she had hidden from those footsteps for a decade. Feigned sleep when they would come into their bedroom.

She turned around.

"Hi, Rachel. Long time no see, as they say."

Seth had finally found her.

SEVENTEEN

Rachel's heart thrummed wildly at the base of her throat. She covered her neck with her hand. It was hard to swallow. The only sound she would likely make was a high squeak, and she didn't want to be timid in Seth's presence. She was trapped in the room she wanted to be pinned in the least.

Prison had not changed his looks for the worse. His blond-brown hair was longer, stylishly mussed up with hair product. A cleanly shaved face. Seemingly, Seth Black had defied the stress that caused some people to age. The weight he had lost defined his musculature. His look was more refined than she'd thought possible. Put a tux on him and he could be the head of the Boston elite without batting an eye. A wolf in Armani. No one would be the wiser. It wouldn't surprise her in the least if he'd gone keto—driving his body fat to single percentage points. His jaw was angular. His green eyes pierced the very essence of her spirit. What woman wouldn't be attracted to him, to his prestige, to his money?

All of it was a facade. The anger she felt toward herself for not realizing at the beginning that he was a shell of a person hiding a dark, dangerous self still lingered.

"Miss me?" he asked, smiling mischievously. He licked his lips—not seductively, but like an animal who had captured long-hunted prey and was hungry to devour it.

He stepped toward her. She refused to back away and broadened her stance to provide more balance and raised her fists. Seth raised his hands in mock surrender, a childlike mask contorting his face.

"Rachel," he said in a singsong voice, like a mother trying to calm a child from a tantrum. "I would never hurt you. Surely you know that by now. You're the only one I ever protected."

"I don't know you, Seth. I never did. Not your true self. Not until the end."

He took two quick steps toward her and grabbed her wrists. She struggled against his grip, trying to turn her wrists into the weakest part of his hand, where his thumb met his index finger. He clamped harder, and she winced at the pressure.

"Just be still," he seethed. "I'm going to check you for a wire, that's all."

He lifted his hands toward her neck and pulled her hair behind her, glancing into her ears. "Guess you ditched the gift from your sister. They served their purpose well."

Thankfully, he missed the tiny device secured in her ear canal.

"Did you threaten her?" Rachel asked.

"Who?"

"Sofia. Did you tell her you would hurt Lyla?"

He smiled snidely. "I never really liked her, anyway. Too homely."

But that had been the very reason he'd picked Rachel. To blend into the background. To give him the cover of having a normal life.

"A woman who cooperates after you threaten her child isn't an ally," she told him. "She's ultimately an enemy."

"Are you sure? Even after all the money I gave her?"

"What are you talking about?" Rachel asked.

"In your absence, I've been keeping tabs on your sister like, well, any good brother-in-law would do. I'm sure you expected me to do nothing less."

"We're not married anymore. You don't owe my family anything. It strikes me as funny that you suddenly had this desire to be close to them only after you went to prison and I was in hiding."

"Well, that may be what you say, but in my heart I'll always be married to you, regardless of what a piece of paper dictates." He waved his hand in front of his face. "Anyway, your sister and her husband got into a bit of a financial bind. There were some debts they couldn't pay off. My mother was more than happy to float her the money for a little help."

"There's no way she would do that."

"Even if she was going to lose her home? Your precious little niece living on the streets? I couldn't bear thinking about it. Even I'm not that coldhearted."

But he was. He just couldn't fathom the evil within himself. He was so smart, yet so emotionally deficient. Seth didn't possess an empathetic Geiger to register what others were feeling.

Rachel pressed her lips together as she considered his statements. This was additional news if true. Part of the game was figuring out if this was one of those moments of brutal honestly or a torturous lie that would get her to doubt her sister and the loyalty they had to one another. Because of WITSEC, she'd lost the ability to know the ins and outs of her sister's life. What sort of trouble Sofia was in.

Seth dug his fingers into Rachel's shoulders and yanked her forward, unbuttoning the top of her shirt and running his fingers across her neckline. Not gently, like a man who loved her would do. Instead he pressed hard enough to make her flinch. He lifted the bottom of her shirt and exposed her belly. Embraced her in an uncomfortable hug and pressed her against him as he patted down her back.

Her stomach roiled. A cold sweat broke out at the base of her neck. He stepped back and ran his hands down her legs. He pushed her to sit on the bed and took off her shoes and socks, reaching up into her loose pants and leaving a slick trail of fear in the wake of his touch. These moves were to both check for a wire and hinder her ability to escape. Running in bare feet across sticks and rocks would slow her down no matter how much adrenaline numbed her nerve endings.

He knelt before her and placed his hands on her lower back and pulled her forward. "I only ever loved you, Rachel. My release from prison—don't you see God's hand in it?"

Another difference between them had been their disparate beliefs in God. He'd often laughed at her faith. Called her weak for putting trust in something that couldn't be seen, felt or heard. Now he was using it to build a bridge back to her. But after having experienced life out from under Seth's shadow, she'd rather be homeless than seek comfort built on a shaky house of cards.

"No, I don't. I see that somehow you manipulated the courts or, at the very least, one juror to rig the system to set you free."

He ignored her taunt. Instead, he eased back and stood up, taking two steps back. He placed his hands on his hips, holding her in his gaze for an uncomfortable length of time. Simply another tactic to exert his power over her. "You look amazing."

The sound of a tree branch breaking drew his attention to the window, and he took two steps toward it to look out. As soon as the exit to the bedroom door was clear, she ran through it. Seth quickly shifted his direction, and in three steps, kicked her feet out from underneath her, sending her face-first into the wood floor. She cracked her chin, blood spurting forth immediately. Lights starred her vision. She rested her cheek against the floor, resisting the lure to close her eyes.

That would be the peaceful path. Surrendering into the darkness. Letting him have his way with her. Wasn't this always going to be the inevitable end?

Then she heard it. A voice in her ear. Kyle.

"Rachel, I'm here. I see you. I'm with you. Get back up. You're okay."

Seth decided her next move for her and grabbed the waistband of her jeans, hoisting her up. "Rachel, Rachel. There's no need to be so dramatic." She tried to look at his face through her blurred vision. "Now, look at what you've done. Marked up that new, shiny face of yours."

He pulled her into the kitchen and plopped her into a chair. Blood dripped onto her shirt, and she used the back of her hand to put pressure on the gash. Seth stepped to the sink and washed his hands, once again the surgeon prepping for the OR.

Stepping in front of her, he placed his thumb and forefinger on her jaw—pressing in, vise-like. Rachel whimpered and knocked his hand away. Without hesitation, he backhanded her across the face, knocking her from the chair.

Her vision blackened.

Kyle's voice crackled in her ear. "Rachel... Rachel..."

Rachel had to move to a sitting position, or he'd storm in. Getting knocked down twice would be hard for Kyle to stand. She had to get back into the game. They didn't have enough information from Seth to lock him away forever. She had to get more.

Her vision was fuzzy. She could see Seth's figure at the window peering out. Rachel pushed up onto all fours, the world spinning, and set her feet to the ground to stand. Grabbing a musty seat cushion from one of the other kitchen chairs, folding and holding it to her body, she rested her head on it. It was funny how one insignificant item seemed to provide enough of a barrier between her and Seth to feel like she had some space to breathe and think. She sat back in the chair.

"You're making me act like a terrible man, Rachel."

In all their years of marriage, he hadn't been violent with her. Now, the gloves were off. Maybe it was the change in her demeanor, her physicality, that told him she wasn't willing to submit to his intimidation anymore.

So he had to prove that he still had power over her.

Her heart ached. She hated the position she was in. She missed Kyle—physically ached for his closeness. Every time Seth touched her, he caused pain. For Seth, Rachel's needs were never considered. Kyle was the opposite. He'd always put her first. She didn't desire to ever be with a man like Seth again.

It was better to be alone if she couldn't be with Kyle.

"I'm here, Rachel. I've got you. You're not alone," Kyle said into her ear.

She wept into the cushion. His words provided strength. There was a panic button placed behind one knee, another item Seth had missed, that she could press if she felt out of control. An exit if she couldn't take what Seth brought on. There was also a word she could say. But they needed more from Seth. More of a confession to put him behind bars for good.

She felt her chin. The wound was open, and it would need stitches. She stretched her neck—it was sore from the impact of the slap and subsequent fall, but nothing a few ibuprofens and a heating pad wouldn't fix.

Seth got down on one knee and took her

hands in his. "I want you, Rachel. I want you to come away with me."

Cool saliva flooded her mouth. She clenched her teeth to keep from vomiting. She didn't know if the feeling was just from his words or the cumulative effects of her recent injury, portending a concussion.

She wiggled her hands free from his and pulled the pillow closer to her body.

"I can make you," he said.

Rachel thought through trying to reason with him. It was always tit for tat. She'd never get ahead, but she also had a job to do. She had to help herself secure her freedom.

"How?" Rachel asked.

"You know about the woman found in the woods with your hair on her body."

"Is that what you really want? To see me go to jail for a crime I didn't commit?"

He pulled a chair from the table and sat down. "If I had known you could be this way, feisty and assertive, I would have never become the man that I was."

Psychopaths always resorted to this— blaming the victim for their own deficits. It pulled her back into his sick emotional web. She would not do it. Three years of being free from it had given her the clarity she needed.

"You're claiming my weight and timidity caused you to be a serial killer?"

"I just needed...more excitement. I hear from the Black Crew that you're quite the fiery one. Like to fight back. Throw a few punches."

Rachel couldn't travel down this road with him. It was a highway too far into the abyss. She wasn't going to cross this line to entertain his morbid fantasies.

"Where is Dr. Allen?" she asked.

"Closer than you think."

Rachel raised an eyebrow. Had Kyle heard that?

"You're using her?"

Seth shrugged. "I may love her, too."

Love to Seth was nothing more than a bargaining chip. Something he used as a weapon to get women to yield to his ways. She could never imagine Kyle using anyone, let alone someone he claimed to love, just to hurt them. In fact, it pained Kyle to feel love for someone that he couldn't give himself fully to.

"What is it you have that makes you think I would go with you?"

"Evidence," he said simply.

"What kind?"

"Signed documents from Dr. Allen from your sessions that you colluded in my crimes.

That we were partners." His green eyes sparkled with pride. "I understand you were fascinated with my work."

How did he know about her murder boards? Someone in the Black Crew must have told him. She closed her eyes and pressed into the conversation. This could be the thing law enforcement needed to make sure Seth never got past the razor-wire fence. Perhaps they'd finally relegate him to the supermax facility in Colorado where he'd only see the outside for an hour a day.

"How many did I have right?" Rachel challenged.

He leaned toward her, taking her hand in his. He wedged his fingers between hers and squeezed, not releasing the pressure.

"Most were correct. A few were outliers, but you discovered some that even law enforcement hadn't found."

Rachel clenched her teeth to keep from crying at the pain in her hands. "What were their names? How long did you torture them?"

Seth rattled off the names of five women like a birthday wish list.

Rachel's heart rammed into her ribs. She found it hard to take a deep breath. How could she get out of this? They had enough now.

He'd admitted to murders that they hadn't yet found him guilty of.

The evidence against Dr. Allen was mounting, too, but would it be enough for people to believe that she'd done things under Seth's influence? Rachel wanted more against Dr. Allen. It was as if Seth was trying to protect her...or maybe just trying to protect the position that she held with WITSEC. If she worked where she did, Seth had a mole at a high level he could depend on.

"They know about the letters," Rachel said. "That you and Dr. Allen were—"

"Exchanging letters isn't a crime. If you had them fully deciphered, you'd realize that there isn't much there."

Rachel bit her lip. He could be right. She didn't fully know what all the documents contained.

"If you come with me," Seth said, "I'll have Nora destroy the evidence. You'll be free."

"All except for my hair that was recently found on one of your victims. How are you going to explain that away?"

He clicked his tongue against the roof of his mouth. "Yeah, that. We might have to put our heads together on that one. Nothing that two smart people can't come up with a solution to.

Does that mean you're in? You'll come with me?" He pulled her into an awkward embrace. "I love you, Rachel. We can start over. We'll go overseas. Europe or something. I won't want the other women if you give me what I need."

Women who were caregivers were at high risk of becoming involved in codependent relationships. It was the first time it was crystal clear in her mind. Maybe this thought had always played in her subconscious. Maybe deep down she'd always known what Seth was and had an inherent desire to fix him. She was a doctor, a smart one, and it shouldn't be beyond her capabilities to do so.

This was the lie she survived on—subconsciously or not. But Seth was the only one who could choose to do the work to fix himself. And he'd never see it. Whether it was nature, or nurture, or an evil seed—it didn't matter. He'd have to strike the match himself, and it was something he'd never be capable of doing.

But right now, Rachel had to get him to believe she was back in this game with him, and she didn't know how good an actress she was.

Rachel tensed the muscles in her arm to keep her hand from trembling as she reached out and settled her palm against his face.

"I'll go with you," Rachel said. "You don't

know how long I've waited for you to say those words to me. Three years was too long to be apart. But if you want me to go with you, tell me the truth about Nora. There will not be another woman coming between us. I must be your one and only."

It was every codependent dream come true. That they had fully encased the partner in the web.

"I'll tell you everything. I don't love her. There's no way I could. She's no match for you. She killed Penelope and put your hair there to frame you for it."

And he pressed his lips against hers.

Kyle was desperate to reach Rachel. The sound of her smacking the floor when Seth tripped her had been one thing. The slap across her face had split his heart in two and simultaneously fueled his blood with anger.

Now it was time to end this interaction. She'd done it. Gotten him to confess enough incriminating evidence to put him away for a lifetime. Cleared herself from the murder they accused her of. They had enough to put Nora Allen behind bars for good, too.

He was constantly scanning the woods for members of the Black Crew. What surprised him was how few there were. As soon as Rachel had gone into the house, WITSEC agents had flooded into the woods to capture those that had approached the car, and all had been secured. Inspector Kruger was now working with Kyle, though he couldn't be seen. They were in radio contact, approaching the cottage from different angles.

"Daniel. Check in."

No response. Had they missed someone? They had accounted for the men who had approached the car. Had Seth hidden Black Crew members farther out? Anything was possible in this situation.

He heard running footfalls behind him. He turned on his belly in that direction, drawing his weapon from his holster, and couldn't fathom what he was seeing. A woman in a business suit, running in heels straight at him, holding a baseball bat above her head.

"Dr. Allen! Drop the bat or I'll shoot."

She didn't listen and began screaming at the top of her lungs. He fired a shot, missed and then raised his hand as she aimed the bat at his head. He blocked the first swing, heard a crack of bone. As he dropped his defensive arm, she clocked him again to the side of the head.

All went black.

EIGHTEEN

"Kyle…"

His name whispered in the distance. The sound of rushing blood in his ears nearly drowning it out. His head pounded, and he felt cold and sweaty. His body felt heavy. Pulling his hands forward, he tried to assess the damage, but found they were bound behind his back.

A foot nudged his knee. The movement made his head pound more.

"Kyle…wake up."

Rachel's voice. Low but insistent. He blinked a few times. Then he turned toward the direction of her voice and opened his eyes. They were sitting side by side in a kitchen, zip-tied to rickety wooden chairs. His vision turned red, and he blinked a few more times to see blood dripping onto his lap. He couldn't remember another situation with a witness where he'd gotten so many injuries—and the crisis wasn't over yet.

He swished saliva around his mouth, his body begging for a drink of water. "Where are they?"

"In the bedroom," Rachel said. "Is anyone else coming?"

Kyle shook his head. "I don't know. On the radio, I couldn't raise Daniel. I don't know where anyone is right now. We... I might have underestimated the number of people Seth had hiding out." He turned to look at her. Her chin was bruised, the laceration open and still oozing blood. Nothing that couldn't be fixed—at least physically. But what he'd asked her to do, and she'd volunteered for— would there be any fixing that? In the woods, praying with everything in him for Rachel's protection, he'd realized one thing.

He loved her.

There was no denying it. She was everything to him. Every injury to her body he could feel on his own, and it tore him to pieces that his actions had caused her to suffer. He had to stop this—stop Seth.

Stop him forever.

And somehow, he had to convince Rachel that he'd been wrong on every level. That she was the one for him. He'd figure out a way for them to be together.

If she would have him.

He held her eyes. "I'm sorry."

"Kyle, it's okay. I knew what I was getting into."

"Can you break free?" he asked.

Rachel wiggled at her bindings and then shook her head.

Kyle did the same, finding them loose enough to break his hands free.

At that moment, Seth and Nora stepped into the kitchen. Kyle kept his hands clasped behind his back. The only explanation for the loose bindings was that perhaps Nora had been the one to tie him up. Seth's fascination with the new Rachel had perhaps made her the biggest prize—the one most worthy of his attention.

"Looks like our sleeping beauty has awakened," Seth said. He stayed out of arm's reach.

"What's your plan, Seth?" Kyle asked.

"For you, it's easy. Looks like your time on earth will end soon."

"That much I gathered."

"What about Nora?" Rachel challenged. "I thought you told me you were done with her."

Rachel was providing the ultimate distraction.

Nora snapped her head toward Seth. "What is she talking about?" she demanded. "You said killing the two of them was the only way to end this situation so we could have the life we've been planning for years."

Kyle eased his arm forward. His holster was empty. That's when he saw his weapon in Seth's hand.

Hopefully, he was a bad shot.

Kyle bolted from his chair and charged Seth. It didn't take Seth more than a second to raise his arm, take aim, and fire off a shot. Searing fire bloomed in Kyle's chest, and the force knocked him backward onto the ancient wood floor. Darkness filled his vision again.

"Kyle!"

Rachel's was not a scream to rouse him, but a cry of desperation, hoping he was still alive. And that's when she knew her feelings had crossed over. It was the sound she heard in the ER only under the direst circumstances. A wail. And now it made sense to her that prayer could happen when words could not be spoken.

When words couldn't be formed because the well of darkness was too deep.

No... No... No... Her thoughts screamed inside her head.

Be calm... She heard another voice break through.

She inhaled sharply and watched for the rise and fall of his chest. Only a momentary reprieve when she saw his ribs heave.

Rachel looked directly at Seth and tried to affect the look of contrition. The words she said next had to be believable. "Seth, you need to untie me right now. Let me help Inspector Reid. If he dies, you and I will always be hunted. We could never be together."

It was a gamble. She was hoping the statements he'd made to her were truthful—one of the few times he'd spoken authentically— or at least what Seth believed to be honesty. Seth walked toward her and clipped the zip ties from her wrists.

Rachel dropped to her knees. She placed her ear above Kyle's mouth and nose while simultaneously slipping two fingers into the crease of his neck. He was breathing. His pulse was quick but relatively strong. She tore his shirt open, buttons flying off into the distance. The bullet had entered the left chest, just above his Kevlar vest, near the shoulder joint. Taking off the vest, she placed a knuckle on his sternum and rubbed hard. It wasn't the kindest thing to do, but she needed him to wake up. Needed him with her.

He inhaled sharply and shoved her hand away. It was the exact response she was looking for. He pushed up to a sitting position, blinking rapidly, and took several deep inhalations, his eyes cringing as he did so. Rachel reached up to the kitchen table and grabbed a towel and put pressure on the wound. It could be a good sign it wasn't bleeding much. It could also mean he was losing a lot of blood internally, hidden from her eyes. If that was happening, it was only a matter of time before shock set in. Just like when he had taken a bullet to the gut.

Kyle met Rachel's eyes with a weary smile, but a spark of light was present in his demeanor. Her heart rate settled a bit.

Kyle reached for his phone in his back pocket and realized it was missing. "Dr. Allen, I suggest you give me my phone. I have something to play for you. It might change your mind about linking your life with Seth's in whatever plans you have made."

He could speak full sentences. Another sign that his lung and large blood vessels were okay. However, he wasn't able to move his left arm much, the bullet likely destroying the joint to the point he would require surgery.

Nora Allen noticed the phone on the table, and both she and Seth reached for it at the same time. She gripped it in both hands and walked slowly to Kyle.

Seth trained his weapon again on Kyle and fired off a shot. Kyle clenched his eyes closed. The gun jammed, and Seth threw it aside in disgust. Kyle exhaled slowly. Without the vest in place, that shot would have proved fatal.

"Nora," Seth pleaded. "This isn't a good idea. He's going to try and turn you against me. I've pledged my love to you. This whole thing was for *you*. So we could be together. The idea was to end these two and go on with life as we wanted it. Don't you remember? All those letters where I said those very things for years?"

Kyle raised his right hand and beckoned Dr. Allen to him. "If you want to know the truth, Nora, you're going to want me to play the things he said to Rachel while you were outside. I think they'll be very enlightening."

Nora hesitated, her eyes darting across the room as she tried to make a decision.

Kyle continued. "Right now, all this is fixable. You have hurt no one. The things you've done…are forgivable, but before you cross that line, you need to understand that what this man has convinced you to be true is a lie."

She squared her shoulders and handed Kyle his phone. He balanced the device on his knee, using the face ID to get inside, and scrolled through a series of voice recordings.

"Nora, you know what the government is capable of. This recording is a fake," Seth said. "This is engineered by WITSEC so you won't believe me anymore. The only reason this man and Rachel are still alive is because the gun jammed."

"Does it surprise you?" Kyle asked the psychologist.

"What?" Nora responded.

"That Rachel is still alive. If he intended to do what he said, why not kill her right away? Why keep her around? It would have been better to make quick work of both of us and be on your way—to the life he promised you."

Nora turned back to Seth. "Yes, why is she still here?"

"She's only been here a short time. We had things to…settle."

Kyle didn't stop. He forged ahead with his argument. "Notice there're no weapons here.

He used my gun against me. Where are the knives? How was he going to kill her?"

A cloudy veil dropped over Nora's face. Kyle's words were having an effect. Doubt had slipped into her mind.

Kyle hit Play, and the conversation that Rachel and Seth had within the last hour filled the cabin. Seth moved toward Kyle, but Nora stayed him with a motion of her hand. As soon as she heard Seth's declaration of love, Nora's face reddened. She paced to where Seth had discarded the gun to and picked it up.

And pointed it at Seth.

"You lied! How could you do this to me?" Nora seethed. "I gave up *everything* for you. My life. My home. You said you loved me."

A smirk spread over Seth's face, his true nature revealed through the facade. What did he care about what Nora thought now? He had done what he most wanted to do. If what Seth had said to Rachel was true, then the relationship Seth had developed with Nora had only been to lure Rachel back to him. Nora Allen had simply been collateral damage.

And Seth knew it.

And now he was going to relish letting Nora know she meant nothing to him.

A weight of darkness fell onto Rachel, and

her skin pricked at its presence. She hadn't felt it in years—not until this moment when Seth let his mask drop and was going to let Nora see the man he really was.

The monster within was going to expose himself.

"How could you be so stupid? You, with your PhD in psychology, and you believed the words of a psychopath over your own training."

Allen was apoplectic. The realization contorted her features. "I'll never get it back." She waved the gun Kyle's direction. "What he says is only partly true. If I stop here, I may not go to jail, but my career is over. The first thing the Bureau of Prisons will do is fire me. The licensing board will yank my credentials. My life…is over."

The last words were whispered in disbelief.

Seth stepped toward her. "You have no one to blame but yourself. You're a pitiful human being. You don't deserve me. My mind. My followers."

Tears ran down her face. Her shoulders dropped, shame overcoming her like a weighted blanket. There was no comfort she could find.

"Nora, it's not you. It's him," Rachel said.

"Yes, you made some mistakes. So did I. Your life can go on. You need to join me in getting him convicted. Your life won't be the same, but regardless of what happens, it will be better when you're free from him."

Nora squared her shoulders. Rachel's heart quickened. The look said she had resigned herself to a course of action that she couldn't be swayed from. A resolve had cemented itself in her mind. The only thing Rachel couldn't calculate was what it meant for the rest of them.

"She's right," Nora said, turning toward Seth. "I need to be free from you. All women need to be free from you."

She raised the gun and fired the weapon. This time a bullet discharged and hit Seth square in the belly. He fell, holding his gut, blood sluicing through his fingers.

And then Nora Allen ran through the door into the woods.

"I've got him," Kyle said. "You're the only one who can go get her."

Rachel stood on her bare feet and took off running.

NINETEEN

Rachel was a good two hundred yards behind Nora when she broke free from the cabin. She glanced from side to side, looking for additional foes, and didn't see any members of the Black Crew trying to annihilate her.

Rocks and sticks punctured into her feet like Legos strewn by a petulant child. She focused her vision on Allen's back. She was gaining on her. The woman's choice of footwear was hindering her. Not spiked heels, but close. Nora had tripped several times, even stopped momentarily, perhaps with thoughts of removing them, turning once in Rachel's direction to fire off a shot before she thought better of it.

Rachel pumped her arms faster. Her legs followed suit. She found herself gaining on Nora, only ten to fifteen steps behind. She picked up her pace and reached her arm out, brushing the back of Nora's worsted wool jacket. The movement dropped her back a few paces. She roared forward, launched herself into the air, and when she came down, she grabbed one of Allen's feet and hung on long enough to trip her.

Allen tumbled, leaves and sticks scratching her face and body. The fall knocked the gun from her hand, and it rolled out of reach. Nora screamed as Rachel scurried and tackled her from behind just as she had gotten up on all fours to take off again. Rachel pulled Nora's arms behind her back and held them tight.

"Rachel, please let me go. I won't ever do anything to you. You know my life is over if the police get hold of me."

Rachel's heart broke for her. Was this manipulation or an honest sentiment? Either could be true. Allen could be closer to Seth's demeanor than Rachel wanted to admit.

"Seth will never let you go," Rachel said.

"Seems like he already did, in favor of you," she grunted between breaths.

Rachel shifted her weight off Allen's back and knelt next to her, continuing to grasp her hands.

"I'm sorry you got tangled in Seth's web."

"I did it by choice, and so did you."

Rachel's mouth dropped. "Hardly—"

"I'm so tired of women claiming to be innocent when they know full well what is happening. You can't tell me that in the years you were with Seth, you did not know what he was up to."

"I didn't."

"But you did. You just didn't want to admit it to yourself."

That dug deep into Rachel's chest. It was the one thing about herself that she dreaded was true. That all along, she'd known the truth somewhere in her subconscious but had pushed it down, through disbelief, through denial, and crafted for herself an alternate reality. When her husband wasn't abusive, he was loving and kind. Those moments were survival respites. She'd been deluded to think that his obsessiveness about her whereabouts, about her dress, were signs he loved her more than anything, when all he was doing was trying to possess her as a cover story. Surely, a woman who had spent so many years with him and went back to him knew to her very core that he wasn't innocent.

"What you say about me might be true—probably is true. That I should have known. That I could have done more if I had just been clear in my thinking and analyzed the situation. But you know what he is, and you want to be with him. You planted evidence on one of his victims to implicate me in crimes that I was never a part of. I might have been foolish. Misled. Eager to hope that my husband wasn't the monster that he is. But you? You're just evil."

One of Nora's hands slipped from Rachel's grip. She rolled away from Rachel, pulled a knife from a sheath at her ankle that had been covered by her slacks and rolled back toward Rachel.

Rachel put her hand up in a defensive move, but the knife plunged through her hand and into her belly. Nora scurried to her feet.

"Seth loves me. And now that you'll be out of the picture, we can move forward with framing you for his crimes. He'll be free and we'll be together."

Rachel blinked as Nora backed away from her and then turned to walk off nonchalantly, as if she had not a care in the world.

Rachel fell back onto her haunches and looked down at her current situation. It wasn't good. It was true—the flood of adrenaline into her system was an amazing painkiller, for a few moments, at least, until her brain registered what had occurred and her abdomen seared with pain. She fell onto her back and pressed her free hand over the impaled one, shoving it against her belly to prevent too much blood loss.

The pain halted her breathing. She clenched her eyes and prayed. Who would find her? Seth was injured. The location of the other agents in the woods was unknown. Probably they were tied up arresting all the members of the Black Crew that surrounded the cabin.

A groan escaped her lips. She didn't want to die this way. She had never wanted to die at Seth's hands—or by an agent directed by him. It was the ultimate folly. She'd done so much to be set free, and now she would be buried because, in her delusion, she'd thought she'd freed herself. In reality, she'd just gone back to ultimately be killed by her great foe.

Her thoughts drifted to Kyle. She yearned for him to find her but in the same breath dreaded his arrival. He would blame himself for her injuries, even though she had agreed to risk her life as part of the plan. As part of fully reclaiming the woman she had transitioned to in the desert. That was important if they were going to have a relationship.

Blood flooded through her fingertips. She

felt it dripping down her sides and pooling behind her back. The wound was close to her left upper side—where her spleen was located. She would bleed out quickly if the organ was injured. She was too far away to get medical help in time if that was the case. She looked at the sky. It was blue, calm. She felt peaceful.

But she didn't want to surrender to it.

Lord, I know You're the author and perfector of life. That each breath and heartbeat is granted at Your pleasure. Please, spare my life. Give me more time to right the wrongs of my past. My death will become Kyle's burden, and I don't want the man I love to feel guilty over a death he had no control over.

A determination rose within her. Seth could not, would not, have the last word on her life. She wasn't meant to die this way. Her work wasn't done. There was one person she loved, and she would not give that up without a fight. Rachel crossed her legs, one over the other, pressing the panic button planted behind her knee.

She spoke—hopefully loud enough for the earpiece to pick up. "Kyle… I'm hurt… I need you."

Turning her head to the side, she scanned

the ground for the gun Nora had left behind. In order to help Kyle find her in time, she had to signal him by firing a shot into the air. With her free hand, she brushed over the forest undergrowth, her fingers inching through dense ground cover. Nothing. Now she had to turn her body the other way to search the other side. Through tears and static breaths, she pivoted, searching the ground for the gun.

Each time she tried to take a deep breath to scream, the pain exploded white-hot through every nerve. Now, each movement was causing the same thing to happen. Whimpering, she made one last attempt and dug her fingers into the dirt, clawing as far out as she could.

Her fingertips touched something metallic and warm.

Kyle heard the words come across his earpiece. Daniel Kruger was with him, putting handcuffs on Seth Black. A team of paramedics who worked with WITSEC in situations like this had made their way to the cottage. Kyle stood and headed to the front door of the cottage. He'd seen the direction that Rachel had darted off in and got a bearing on the tree line.

"Inspector Reid, you can't go after her. You're injured," Daniel said.

Ignoring Daniel, Kyle motioned for the paramedics to follow him. He drew his weapon and raced into the woods. His left arm was in a sling, hindering his running, but nothing was going to stop him from finding Rachel. He had to. He wasn't going to let this happen again. This time it was more than losing a witness.

It was losing someone he loved and couldn't live without.

He ran faster. There were signs someone had gone this way. A trail of stomped grass. Newly broken twigs. He climbed over a few fallen logs.

"Rachel, I'm coming! Stay with me. Call out. I need to hear your voice so that I can find you."

He stopped to listen for the sound of her voice. Hearing nothing, he continued to run, trying to fine-tune his hearing for any vocalization she might make. If she was injured too badly, her voice would not be strong enough to be heard.

Lord, please. I know I'm horrible at this whole prayer thing, but I need You to keep her alive. Rachel needs You. Help me find her. Guide my steps in the right direction.

A gunshot broke through the silence of the woods. A flock of birds scattered into the air to his right. It was Rachel. It had to be.

And if it wasn't, he was willing to risk it.

"This way!" He motioned to the medics.

They followed without question, and Kyle couldn't help but feel astonished by their actions. He knew their edict—they could only help a patient when the scene was safe and there wasn't any question they were heading into unknown danger. Even though Kyle felt assured that it was Rachel trying to signal for help, they didn't, and it would have been within their rights to stop and wait.

Finally, he saw Rachel lying in the distance, perhaps one hundred yards away. Sharp pains zinged through his chest, but he ran harder. If the worst outcome happened, he would not let her die alone.

Kyle pulled up to a stop when he found her, and his breath left him, as if he'd fallen straight onto his back from a high roof. She was on her back, her left hand pinned to her abdomen, a knife thrust through it.

She was pale. The gun lay at her right side, her hand covering it but not gripping it. He walked the last two steps and knelt next to her, reaching underneath her head to cradle it with his good arm.

"You found me." Her words were a whisper. She was breathing rapidly, her face contorted in pain.

"Of course I did. There are two medics with me... I need you to stay with me so they can help you." The pair, a man and a woman, reached them then and opened their trauma packs. One grabbed an oxygen mask and began connecting the end to a tank. He could hear the hiss as the man turned it on. The female EMT grabbed a package of gauze and started stringing together some IV fluids.

The woman grabbed her radio. "I need the cooler from our rig to our location ASAP. I mean, run it here." A pair of trauma shears flashed, and they cut the bottom of Rachel's shirt open to the hand that was impaled.

"Kyle..."

His heart knew what was happening, and he shook his head and leaned it next to hers. He couldn't bear to witness the look in her eyes. He'd been in too many of these situations not to know what that look meant. The overwhelming desire to utter those last words when a person didn't think they were going to make it. Once those words were uttered, death soon followed, the spirit considering the work complete and moving on to other realms.

"No—" Kyle moaned. "Stay with me."

"Thank you." The words split him in half. What did she really have to thank him for? For allowing her to put herself in this situation? For him not protecting her? For not keeping her from Seth Black's evil ways? From the Black Crew?

"I'm free…it's okay," Rachel said. "Get him…jail. You have enough."

But he needed her. Not just to testify. He needed her always.

Kyle rested her head onto the ground and reached for her free hand, squeezing it hard. Sobs racked his body, and he pressed his head into the side of her chest and pleaded. "Rachel, stay with me. You can't leave me. Not like this." In his mind, if he gripped her hand hard enough, he could anchor her to the earth. Keep her from leaving.

Keep her from leaving him.

Her eyes closed—but there was one more phrase.

"I love you."

TWENTY

Kyle stood outside Rachel's hospital room. She was back at the hospital where her career started, except on the other side of the experience. She was alive…stable, but not yet ready to wake up. Her eyes would briefly flirt with opening and quickly close. Her hand was repaired and bandaged. A central line snaked into her chest. The nurse discontinued the last bag of blood that hung on the IV pole. He'd lost count of how many bags there had been.

She was in a tenuous position. Her injuries were extensive. The knife had sliced through several sections of bowel and lacerated her spleen; the only way they could save her life was to take it out. Her medical team credited the paramedics with saving her life. They'd had four pints of O-negative blood on their rig—enough to replace the lost volume to keep her clinging to life and get her to the OR. Her blood counts were finally stabilizing.

Rachel looked completely washed out. The color of her face was indistinguishable from the starched pillow it rested upon. Word had spread throughout the hospital of her presence. A HIPAA violation for sure, but there was little that could stop the furtive whispers of hospital gossip when one of their own was within their walls. Particularly one who'd been married to the infamous Seth Black and had been accused of murder herself.

The ER team and surgical staff had evaluated Kyle's injury. Surgery to his left shoulder was necessary, but he'd been putting the doctors off until he felt Rachel was out of the woods. That time hadn't come yet. He'd made so many mistakes and wasn't going to leave her side until he could rest assured she'd live.

A man approached. Kyle assumed he was a member of Rachel's medical team. The semblance of a suit filled his peripheral vision. When he turned, it was Inspector Armijo.

Kyle faced him. "You're the last person I'd thought I'd see."

"How is she?" Javier asked.

Kyle turned back to the window. "Stable, but she hasn't really woken up yet. Her eyelids will flutter, but that's about it. They had to remove her spleen and part of her bowel. Several tendons in her hand needed repair."

"She's alive. She'll work her way back—of this I have no doubt. I heard they found Dr. Allen. Once Seth is out of the hospital, he'll be back in jail. Those are all wins."

Kyle swallowed hard. Yes, they were. On the law enforcement side. But was it a win in the personal sense? Was it ultimately a win that mattered? To those women who wouldn't fall victim to Seth, of course it was. But was there any stopping Seth's particular brand of evil? Could his metastatic reach ever be stopped? Could they restrict his rights to where he wouldn't ever be able to communicate with a person again?

"It was risky, what you did," Javier said.

"I know. She begged me. I didn't feel like anyone else in the agency believed me as far as her innocence. I couldn't trust anybody. I made a judgment call. A bad one, maybe. Probably."

Armijo shoved his hands in his pocket, turned and leaned against the window so he was face-to-face with Kyle.

"I was one of them who didn't believe you or her, but those tapes are convincing. Yes, it was risky. I don't think WITSEC will forgive you for the judgment call. If they do, I'm not sure what kind of job you'll have. Fieldwork may be out of the question."

"It's okay. I don't expect WITSEC to ever take me back, to be honest."

The man nodded. "Looks like we're both out of a job...for the same reasons."

"The same?" Kyle questioned. "I didn't betray a witness."

"Didn't you, though? You chose to put her in harm's way...because you loved her. You knew the only way you could save her was to clear her name. And the only way to do that was to risk her life."

Kyle looked at Rachel's sleeping form. Javier was right. They had acted for the same basic reason, even though Javier had twisted his version to a story he could tell himself that exonerated him from some truly abhorrent actions. As Rachel had said to him on many occasions, denial was the most powerful human defense mechanism.

"Don't you think it's time you tell her how you really feel?" Javier asked.

Kyle pressed his lips together.

"Once you find the woman you can't live without, do everything in your power to keep her with you. Even if it means losing everything." He laid a hand on Kyle's shoulder. "Sometimes, the very things we think we can't live without are those things we should lose in order to have the life that was meant for us."

Rachel shifted. Her last memory was of the woods. The knife. All the blood. Kyle... begging her to stay with him. She'd wanted to, for a moment, but some injuries were too devastating for a person no matter their will to live.

She opened her eyes to a dark room. Shapes were blurry. The soft beeping of a monitor tickled her ears, the sound quickening as she focused on it—it was her heartbeat. She was alive. Still on earth. Her mouth was dry, sticky. Her lips chapped. She pulled her shoulders down. Her left hand ached as she lifted it. It was heavily bandaged, with small drops of dried blood on the outside of the Kerlix gauze. Her other hand was free, and she felt her abdomen. A large dressing was present, and she wondered how many organs she still had left. Enough to ensure her survival? There was a tug at her neck as she looked out the window. She reached for it. A central line. Looking up, she saw the bag of IV fluids hanging. There'd be no need for a central line unless she'd been a critical patient. Likely for blood. How many pints? She wasn't sure she wanted to know.

When she rested her hand back down, it landed on a head of hair.

It was as if a bolt of electricity plowed through Kyle's body. He sat up ramrod straight and looked at her. A look of utter relief washed over his face. He grabbed her uninjured hand and pressed it against his lips, kissing it softly.

She felt a warm tenderness spread through her body. A sense of peace washed over her.

"I'm so glad I get to see your blue eyes again," he whispered softly. "You're beautiful."

She tried to laugh, but the slight movement of her abdominal muscles sent waves of pain through her midsection.

Kyle caressed her arm with his hand. "Shh…that wasn't meant to be funny."

Rachel inhaled. Kyle rustled through her covers and handed her a button. "Here." He pressed it into her palm. "The nurse said when you woke up to give you this. To press it if you're hurting."

That said a lot. The medical team had expected her to wake up. That was a good sign.

"Seth's in jail. Nora, too. He's never getting out again. They found more evidence in Nora's home that she framed you for Penelope Schmidt's murder. That she and Seth were…having an affair, I guess is the safest way to say it." He paused a second, then said, "There's one more thing I need to tell you."

Rachel shifted, trying to find a comfortable spot. "What is it?"

"In hopes of securing a deal with the prosecutor, Nora disclosed what happened to Dr. Lewis—Seth's previous partner."

"Let me guess, he's not alive anymore."

"No." Kyle smoothed his hand over her lower leg. "At least his family will have closure. Nora will replace him in providing testimony against Seth."

"I don't care about the two of them anymore. I only care about the life I have left and what that looks like."

What would become of her? WITSEC was optional, but she didn't know if she could endure that prison again. Not alone. She'd rather risk the threat from the Black Crew and go back to her old life—or what remained of it—and live with the risk if she could be with those she loved. The loneliness of the last three years had been too much.

"I can't go back."

"Rachel, you'll be killed if you don't. The Black Crew—we might be able to stop them if we hide you, but if we don't, there will be no protecting you. I can't let that happen. I won't let it happen."

She turned and looked at him. "Kyle, you can't force me. You're the one who told me WITSEC was a choice. Maybe my only choice, but still a choice. You can't force me against my will. I won't stay...not alone anymore."

"What if you weren't alone?" Kyle asked.

"Who's going to be with me?"

He stood, pushed the chair away and knelt next to her bed. "Me. I want to live the rest of my life with you." He edged up and brushed his lips against hers. A soft sigh escaped her lips.

"You can't."

"I can," he said, trying to convince her. "I'm going to leave WITSEC."

Rachel tried to sit up but winced. "No, you can't. It wouldn't be right."

He gripped her hand between his. "It is right." He implored her eyes with his. "Because I love you...am in love with you. I don't want to—no, I *can't* live without you. I'm going to give it all up if you'll have me. Please, say you'll have me."

They were words she'd longed to hear her entire life. A man, a trustworthy and honorable man, speaking sincere truth from his heart, willing to put himself aside—for her.

She cried. He stood up and kissed her eyelids ever so gently. Her cheeks next. And then their lips met. She reached her hand up, placed it around his neck and pulled him into her, kissing him back.

Kyle eased back. "Can I take that as a yes?"

"Yes, Kyle. I love you. You're the one who made me believe in love again. Who taught me what love truly is. There's no one else I'd spend my life with."

EPILOGUE

Rachel and Kyle stood at the top of Angel's Landing in Zion National Park. The hike had started in the early morning. Once at the top, Rachel had changed into a simple floral sundress. Kyle was in jeans and a white button-up shirt.

She'd had pomp and circumstance before when she married Seth. She didn't need or want it now. All she needed was Kyle. She reached out for his hand. Heather and Sofia were her bridesmaids. Forgiving Sofia for colluding with Seth hadn't been easy but once Rachel understood how Seth had trapped her and threatened her family it became a necessity. Rachel would never allow Seth to tear her family members away again.

Kyle stood with his brother and Rachel's brother-in-law. A soft breeze rustled Rachel's hair, and Kyle reached up and tucked the way-ward blond strands behind her ear.

So much had happened in the last year. It had been dizzying. Terrifying at times. Ultimately the most trying, yet rewarding, time of her life. Kyle had done what he said. He'd left WITSEC and entered witness protection with her. At first, they'd been sepa-rated, in different locations, but they were allowed to communicate with one another. It was the only way Rachel had agreed to coop-erate with their plan. She also insisted that if WITSEC wanted her to testify against Seth again and remain in the program, she was bringing her sister's family and her parents with her. To Rachel, it was a small price to pay for convicting one of the most prolific serial killers of present times. The trial had taken place six months after the incident at the cottage. Prosecutors and WITSEC were eager to get the episode behind them. The trial had taken three months. As soon as the prosecutors achieved a guilty verdict and sen-tenced Seth to life in prison for the second time, Kyle had proposed on the courthouse steps as they left.

Now it was time to move forward. Rachel could hardly hear the words the minister said during the ceremony. She held a bouquet of white and pink daisies. Kyle caressed her fingers as they said their vows. She couldn't tear her eyes away from the way her ring sparkled under the sunlight or the pure joy on his face as he leaned in to kiss her.

Next was Alaska. During the trial, she'd worked to get a medical license there. Kyle had secured a job in law enforcement. Her sister would continue to be a stay-at-home mom while her husband worked at the local high school. Her parents would be tucked away in a retirement community.

At the end of the ceremony, Kyle and Rachel let their guests drift away to start the hike down. Kyle pointed to her hiking boots. "Ready for our new life?"

"When did you know?" Rachel asked him.

"Know what?"

"That you loved me?"

"There was never just one moment. It was an accumulation of many moments, to where I couldn't deny my feelings any longer. But if I look back, I'd have to say my feelings for you started during Seth's first trial."

"What?"

"I didn't understand then what I do now. I was so proud of you. For surviving. For facing Seth. *Noble* was never a word I'd used to describe any other witness."

Rachel smiled coyly. "All the papers were right. Remember? How they'd speculate that I was falling in love with you? At the time, I thought it was knight-in-shining-armor syndrome—like how some people will fall in love with their doctors. That's what I chalked it up to."

He leaned into her, pressing his cheek to hers. "This has been the hardest year for me, Rachel. Being separated from you. Hoping they would believe our stories. Hoping they wouldn't assume we were lying for a cover story."

"We can't look back. No matter what happens, we're not living under Seth's shadow anymore."

He kissed her. "That was when I really knew I was done for. When you kissed me at the cottage." He placed his palms to her face. "I tried to hide it…maybe a little too successfully. I'm glad you found your way back to me."

"I'm never letting anything separate us again."

He took her hands in his. "Ready to start?"

"I have been…forever."

* * * * *

If you enjoyed this story, look for these other books by Jordyn Redwood:

Taken Hostage
Fugitive Spy
Christmas Baby Rescue

Dear Reader,

Many of my novels are based on inspiration from non-fiction books and *Eliminating the Witness* was no exception. If you want to know more about WITSEC I highly suggest you read *WITSEC: Inside the Federal Witness Protection Program* by Pete Earley and Gerald Shur. Gerald Shur is the man that started the program and came up with the name WITSEC Inspector, which was meant to elevate the position to be more esteemed.

I'm also fascinated in general by people. Perhaps that's just one of the many reasons I am an author. I'm intrigued by how we move through life. How we weather difficulties. The defense mechanisms we use to deal with stress and trauma. Denial is by far the most prominent and humans are experts at it. What is it that we might know but we hide from ourselves? If we confronted our own secrets—could we be better at relating to, loving, and forgiving others? In my own life, I have found the things I'm most critical of in others are often things I need to work on myself, and those judgments have become guideposts for me to pay attention to.

I hope you love Kyle and Rachel's story as much as I loved writing it. I love to hear from my readers. You can reach me via email at jredwood1@gmail.com or PO Box 1142, Parker, Colorado 80134.

Many Blessings,
Jordyn

Get 3 FREE REWARDS!

We'll send you 2 FREE Books <u>plus</u> a FREE Mystery Gift.

FREE
Value Over
$20

Both the **Harlequin®** Special Edition and **Harlequin®** Heartwarming™ series feature compelling novels filled with stories of love and strength where the bonds of friendship, family and community unite.

YES! Please send me 2 FREE novels from the Harlequin Special Edition or Harlequin Heartwarming series and my FREE Gift (gift is worth about $10 retail). After receiving them, if I don't wish to receive any more books, I can return the shipping statement marked "cancel." If I don't cancel, I will receive 6 brand-new Harlequin Special Edition books every month and be billed just $5.49 each in the U.S. or $6.24 each in Canada, a savings of at least 12% off the cover price, or 4 brand-new Harlequin Heartwarming Larger-Print books every month and be billed just $6.24 each in the U.S. or $6.74 each in Canada, a savings of at least 19% off the cover price. It's quite a bargain! Shipping and handling is just 50¢ per book in the U.S. and $1.25 per book in Canada.* I understand that accepting the 2 free books and gift places me under no obligation to buy anything. I can always return a shipment and cancel at any time by calling the number below. The free books and gift are mine to keep no matter what I decide.

Choose one: ☐ **Harlequin**   ☐ **Harlequin**   ☐ **Or Try Both!**
                Special Edition   **Heartwarming**   (235/335 & 161/361
                (235/335 BPA GRMK)   **Larger-Print**   BPA GRPZ)
                                       (161/361 BPA GRMK)

Name (please print)

Address   Apt. #

City   State/Province   Zip/Postal Code

Email: Please check this box ☐ if you would like to receive newsletters and promotional emails from Harlequin Enterprises ULC and its affiliates. You can unsubscribe anytime.

Mail to the Harlequin Reader Service:
IN U.S.A.: P.O. Box 1341, Buffalo, NY 14240-8531
IN CANADA: P.O. Box 603, Fort Erie, Ontario L2A 5X3

Want to try 2 free books from another series? Call 1-800-873-8635 or visit www.ReaderService.com.

*Terms and prices subject to change without notice. Prices do not include sales taxes, which will be charged (if applicable) based on your state or country of residence. Canadian residents will be charged applicable taxes. Offer not valid in Quebec. This offer is limited to one order per household. Books received may not be as shown. Not valid for current subscribers to the Harlequin Special Edition or Harlequin Heartwarming series. All orders subject to approval. Credit or debit balances in a customer's account(s) may be offset by any other outstanding balance owed by or to the customer. Please allow 4 to 6 weeks for delivery. Offer available while quantities last.

Your Privacy—Your information is being collected by Harlequin Enterprises ULC, operating as Harlequin Reader Service. For a complete summary of the information we collect, how we use this information and to whom it is disclosed, please visit our privacy notice located at corporate.harlequin.com/privacy-notice. From time to time we may also exchange your personal information with reputable third parties. If you wish to opt out of this sharing of your personal information, please visit readerservice.com/consumerschoice or call 1-800-873-8635. **Notice to California Residents**—Under California law, you have specific rights to control and access your data. For more information on these rights and how to exercise them, visit corporate.harlequin.com/california-privacy.

HSEHW23